Sophocles and Alcibiades

Sophocles and Alcibiades

Athenian Politics in Ancient Greek Literature

Michael Vickers

Cornell University Press
Ithaca, New York

For
Gerald, Sophie, James, Philip,
Lika and Sandro

Copyright © Michael Vickers 2008

First published in the United States of America in 2008 by Cornell University Press

First published in the United Kingdon in 2008 by Acumen Publishing Limited

Library of Congress Cataloging in Publication Data
A CIP catalog record for this book is available from the Library of Congress.

ISBN 978-0-8014-4732-7 (cloth)

Designed and typeset by Kate Williams, Swansea.
Printed and bound by Biddles Ltd., King's Lynn.

Cloth Printing   10 9 8 7 6 5 4 3 2 1

Contents

Preface

Greek politics were highly personalized. The very existence of the institution of ostracism, for example, whereby individuals were sent into exile by means of a popular vote, attests to the fact. Pericles owed his dominance of Athenian political life in large part to the fact that he had successfully rallied opposition to Thucydides (son of Milesias, to distinguish him from the historian) in the 440s BCE. Thucydides had been the first to create anything like a political party in Athens, encouraging his partisans to sit together in the assembly. Thucydides' power came to an abrupt end when he was ostracized in 443 BCE, and Pericles was pre-eminent for the next decade or more. On Pericles' death in 429 there was a struggle for the succession, at the level of succeeding to the grip on Athenian politics that Pericles had enjoyed, rather than any formal position beyond an annual election to a generalship. There were ten generals each year, and any pre-eminence was due to the Athenian public's view as to who appeared to carry the most influence. Cleon (who was not at first a general) succeeded for a time in laying claim to Pericles' mantle, and after his death Nicias came to the fore. Both were challenged, either overtly or in the most under-hand fashion, by Pericles' ward Alcibiades (c.452–404 BCE), an individual who regarded himself from a very early age as his guardian's true successor.

Alcibiades' conduct attracted innumerable anecdotes, many of which have come down to us. These go far beyond the story of his generalships, his joint command on the ill-fated Sicilian campaign (an expedition he had done much to foster), his desertion to Athens' Spartan enemies, and his triumphant return to Athens towards the end of his life. They tell of his irrationality, his selfishness, his greed, his flamboyance and above all his ambition. It was this aspect of his personality that polarized Athenian opinion. Some were for tolerating the extraordinary individual whose persuasiveness camouflaged many of his failings, while others were scandalized by his excesses and saw in the person of Alcibiades the emergence of a new tyrant, of a kind that their ancestors had successfully sent into exile decades earlier.

Alcibiades' dissolute way of life – he was accused by a contemporary of "lying with his mother, his sister and his daughter" – contributed to widespread mistrust.

No other Athenian politician during the Peloponnesian War was as controversial as Alcibiades. In *Frogs*, Aristophanes famously makes Dionysus ask Aeschylus and Euripides: "what would you do about Alcibiades?" In the same play, he says of the Athenian populace and Alcibiades: "They love him, they hate him, they cannot do without him" (*Ra.* 1422–5). It will be argued here that this tense relationship was monitored by the tragedians, who treated it through the medium of myth. They included Sophocles and Euripides, who in the plays to be discussed here display the reaction of, respectively, a wise and a subtle spectator to the excesses that Alcibiades perpetrated from his early teens to his maturity, if that word could ever be used in his case. It would seem that both writers extrapolated from whatever the current situation might have been and showed on stage, according to Aristotle's definition of tragedy, the sorts of things that a person with certain tendencies and predilections "would inevitably say or do" (Arist. *Po.* 1451b). The "love" and "hate" of Aristophanes' Athenians, moreover, will have done much to charge the plays of Sophocles and Euripides with the "pity" and "fear" that, again according to Aristotle, characterized the best sort of Athenian tragedy (*ibid.* 1449b).

These emotions were felt by the audience in the context of real people, not of disembodied idealizations. No one really cared if the son of Laius was given a hard time on the stage; still less did they project their own fantasies about their mothers onto his peculiar situation. What people were seriously concerned about was what Alcibiades might do next, given his tendencies and proclivities. To have the way that things might go exaggerated on stage in an extraordinary but admonitory fashion might serve, it was felt, as a brake on, among other things, Alcibiadean excess and ambition. And when Alcibiades was away from Athens, debates between him and other exiles could be safely conducted beneath the veil of legend. There will of course have been many other butts of dramatists' criticism (Pericles was one such, as was Critias, as we shall presently see), but Alcibiades was the principal target during the later fifth century.

"Hidden meanings" have had a bad name in classical studies. Quite why this should be is a subject worthy of study in its own right. Any relationship Sophocles' plays might have had to contemporary history has been strenuously, and influentially, denied. Euripides was, however, famously adept at writing one thing while intending another. Quintilian describes him as the master of oblique reference for good reason, as we shall see in the discussions of *Cyclops* and *Bacchae*, which cover the same ground as plays of Sophocles, but from a different viewpoint. The practice was not restricted to playwrights, but was employed by writers of prose as well.

Thucydides employed it, as did Plato, and specifically in the context of Alcibiades. The Melian Dialogue, Thucydides' supposed "digressions" and the personality of Callicles in *Gorgias* are discussed in further chapters, with a view in part to demonstrating how strong was Alcibiades' grip on the Athenians' imagination even after his death, and in part to elaborate on themes already broached by Sophocles and Euripides.

This book is a by-product of work done in connection with a revision of my 1997 publication *Pericles on Stage: Political Comedy in Aristophanes' Earlier Plays.*[1] My forthcoming work, which covers the later plays, is twice as long and makes much use of the technique the late Keith Hopkins called the "wigwam argument": "each pole would fall down by itself, but together the poles stand up, by leaning on each other; they point roughly in the same direction and circumscribe 'truth'".[2] The "wigwam argument" differs from traditional philological debate, where it is fair game to sniff out any apparently weak evidence, to imply that even to think of using it is a sign of madness, and to declare gleefully that any conclusions based on it must be inherently flawed. Here, I shall frequently be taking note of hitherto unconsidered scraps which, when combined, amount to something substantial. For some pieces of evidence are stronger than others, but the "wigwam" approach enables all kinds to be taken into account.

If the plays discussed here do indeed prove to have a political content, what might the consequences be? Are we to think in terms of the worst-case scenario once adumbrated by Terry Eagleton in his *Literary Theory*?

> Let us imagine that by dint of some deft archaeological research we discovered a great deal more about what Greek tragedy actually meant to its original audiences, recognised that these concerns were utterly remote from our own, and began to read the plays again in the light of this deepened knowledge. One result might be that we stopped enjoying them. We might come to see that we had enjoyed them previously because we were unwittingly reading them in the light of our own presumptions; once this became less possible, the drama might cease to speak at all significantly to us.[3]

---

1. M. Vickers, *Pericles on Stage: Political Comedy in Aristophanes' Early Plays* (Austin, TX: University of Texas Press, 1997).
2. K. Hopkins, *Conquerors and Slaves: Sociological Studies in Ancient History* (Cambridge: Cambridge University Press, 1978), 19.
3. Terry Eagleton, *Literary Theory: An Introduction* (Minneapolis, MN: University of Minnesota Press, 1983), 12.

What follows is an argument for a different position, and it will be suggested that Sophocles' enterprise was essentially the same as that of modern writers who have used aspects of the history of the house of Laius, for example, to make incisive comments on contemporary events, whether it be in the form of resistance to authority or to totalitarianism, of national aspirations, postcolonialism or even of anti-Americanism. For Sophocles and Euripides, as for them, the tales were already there, and they, like them, exploited the possibilities inherent in the traditional plots for creating fruitful resonances with the contemporary scene. The concerns of the ancients were different, of course, but not in essence "utterly remote". It is diverting to note that it has been playwrights such as Anouilh, Brecht and Heaney, and not scholars of classical literature, who have been most alert to the close parallels between ancient and modern dramatic practice. But a new understanding of first meanings and an awareness that they were political before they were anything else can only enhance our enjoyment of the ancient plays, and help us to see them as part of a continuum that links the past with the present.

This book was written during leave from my employment at the Ashmolean Museum, when I was wearing another hat, namely, that of Senior Research Fellow in Classical Studies at Jesus College, Oxford. Debts of gratitude are owed to the librarians of the Bodleian, Sackler, Norlin and Jesus College libraries for their unfailing courtesy. The *Thesaurus Linguae Graecae* proved to be an invaluable tool. Many thanks are also due to friends and colleagues who have encouraged (or attempted to restrain) my interest in history and tragedy; in particular, Frederick Ahl, Maureen Alden, Michael Allen, Włodzimierz Appel, Ernst Badian, Laura Biondi, Edmund Bloedow, Daphne Nash Briggs, William M. Calder III, Mortimer Chambers, Armand D'Angour, the late Peter Derow, Mamuka Dolidze, Elspeth Dusinberre, Pat Easterling, Joel Eis, Joseph Farrell, Clive Foss, John Gibert, David Gill, David Gribble, Rismag Gordesiani, Keti Gurtshiani, Gabriel Herman, Mira Hofmann, David Konstan, the late Pierre Lévêque, the late D. M. Lewis, Andreas Markantonatos, Mark Munn, Manana Odisheli, Martin Ostwald, Richard Seaford, Nicholas Sekunda, Susan Sherratt, Barry Strauss and Christopher Tuplin. John Richmond generously applied a critical eye to earlier versions of most chapters, and Daphne Briggs and Andreas Markantonatos very kindly read through the text at a late stage. I am also grateful for ideas and feedback from audiences in Oxford, Birmingham, Belfast, Toruń, Tbilisi and Batumi. Several chapters are based on material that has appeared elsewhere in various guises: in *Historia*, *Phasis*, *Classics Ireland*, *Dialogues d'histoire ancienne* and *Xenia Toruniensia*. I am grateful to the respective editors for having entertained these contributions in the first instance. Anonymous readers for the press made many valuable comments and suggestions for improvement. My thanks also go to Steven Gerrard at Acumen for being the most efficient and businesslike editor one could ever have hoped for, and to Kate Williams, whose editing made a chore into a pleasure. I owe immense intellectual debts to the late E. D. Francis, who taught me how to read Greek with understanding, and to the late William S. Heckscher, who taught me how to think about the past. If there are any remaining shortcomings, they are to be laid at my door.

Michael Vickers,
Jesus College, Oxford

Abbreviations

Abbreviations used in the text and notes are based on H. G. Liddell, R. Scott & H. S. Jones, *A Greek–English Lexicon*, 9th edn (with supplement) (Oxford: Clarendon Press, 1968) [LSJ] and S. Hornblower & A. Spawforth, *The Oxford Classical Dictionary*, 3rd edn (Oxford: Clarendon Press, 1996) [*OCD³*].

1
The mythologizing of history

The case to be made in this book is that Sophocles (and Euripides) took traditional legends and employed them to make highly pertinent observations on contemporary military and political events. That this sort of investigation is supposed to be off-limits only adds to the interest of the exercise. For more than a hundred years now, most students of Sophocles, for example, have followed unquestioningly the dictum of the highly respected Ulrich von Wilamowitz-Moellendorff (1848–1931) that "no Sophoclean tragedy has any immediate connection with a contemporary event".[1] Students of Euripides have only gingerly followed Günther Zuntz in admitting that some at least of Euripides' plays might be political.[2] There has been, it is true, a vogue more recently for ascribing definitive political messages to the tragic poets.[3] This development has been criticized,[4] in some respects rightly, for it has led to a proliferation of disparate political interpretations, most of which are inevitably off-

1. "Es ist auf das schärfste zu sagen, dass keine sophokleische Tragödie eine unmittelbare Beziehung auf ein Factum der Gegenwart enthält" (U. von Wilamowitz-Moellendorff, "Excurse zum Oedipus des Sophokles", *Hermes* **34** [1899], 55–80, esp. 59). Respect for Wilamowitz has verged on the hagiographical, for example, W. Appel (ed.), *Origine Cujavus. Beiträge zur Tagung anläßlich des 150. Geburtstags Ulrich von Wilamowitz-Moellendorffs (1848–1931)* (Toruń: Wydawnictwo Uniwersytetu Mikołaja Kopernika, 1999). See too G. Müller: "Grundsätzlich muss jedes zeitgeschichtliche Moment an Conception und Durchführung der sophokleischen Tragödien geleugnet werden" (Any contemporary factor in the conception and implementation of the Sophoclean tragedies must be denied on principle) (*Sophokles, Antigone* [Heidelberg: Winter, 1967], 245).
2. Cf. G. Zuntz, *The Political Plays of Euripides* (Manchester: Manchester University Press, 1963). C. Collard (ed.), *Euripides Supplices* (Groningen: Bouma's Boekhuis, 1975), 13, for example, speaks of the "impropriety" of a political reading of *Supplices*.
3. See, for example, the essays in C. B. R. Pelling (ed.), *Greek Tragedy and the Historian* (Oxford: Clarendon Press, 1997).
4. For example, by J. Griffin, "Sophocles and the Democratic City", in *Sophocles Revisited: Essays Presented to Sir Hugh Lloyd-Jones*, J. Griffin (ed.), 73–108 (Oxford: Oxford University Press, 1999).

target. Many fail because they speak in generalities about macro-political themes: for example, the endorsement of aristocratic paternalism and imperial hegemony,[5] competing models of elite leadership[6] or "a [strong] contemporary application to the problems of the Athenian *polis*".[7] But both they and their critics go astray in overlooking – or rejecting – the possibility that the themes might be micro-political and be concerned with the role played in politics by specific individuals.

Given the intensely personal nature of Athenian politics, this should not be surprising. Even history, according to Aristotle, might be personal: for him it dealt with particulars, such as "what Alcibiades actually did, or what was done to him" (*Poet.* 1451b.11). Given Alcibiades' stature as a public figure, we might speculate that if Greek tragedy did deal with politics at the personal level, then he might figure as large on the tragic stage as he apparently did in comedy: for Plutarch, Alcibiades was "a powerful speaker, as the comic dramatists bear witness" (*Alc.* 10.4), while Libanius posed the rhetorical questions, "What play did not include [Alcibiades] among the cast of characters? Did not Eupolis and Aristophanes show him on the stage? It is to him that comedy owed its success" (Lib. Fr. 50.2.21; generally overlooked by modern critics). Much the same might be said of older members of the household in which Alcibiades grew up, and who will be prominent in some of the plays to be discussed here. Pericles had "many songs and jests written about him" (Plut. *Per.* 33.7–8), and Aspasia "figured large in the work of comic writers" (Did. ap. Clem. Al. *Strom.* 4.19.122). Once we penetrate the veils of allusion and oblique reference woven by the playwrights we shall find that both Pericles and Aspasia – like Alcibiades – also figured large in tragedy. At least, this is the working hypothesis of this book.

It was said of Alcibiades' relationship with the Athenians that "they love him, they hate him, they cannot do without him" (Ar. *Ra.* 1425). The relationship between "love" and "hate" might be closely observed by the tragedians, who reflected on it by means of lightly disguised reworkings of legendary tales. Sophocles and Euripides were prominent among them, and in several of their plays they display the reactions of

5. P. Rose, "Historicizing Sophocles' *Ajax*", in *History, Tragedy, Theory: Dialogues in Athenian Drama*, B. Goff (ed.), 59–90 (Austin, TX: Texas University Press, 1995).

6. D. Rosenbloom, "From *Ponêros* to *Pharmakos*: Theatre, Social Drama and Revolution in Athens, 428–404 BCE", *Classical Antiquity* **21**(2) (2002), 283–346.

7. P. E. Easterling, "Tragedy, Greek", in *OCD*³, 1541; contrast "Nowadays the polis and its collectivity gets in everywhere" (Griffin, *Sophocles Revisited*, 48, n. 30). Indeed it does; see R. Buxton, "Time, Space and Ideology: Tragic Myths and the Athenian Polis", in *Mitos en la literatura griega arcaica y clásica*, J. López Férez (ed.), 175–89 (Madrid: Ediciones clásicas SA, 2003); P. E. Easterling, "The Image of the *Polis* in Greek Tragedy", in *The Imaginary Polis*, M. H. Hansen (ed.), 49–72 (Copenhagen: Royal Danish Academy of Sciences & Letters, 2005) and D. M. Carter, *The Politics of Greek Tragedy* (Bristol: Phoenix, 2007), 73–8.

concerned spectators to Alcibiades' tumultuous career. It would seem that Sophocles inferred the worst from whatever Alcibiades had most recently done and gave voice in his allusive but highly effective way to public distaste and displeasure. Euripides, at least after he had been bought by Alcibiades, tended to give a rosier view.

The Theban plays of Sophocles did not, as is often assumed, form part of a trilogy (i.e. plays that were originally presented one after the other on the same day as part of the same Athenian dramatic festival). Rather, they were written over many years, and it will be argued here that they were performed in 438, 425 and 401 BCE. There is a connecting theme, as we shall see, but it lies in a somewhat unexpected quarter. If the arguments presented here are correct, there will be considerable ramifications.

The earliest is *Antigone*, in which a girl defies her uncle's command that her brother should be denied a decent burial. The play has attracted a variety of critical reaction. In the nineteenth century, for Hegel, *Antigone* was "the most accomplished of all aesthetic works of the human spirit"; Kierkegaard created an analogy between the tragedy of Antigone and his own tortured personal circumstances, while Hölderlin took her to be "a terribly impatient human being". In the twentieth century Anouilh was inspired to show Antigone as a martyr of the French Resistance, Brecht to regard her strength and courage as a reproach to Nazi collaborators and Heinrich Böll to write a screenplay identifying her with the terrorist Ulrike Meinhof.[8] More recently, Zbigniew Rudziński has shown the dead unburied brother looking like a Chechen shot by the Russian army.[9] There seems to be no end of ways to interpret the play, and it has been said that "inexhaustibility explains its classic status".[10] The position taken here is closest to that of Seamus Heaney, thanks to whose work we can begin to understand what Sophocles was doing when he first presented his plays to an Athenian audience in the fifth century BCE. Heaney recycles the stories once told by Sophocles in order to make pointed statements about present-day politics.[11] I have come to believe that Sophocles was doing precisely the same, in taking old legends and recasting them in order to comment on the contemporary scene.

---

8. G. Steiner, *Antigones* (Oxford: Clarendon Press, 1984).
9. In his chamber opera *Antigone*, which received its première at the Lower Silesian Opera in Wrocław on 7 February 2003. For recent performances in Georgia, see K. Gurchiani, "Sophocles on the Georgian Stage", in *Proceedings of the 1st International Symposium "The Theatre and Theatrical Studies at the Beginning of the Twenty-first Century", Athens 2005* (forthcoming); performances elsewhere, Carter, *The Politics of Greek Tragedy*, 145–6.
10. B. Morrison, "Femme Fatale", *Guardian* (4 October 2003), http://arts.guardian.co.uk/features/story/0,11710,1055507,00.html (accessed Mar. 2008).
11. S. Bishop, "An American Antigone: Seamus Heaney's Version of Antigone", *Harvard Book Review* 6(1) (Winter 2004), www.hcs.harvard.edu/~hbr/issues/winter04/articles/heaney.shtml (accessed Mar. 2008); M. Denton, Review of *Antigone*, 27 July (2004), www.nytheatre.com/nytheatre/archweb/arch2005_02.htm (accessed Feb. 2008).

But before we can approach the first meaning of Sophocles' (or Euripides') plays we must first remove a huge obstacle to understanding best exemplified by a dictum of E. R. Dodds. In an article perhaps appropriately entitled "On Misunderstanding the *Oedipus Rex*", Dodds wrote that "it is an essential critical principle that *what is not mentioned in the play does not exist*" (italics original),[12] and this is still the approach adopted by most professional critics of Greek drama. It will be argued in what follows that *Oedipus Tyrannus* (= *Oedipus Rex*) makes rather better sense, and inconsistencies disappear, when it is viewed against its likely historical background (see Chapter 3). The same applies to Sophocles' *Oedipus at Colonus*, discussed in Chapter 7. It will be argued there that there is a precise historical, indeed political, basis for the plotting of the ancient Greek play that accounts for its somewhat optimistic outcome. Chapter 8 is concerned with *Bacchae,* a play that deals with the same political situation, but seen from Euripides' rather different standpoint. And in a play that was produced in Athens only a few years before Sophocles wrote the Colonus play, namely his *Philoctetes* of 409 BCE, Sophocles was apparently again using an ancient story as a screen behind which he could make pertinent observations about the contemporary scene (see Chapter 5). The play was not "a romantic holiday".[13] Odysseus figures large in *Philoctetes,* and the same applies to *Ajax* (Chapter 4), of hitherto unknown date, and it used to be the case that the two plays were grouped together on the not unreasonable grounds that Odysseus "appears as the leading instrument in the development of the plot".[14] Although it is customary today to date *Ajax* to the 440s BCE, it will be argued presently that in the absence of any firm support for such a date (and there is none), there may be sufficient historical evidence to justify a date of 410 BCE. I concur with Hugh Lloyd-Jones in regarding the play as a "mature masterpiece".[15] There will be no discussion of *Trachiniae* or *Electra,* for the good reason that they do not appear to concern Alcibiades. *Trachiniae* is, I believe, certainly historical, and I have argued elsewhere that it was an Athenian reaction to the foundation in 427/6 of the Spartan colony of Heraclea in Trachis (cf. Thuc. 3.92–3).[16] *Electra,* however, is impenetrable by the

---

12. E. R. Dodds, "On Misunderstanding the *Oedipus Rex*", *Greece and Rome* **13** (1966), 37–49, esp. 40, (reprinted in his *The Ancient Concept of Progress and other Essays on Greek Literature and Belief,* 64–77 [Oxford: Clarendon Press, 1973], 68, and in *Oxford Readings in Greek Tragedy,* E. Segal [ed.], 177–88 [Oxford: Clarendon Press, 1983], 180).

13. C. Whitman, *Sophocles: A Study of Heroic Humanism* (Cambridge, MA: Harvard University Press, 1951), 172.

14. J. W. Donaldson, *Theatre of the Greeks,* 7th edn (London: Longman, 1860), 125.

15. H. Lloyd-Jones (ed.), *Sophocles: Ajax, Electra, Oedipus Tyrannus* (Cambridge, MA: Harvard University Press, 1994), 9.

16. M. Vickers, "Heracles Lacedaemonius: The Political Dimensions of Sophocles *Trachiniae* and Euripides *Heracles*", *Dialogues d'histoire ancienne* **21** (1995), 41–69.

techniques employed on the five Sophoclean plays discussed in this book, and so is not treated here. Rather than being a cause of disappointment, this is a welcome state of affairs, for it renders futile the charge that Alcibiades can be seen anywhere by the gullible or misguided.

Euripides was more oblique in his approach to history, but again it was the contemporary scene that came first; as with Sophocles, the political situation gave rise to his plotting. This might be at the most general level, as in the way in which *Medea* (of 431 BCE) treats of an exotic foreign wife with a faithless husband at a time when Pericles was under attack via his exotic, foreign, and perhaps faithless, mistress. The same motif, of an exotic foreign wife causing embarrassment to her Greek consort, occurs in *Hippolytus* (of 428 BCE), and I have argued elsewhere that the situation may reflect gossip relating to the Periclean ménage.[17] There is not a one-to-one correspondence between the individuals involved, but the flavour is the same: deniable ambiguities are the order of the day – a chaste hero and uncon-summated lust on stage, but profligacy and (perhaps) indulgence in real life. Such was the essence of a Euripides who was *sententiis densus* ("the master of oblique allusion": Quint. *Inst.* 10.1.68). The imputation that Pericles' consort might have been unfaithful with someone with whom she had a maternal relationship, true or not, and invented by Euripides or not, probably provided the basis for the theme of matrophilia that underlies *Oedipus Tyrannus*.

By the time of his later plays, two of which are discussed here, Euripides could be thought to be in Alcibiades' pocket. He had written verses in praise of Alcibiades' remarkable victory in the chariot race at the Olympic games of 416 (Plut. *Alc.* 12.3–5), and was doubtless, like Simonides, Bacchylides or Pindar in their day, generously rewarded for his trouble. Pindar earned 100 *minae* (or more than 43 kilos of silver) for his *Dithyramb for Athens* in the 470s (Isoc. 15.166). The Theban neighbour charged with the responsibility of looking after Pindar's possessions in his absence (Pind. *Pyth.* 8.58) was probably the curator of a choice collection of plate.[18] Euripides' indebtedness to his patron could account for his light touch where Alcibiades was concerned, in contrast with Sophocles' more sceptical and robust position. The "love" and "hate" of which Aristophanes speaks (*Ra.* 1425) were simply exaggerated versions of Euripidean and Sophoclean standpoints. Chapters 9–12 discuss further various ways in which Thucydides and Plato treated

17. M. Vickers, "Alcibiades and Aspasia: Notes on the *Hippolytus*", *Dialogues d'histoire ancienne* **26** (2000), 7–17, following B. S. Strauss, *Fathers and Sons in Athens: Ideology and Society in the Era of the Peloponnesian War* (Princeton: NJ: Princeton University Press, 1993), 166–75; M. Vickers, *Alcibiades on Stage: Political Comedy in Aristophanes* (in preparation).
18. Cf. M. Vickers & D. Gill, *Artful Crafts: Ancient Greek Silverware and Pottery*, 2nd edn (Oxford: Clarendon Press, 1996), 102.

Alcibiades' heroically flawed career. Alcibiades is also frequently the principal κωμῳδούμενος in Aristophanes' extant plays, but these are discussed elsewhere.[19]

There is enough information – of an anecdotal, often gossipy, nature that has tended to be overlooked, being "outside the play" and often based on late (therefore "suspect") sources – to enable a reconstruction of the original significance, the first meaning, of tragedies that relate to Alcibiades. Our principal sources of historical information are Thucydides and Plutarch. Although Plutarch was writing centuries later, he made substantial additional use of contemporary sources.[20] He:

> had an excellent library containing many works now lost to us, some written by contemporaries of Pericles and by men of the next generation. He read the inscriptions and ancient documents and saw paintings, sculptures, and buildings that no longer exist. When used with care, his work is an outstanding source of authentic information.[21]

That was written in the context of the *Life of Pericles*, but much the same might be said of the *Life of Alcibiades*, which quotes from contemporary playwrights, and writers such as Antisthenes, Antiphon and Lysias, who knew Alcibiades personally. Other sources used by Plutarch include the work of later writers such as Satyrus and Duris of Samos.[22] Other useful sources include Andocides, Lysias, Plato, Xenophon and Isocrates (who were roughly contemporary with Alcibiades), and others such as Libanius,[23] and later grammarians and encyclopaedists. The latter preserve many

---

19. Vickers, *Pericles on Stage* and *Alcibiades on Stage*.
20. P. A. Stadter, *A Commentary on Plutarch's* Pericles (Chapel Hill, NC: University of North Carolina Press, 1989), lix; cf. lviii–lxxxv.
21. D. Kagan, *Pericles of Athens and the Birth of Democracy* (London: Secker & Warburg, 1990), xii.
22. Cf. D. A. Russell, *Plutarch* (London: Duckworth, 1972), 117–29; L. Prandi, "Introduzione", in Plutarch, *Vite parallele, Coriolano/Alcibiade*, 255–317 (Milan: Biblioteca Universale Rizzoli, 1992), 281–92 (on sources); T. Duff, "Plutarch on the Childhood of Alkibiades (Alk. 2–3)", *Proceedings of the Cambridge Philological Society* 49 (2003), 89–117 (on Alcibiades' childhood); C. B. R. Pelling, "Plutarch and Thucydides", in *Plutarch and the Historical Tradition*, P. A. Stadter (ed.), 10–40 (London: Routledge, 1992) (on Plutarch's artistry). In general, cf. M. A. Levi, *Quattro studi spartani e altri scritti di storia greca* (Milan: Istituto Editoriale Cisalpino, 1967), 132: "The sources for the history of Alcibiades are of the best quality". There is a useful collection in M. E. Rodríguez Blanco, *Alcibíades: Antología de textos con notas y comentarios* (Madrid: Ediciones de la Universidad Autónoma, 1988). Duff makes a very telling comparison between Plutarch's approach and the cinema: "the camera focuses, as it were, on a set-piece tableau, striking, colourful and memorable" ("Plutarch on the Childhood of Alkibiades", 112–13).
23. A. Schouler, *La Tradition hellénique de Libanius* (Lille/Paris: Atelier national reproduction des thèses, Université de Lille III/Belles Lettres, 1984), esp. 626–34.

anecdotes that are otherwise unknown. It will be assumed that such anecdotes are usually the expression of quintessential truths, distilled over centuries, rather than the products of later scholars intent on muddying the waters; at least if there appears to be a prefiguration in an early source of a story told in the anecdotal tradition, then it will be taken for granted that the two are related. In fact the anecdotes relating to Alcibiades are rarely fanciful, Alexander the Great having supplanted him in the imaginations of all except the learned.[24]

If the approach employed in this book is correct, then the role of Greek drama, which is often couched in myth, may require reappraisal. It is customary to say, for example, that "we can make a number of fairly confident assumptions without having to argue from scratch about the nature of Sophocles' methods",[25] and much the same approach is generally taken towards Euripides; but a reassessment is perhaps called for, and a good place to start is with the work of the late E. D. Francis, who once wrote:

> For the Greeks, myth was an exceptionally powerful form of metaphor, a code through which human events, indeed contemporary experience, could be expressed, interpreted, analyzed in symbolic terms .... The expression of an historical event in mythological terms – or alternatively, the mythologizing of actual history – are processes thoroughly characteristic of Greek thought and closely comparable with that tendency in Greek art to represent the specific in the light of the generic.[26]

While most would pay lip service to this statement, few apply it in practice. Historical allegory is not now in favour; for example, "clear contemporary references [in tragedy] seem to be limited to a few exceptional events".[27] Athenians in the period following the Persian attacks on their city expressed their deepest feelings in the form of myth, Phrynichus' fine of 1000 drachmae for reducing an audience

---

24. Cf. R. Stoneman, *Alexander the Great: A Life in Legend* (London: Yale University Press, 2008).
25. P. E. Easterling, "*Philoctetes* and Modern Criticism", *Illinois Classical Studies* 3 (1978), 27–38, esp. 27; reprinted in *Oxford Readings in Greek Tragedy*, E. Segal (ed.), 217–28 (Oxford: Oxford University Press, 1983).
26. E. D. Francis, "Greeks and Persians: The Art of Hazard and Triumph", in *Ancient Persia, the Art of an Empire*, D. Schmandt-Besserat (ed.), 53–86 (Malibu, CA: Undena Publications, 1980), 62.
27. Pelling, *Greek Tragedy and the Historian*, 216. Some exceptions to the general rule are: A. J. Podlecki, *The Political Background of Aeschylean Tragedy* (Ann Arbor, MI: University of Michigan Press, 1966); P. J. Bicknell, "Themistokles, Phrynichos, Aischylos, Ephialtes and Perikles: Political Dimensions of Attic Tragedy", *Ancient History: Resources for Teachers* 19 (1989), 120–30; Strauss, *Fathers and Sons in Athens*; M. Munn, *The School of History: Athens in the Age of Socrates* (Berkeley, CA: University of California Press, 2000).

to tears in 493/2 with harrowing descriptions in his *Sack of Miletus* of the fate of the Athenians' kith and kin (Hdt. 6.21)[28] having shown the perils of the realistic representation of tragic events. Myth was employed in antiquity much as it was in the Renaissance: "Throughout the fifteenth and sixteenth centuries subjects from antique mythology, poetry and history remained popular ... with allegorical meanings that could be deciphered only by some élite group united around a particular common interest or belief";[29] the only difference being that in antiquity knowledge of the mythical code was general, not esoteric. In the Renaissance myths in both art and literature were transformed to express new realities. Transformations were, however, normal practice in antiquity too, as the following readings of Sophocles (and Euripides) suggest. Myths were mutable, as Aristotle noted: "all poets err who have written a Heracleid, a Theseid, or similar poems. They imagine that since Heracles was one, the plot should also be one" (Arist. *Po.* 1451a, 21–22). This principle should, for example, explain the different treatments of Creon in three of the plays discussed here. A related principle accounts for the vast number of discrepancies to be found between one treatment of an ancient myth and another: the versions we have were frequently composed to meet specific (and different) historical situations; but history never repeats itself (although it might well rhyme, as Mark Twain is supposed to have said) and consequently no two myths are quite the same.

It should not be forgotten that plays were composed for performance on a single occasion, or if there were repeat performances they usually took place shortly afterwards. This suggests that their content might be occasional, that is, it reflected recent historical events. Writers frequently achieved this end by means of allusion or *emphasis*, a technical term meaning "innuendo", or even "subliminal suggestion", rather than "explicitness" as it does today: "We [today] are simply not attuned to writing which proceeds by indirect suggestion rather than by direct statement ... When we 'emphasize' something, we proclaim it to our readers, leaving no doubt that we want its presence known. The ancient writer does the exact opposite".[30] *Emphasis* was defined by Quintilian as "the process of digging out some lurking meaning from something said" (Quint. *Inst.* 9.2.64),[31] and a contemporary of Demetrius the rhetorician (writing in the second or first century BCE)

---

28. Bicknell, "Themistokles, Phrynichos, Aischylos", 124–5; for a later date for the performance, see E. Badian, "Archons and *strategoi*", *Antichthon* 5 (1971), 1–34, esp. 15–16 n.44.

29. W. S. Sheard, "Antique Subjects and their Transformations", in her *Antiquity in the Renaissance* (Northampton, MA: Smith College, 1979).

30. F. Ahl, "The Art of Safe Criticism in Greece and Rome", *American Journal of Philology* 105 (1984), 174–208, esp. 179, and *Sophocles' Oedipus: Evidence and Self-Conviction* (Ithaca, NY: Cornell University Press, 1991), 22–4.

31. Translated by Ahl, "The Art of Safe Criticism", 176.

stated that "the effect of an argument is more formidable because it is achieved by letting the fact make itself manifest rather than having the speaker make the point for himself" ([Demetr.] *Eloc.* 288).[32] A modern example of *emphasis* has been observed in the past few years when the Welsh rugby team plays in France. Welsh players sport the logo for their current sponsor Brains Beer on their shirts, but since it is forbidden to advertise alcohol in such contexts in France, it has been substituted with a logo reading "Brawn". *Emphasis* in the technical sense was the principal means by which a tragedian could play on recent events without referring to them directly.

Ancient Greeks were in fact very keen on ambiguity and on concealing (or enhancing) fact with fiction. "Ambiguous words" were frowned on in business or in court, but their use "when one discourses on the nature of man and things, [was] fine and philosophical" (Isoc. 12.240). Ambiguity might exist in poetry, however:

No *genre* of Greek poetry is entirely free from deliberate ambiguities, whether trivial puns, superstitious or sophistical etymologies, cryptic oracles, diplomatic evasions, cunning and deceptive equivocations, humorous or cacemphatic *doubles entendres*, unconscious foreshadowings of catastrophe, allusive phrases, associative meanings and vaguenesses, or any other of the manifold devices of ambiguity in its widest sense. Simpler lyric poetry had least of it, drama most.[33]

Athenian dramas were written for performance before Athenian audiences and can fairly be taken to reflect the concerns and preoccupations of those audiences. They also served as a kind of civic sanction, on the same spectrum as execution or ostracism (a ten-year exile) but milder, whether as ridicule in comedy or condemnation in tragedy. The comparative rarity of themes from the tragic stage in extant Athenian art provides indirect support for such a view. The epinician function of most public art is obvious, and the scenes on painted pottery, for example, reflect – albeit at one remove[34] – the values of a plutocratic elite intent on celebrating

---

32. Translated by Ahl, *Sophocles' Oedipus*, 22–5.
33. W. B. Stanford, *Ambiguity in Greek Literature* (Oxford: Blackwell, 1939), 181–2; cf. the Yeatsian doctrine of "the half-said thing": L. MacNeice, *The Poetry of W. B. Yeats* (London: Faber & Faber, 1967), 41ff., and D. Kiberd, *Inventing Ireland* (London: Cape, 1995), 128. On puns in Sophocles see B. M. W. Knox, *Oedipus at Thebes* (New Haven, CT: Yale University Press, 1957), 264.
34. Vickers & Gill, *Artful Crafts*; and M. Vickers, "Art or Kitsch?", *Apollo* (January) (2007), 98–9 (on the subsidiary role of painted pottery with respect to silverware).

military or athletic victory. The visual arts thus stress the positive qualities of victory, whereas tragedy dwells on the negative aspects of weakness and defeat. In essence, artists praise, tragedians criticize.

G. M. Young once observed that "the real, central theme of History is not what happened, but what people felt about it when it was happening".[35] And the role of gossip in a "shame-honour" culture such as that of ancient Athens should not be underestimated. If gossip did indeed "play with reputations",[36] how much more effectively could this be achieved on the stage? If "talk dragged details of men's private lives into the public arena for inspection and condemnation",[37] and if the arguments presented here are correct, then writers of tragedy will have capitalized on the fact. In a society that "lacked organized news media",[38] the theatre will have served as an effective means of dissecting rumour and gossip. The theatre emerges as the venue for experimental politics, where policies could be debated, or prominent personalities supported or ridiculed in ways that would not be possible in more conventional political meetings, not least because some of the protagonists might be absent from Athens. This was probably the case in 409 and 406, when Sophocles' targets were all in exile. The only way that the Athenian public could witness a debate between exiles was for it to be represented on the stage.

The civic aspect of the great dramatic festivals cannot be overemphasized, with (at least at the Great Dionysia) libations poured by the ten generals, the public display of the annual tribute in the theatre, the announcement of the names of civic benefactors, and the parade in full armour of young men whose fathers had died in battle and who had been raised at public expense.[39] This was not a likely setting for escapist drama but for plays – like those discussed here – that were fully integrated into political life. Euripides' financial involvement with one of Athens' most prominent politicians has already been noted. Sophocles' role as a politician is rarely given the prominence it deserves. Indeed, few individuals in recorded history have had such a long public career, much of it in what passed in the fifth century

35. G. M. Young, cited in S. Marcus, *The Other Victorians* (London: Weidenfeld & Nicolson, 1966), 111. Cf. B. S. Strauss, "The truth of [the anecdotes about Alcibiades' youthful adventures] hardly matters; much more important is that Alcibiades elicited them" ("*Oikos/Polis*: Towards a Theory of Athenian Paternal Ideology 450–399 BC", *Classica et Mediaevalia* **40** [1990], 101–27, esp. 122).

36. P. M. Spacks, *Gossip* (Chicago, IL: University of Chicago Press, 1985), 4; cf. V. Hunter, "Gossip and the Politics of Reputation in Classical Athens", *Phoenix* **44** (1990), 299–325.

37. Hunter, "Gossip and the Politics of Reputation", 322.

38. J. Ober, *Mass and Elite in Democratic Athens* (Princeton, NJ: Princeton University Press, 1989), 148. For comedy, see my *Pericles on Stage, passim*.

39. S. Goldhill, "The Great Dionysia and Civic Ideology", *Journal of Hellenic Studies* **107** (1987), 58–76.

BCE for political life. In 480 BCE, at the age of sixteen Sophocles was chosen to lead a choir of boys at the celebrations of the victory over the Persians at Salamis. He was the chairman of the board of *hellenotamiai* in 443/2, general in 441/0, and perhaps again in either 438/7 or 437/6. Then, in 412/11 BCE, nearly 70 years after his first appearance in public life, he was a *proboulos*, one of the board of ten officials appointed during a political emergency (Arist. *Rh*. 1419a).[40] Those who maintained that Sophocles was apolitical when it came to the theatre should never have been able to get away with it.

Athenian tragedy is of course great literature that provides magnificent poetry and powerful drama on timeless themes, but before doing this it required a basis in a contemporary historical situation. In essence, although not perhaps in esteem, the writer for the Athenian stage, whether of comedies or tragedies, resembled today's political cartoonist. Some cartoonists employ slapstick in order to ridicule a certain politician, while others might use austere and sombre means to make even more incisive comments on contemporary events; and it is essentially in the latter role that one would view the ancient tragedian. A clever device employed by writers for both the tragic and comic stage is what I have called "polymorphic characterization",[41] whereby different facets of an individual's personality or public image could be played by a different character on the stage.[42] Politicians today are colourless creatures for the most part, but within living memory we might perhaps have seen (had such a dramatic technique still been in use) a dramatic exploration of the political career of, for example, Lady Thatcher by means of an Iron Lady, St Francis of Assisi and Queen Boadicea (embodying the belligerent, sanctimonious and patriotic *personae* of the former British prime minister). Two or more of these individuals might be on the stage at the same time, sometimes interacting with each other, and sometimes playing opposite an assortment of equally varied caricatures of someone

---

40. Cf. P. Foucart, "Le Poète Sophocle et l'oligarchie des Quatre Cents", *Revue Philologique* **17** (1893), 1–10; U. von Wilamowitz-Moellendorff, *Aristoteles und Athen* 1 (Berlin: Weidmann, 1893), 102 n.6; W. M. Calder III, *Theatrokratia: Collected Papers on the Politics and Staging of Greco-Roman Tragedy*, R. Scott Smith (ed.) (Hildesheim: George Olms, 2005), 219–20 (with further literature); F. Ahl, *Two Faces of Oedipus: Sophocles'* Oedipus Tyrannus *and Seneca's* Oedipus (Ithaca, NY: Cornell University Press, 2008), 5–10.

41. Vickers, *Pericles on Stage*, xxvi–xxvii; 15–16.

42. The same technique was used by the psychotherapist and playwright Nikolai Nikolaivich Evreinov (1879–1953) in his *Theatrical Soul* (1912) (S. Carnicke, *The Theatrical Instinct: Nicolai Evreinov and the Russian Theater of the Early Twentieth Century* [Frankfurt: Lang, 1991]). It was also employed by W. B. Yeats, who adopted it from William Hale White, who had introduced "characters whose function it was to speak for another side of his own mind and test ironically the strength of his developing convictions" (D. Daiches, *Some Late Victorian Attitudes* [London: Deutsch, 1969], 97; Kiberd, *Inventing Ireland*, 446).

else. The message of tragedy was usually couched in mythical terms. It is thanks to the existence of polymorphic characterization that in *Antigone* we can recognize evocations of different facets of a single individual in Creon and the Chorus, or of another in *Oedipus at Colonus* in the characters of Theseus and Creon. There is, incidentally, much use of the technique in comedy, where an awareness of its presence removes at a stroke the problem of continuity that is said by some to disfigure some of Aristophanes' plays,[43] for the principal targets of the playwright's humour are in effect on stage throughout, in one evocation or another. It was, moreover, an especially useful technique for the exploration of complex personalities, such as that of Alcibiades.[44]

---

43. Aristophanes' plot construction has thus been described as "loose and faltering" (G. Norwood, *Greek Comedy* [London: Methuen, 1931], 302) and "inconsequential" (J. Henderson [ed.], *Aristophanes Lysistrata* [Oxford: Clarendon Press, 1987], lx). But with the aid of polymorphic characterization, Aristophanes' plots can be seen to be tightly constructed, rather than rambling and lacking in unity.

44. For example, Alcibiades was compared in antiquity to a chameleon (Plut. *Alc.* 23.4). G. F. Hertzberg writes of Alcibiades' "intellectual elasticity" (*Alkibiades: Der Staatsmann und Feldherr* [Halle: C. E. M. Pfeffer, 1853], 14).

2
Antigone, Pericles and Alcibiades

If modern interpretations of *Antigone* seem to be inexhaustible,[1] there is no end
to the problems of interpretation within the play itself either. Perhaps the most
notorious is the status of Antigone's speech just before she goes off to prison (904–
20). The problem was very well expressed by Goethe in 1829, in these words:

> There is a passage in Antigone which I always look upon as a blemish, and I
> would give a great deal for an apt philologist to prove that it is interpolated
> and spurious.
>
> After the heroine has, in the course of the piece, explained the noble motives
> for her action, and displayed the elevated purity of her soul, she at last, when
> she is led to death, brings forward a motive which is quite unworthy, and
> almost borders upon the comic.
>
> She says that, if she had been a mother, she would not have done, either
> for her dead children or for her dead husband, what she has done for her
> brother. "For," says she, "if my husband died I could have had another, and
> if my children died I could have had others by my new husband. But with
> my brother the case is different. I cannot have another brother; for since my
> mother and father are dead, there is no one to beget one."
>
> This is, at least, the bare sense of this passage, which in my opinion, when
> placed in the mouth of a heroine going to her death, disturbs the tragic tone, and
> appears to me very far-fetched to save her too much of dialectical calculation.
> As I said, I should like a philologist to show us that the passage is spurious.[2]

---

1. Cf. Morrison, "Femme Fatale", and p. 3 above.
2. R. Otto & P. Wersig, *Gespräche mit Goethe in den letzten Jahren seines Lebens/Johann Peter
   Eckermann* (Berlin: Aufbau-Verlag, 1982), 28 March 1827, translated by J. Oxenford as
   Conversations of Goethe with Eckermann and Soret (London: George Bell, 1874), 227–8.

He was not the first to make this observation, but his was the most influential. The lines are often deleted by editors, and paradoxically by those who want to see Antigone as the heroine, played by the most important actor.[3] But Antigone has comparatively few lines in any case and to rob her of these is to give her even less to say. In fact, as we shall see, Sophocles has portrayed the mentality of an adolescent with exquisite accuracy, and any parent having a row with a teenager, then or now, would recognize the situation and the quality of Antigone's reasoning.

Antigone as a production of 438 BCE

The fundamental problem is the date of *Antigone*. It is conventionally dated to one of the years 443–441 BCE, but powerful arguments exist for 438 BCE, when we know in any case that Sophocles won a dramatic victory (Eur. *Alc.* Arg. 2). More support may be found for a date of 438 in the way the outline of the plot, involving an unburied corpse, seems to echo the events after the fall of Samos to Pericles in 439, when prisoners were allegedly crucified, clubbed and left unburied (Plut. *Per.* 28.2). These events were so shocking that Thucydides chose to pass them over in silence, and Plutarch to dismiss the reports as irresponsible Samian propaganda. Modern scholars are divided between those who go for the "plaster saint" version of Pericles' career, according to which he could do no wrong, and those who accept that something rather nasty happened to the Samian prisoners.[4] Assuming for a moment that Pericles did punish the captives, the law would in fact have been on his side. The crucified Samians had been traitors, and thus did not merit burial.[5] The cruel punishment to which they were subjected (*apotympanismos*, whereby they

---

3. For example, Müller, *Sophokles, Antigone*.
4. G. Grote, whose aim was to rehabilitate Pericles, omits the story of the punishment of the Samians altogether (*A History of Greece*, new edn [London: John Murray, 1870], 5.292); cf. "calumnies" (Kagan, *Pericles of Athens*, 142 n.2); "exaggeration" (A. J. Podlecki, *Perikles and his Circle* [London: Routledge, 1998], 125–6); "The character of Pericles contradicts such a story without discussion" (C. Mackenzie, *Pericles* [London: Hodder & Stoughton, 1937], 233). For R. Meiggs, however, "the substance of the story rings true" (*The Athenian Empire* [Oxford: Clarendon Press, 1972], 192). Stadter also believes that archaeological evidence for *apotympanismos* "makes it likely that Duris' story is at least partially true" (*A Commentary on Plutarch's Pericles*, 258–9). The most satisfactory solution to the problem is that of F. Landucci Gattinoni, *Duride di Samo* (Rome: 'L'Erma' di Bretschneider, 1997), 231–4, who believes that Thucydides' silence in the matter can be accounted for by his wish to put Pericles in a favourable light, and that Duris' testimony comes from an independent Samian anti-Athenian source.
5. R. G. Lewis, "An Alternative Date for *Antigone*", *Greek, Roman and Byzantine Studies* 29 (1988), 35–50, esp. 47–8; cf. W. B. Tyrrell & L. J. Bennett, *Recapturing Sophocles' Antigone* (Lanham, MD: Rowman & Littlefield, 1998), 3–4.

were tied to boards and exposed until they died) existed, strange to say, because it absolved the perpetrators of the charge of murder in that the victims, like Antigone in the play, in effect committed suicide.[6] Nevertheless, it was held in some quarters that Pericles' action was somehow "not cricket". Perhaps exception was taken to Pericles' having allegedly hit the dying men (who had already been exposed for ten days) over the head with clubs.

Some confirmation that Pericles was guilty of awful things may be found in an anecdote that has Cimon's sister Elpinice chiding Pericles for his cruelty after the commemoration of the Athenian war dead (Plut. *Per.* 28, 5–7). According to Plutarch, Pericles' Samian victories "wonderfully flattered his vanity" (θαυμαστὸν δέ τι καὶ μέγα φρονῆσαι; *ibid.*); he claimed that since he had successfully besieged Samos in eighteen months his victory outranked the Greek achievement at Troy, which had taken ten years to achieve. It will presently be suggested that Sophocles might have wanted to diminish Pericles' reputation while at the same time distancing himself from the excesses (with which he was still, however, being associated centuries later; Strab. 14.1.18).

It is a commonplace to say that Sophocles was a personal friend of Pericles. But even a superficial reading of the relevant sources reveals that their relationship perhaps had an edge to it. One of Pericles' "very few recorded sayings" (Plut. *Per.* 8.7) was a rebuke to the playwright (who had cast lustful looks at a young cup-bearer) that "a general ought to keep not only his hands clean, but his eyes" (*ibid.*; Cic. *Off.* 1.40; Val. Max. 4.3. ext.1). And in the context of another homoerotic encounter, in which he outwitted a foolish youth, Sophocles said, "I am practising strategy [μελετῶ στρατηγεῖν], gentlemen, because Pericles said that while I could write poetry, I did not know how to be a general [στρατηγεῖν]" (Ion Chius *P* 392 F 6, ap. Ath. 13.603e–604e). Neither of these tales (which are the sum total of the testimonia) suggests friendship; rather, they suggest the polite face of a fundamental antipathy. Pericles' personal tastes ran in a completely different direction. It will be argued later that Sophocles' position was highly unsympathetic towards Pericles; in particular on account of what Pericles is said to have done to the Samian prisoners after the war.

R. G. Lewis has shown how vulnerable is the traditional dating to 443–441 BCE, and how, given that Sophocles was the chairman of the board of *hellenota-miai* in 443/2, and general in 441/0, he would probably have been too busy to have written three tragedies and a satyr play and seen them into production before

---

6. W. M. Calder III, "Sophokles' Political Tragedy, *Antigone*", *Greek, Roman and Byzantine Studies* **9** (1968), 389–407, esp. 400 n.48.

439.[7] He did not serve as general in 439/8, and perhaps then having more time for writing composed the works that definitely won the dramatic competition for 438.[8] This, on balance, is the likeliest date for *Antigone*.[9] The implications would be considerable. Not least, Wilamowitz's dictum about Sophoclean tragedies bearing no relation to contemporary events[10] is called into question. Rather, contemporary issues will have had a substantial influence on the plot. The audience did not go to the theatre to learn yet more of the history of the House of Laius, any more than we read *Animal Farm* to learn about the everyday lives of countryfolk. Rather, they went to see dramas couched in myth and which might also play allusively on current events, often via personalities who were at the forefront of everyone's minds. One would not claim that there was a one-to-one correspondence between Sophocles' characters and historical figures, but that his rich and subtly symbolic language and plotting would have inevitably recalled situations well known in their day, some of which are preserved in the anecdotal record relating to Pericles and his extended family. The year 438 was a time of general unease at home and abroad, with the effects of the pacification of Samos not altogether worked through. The curbs on comedy (Schol. Ar. *Ra.* 67) that lasted from 440/39 until 437/6 suggest that Pericles was unsure of public reaction to the Samian war, which, it was popularly believed, was started at the urging of his mistress Aspasia,[11] the woman for whom he had cast aside his wife, the mother of his sons Xanthippus and Paralus.

The tragedy of Creon

In the play, by far the biggest part is that of Creon. He has most lines to deliver and, unlike Antigone, is on stage for most of the action. There are arguments for his having been the protagonist, and for the role having been played by the leading actor.[12] It

---

7. At some time before 443 BCE all but one of a board of *hellenotamiai* were executed. The event "was unlikely to encourage negligent insouisance in later boards" (Lewis, "An Alternative Date for *Antigone*", 37).
8. Eur. *Alc.* Arg. 2; Lewis, "An Alternative Date for *Antigone*", 43.
9. The sources allow for a second generalship in either 438/7 or 437/6 BCE against the Anaeans, for which the base was Samos (Lewis, "An Alternative Date for *Antigone*", 40–41). This might be Sophocles' "appointment as general on Samos", earned by "esteem from his production of *Antigone*" (Soph. *Ant.* Arg. 1).
10. Wilamowitz, "Excurse zum Oedipus des Sophokles", 59. See above, p. 1.
11. Lewis, "An Alternative Date for *Antigone*", 44.
12. K. Frey, "Der Protagonist in der Antigone des Sophokles", *Neue Jahrbücher* 1, **117** (1878), 460–64; Calder, "Sophokles' Political Tragedy, *Antigone*", 390. G. M. Sifakis, "The One-actor Rule in Greek Tragedy", in *Stage Directions: Essays in Ancient Drama in Honour of E. W. Handley*, A.

has often been noted that Creon's insistence that the interests of the state should always come before those of family (182–90) resemble the views that Thucydides puts into Pericles' mouth (Thuc. 2.38–46 and 2.60). But there is more to say on this particular point, for just as Creon's first speech (162–210) contains obtrusive references to himself and his personal opinions ("ἐγώ, ἐμός, κ.τ.λ. occur nine times ... often in emphatic positions"),[13] the same is true of Pericles' second Thucydidean speech, where ἐγώ, ἐμόν and ἐμοί occur twelve times between them.[14]

According to Aristotle, Pericles' oratory was characterized by the frequent use of striking metaphor. He left no writings (Plut. *Per.* 8.7), and while extant examples of his sayings are few, they are impressive: the Samians were "like children who have been given food, but cry nevertheless" and the Boeotians "like holm-oaks that batter their limbs against one another" (Arist. *Rh.* 1407a). Aristotle, in analysing the different kinds of metaphor, begins with "those by analogy, such as when Pericles said that the youth fallen in battle was like the spring taken from the year" (*ibid.* 1411a). A recent account of Creon's language is identical:

> [Creon] habitually starts out and ends his speeches with generalizations, and relies heavily on analogies and abstractions, often in the form of simile, metaphor or γνώμη. His use of harsh metaphors drawn from coinage and metal-working, from military organization and warfare, from the commanding and steering of a ship, and from the breaking and yoking of animals, lends an especially rigid and domineering tone to his utterances.[15]

Our view of Pericles is for the most part derived from the rather sympathetic figure that Thucydides gives us, and he is sparing in the images he includes in his Periclean speeches; the only one being his injunction to view the Athenians' loss of the use of their land in the light of such transitory possessions as "a garden and other embellishments of wealth" (κηπίον καὶ ἐνκαλλώπισμα πλούτου; 2.62.3).[16] Plutarch, however, cites Ion of Chios, who knew Pericles and was less than impressed with

---

Griffiths (ed.), 13–24 (London: Institute of Classical Studies, 1995) argues that different actors may have shared the parts of Antigone and Creon, greatly aided by the fact that masks were worn.

13. M. Griffith (ed.), *Sophocles* Antigone (Cambridge: Cambridge University Press, 1999), 156.
14. ἐγώ (Thuc. 2.60.2, 2.61.2 [καὶ ἐγὼ μὲν ὁ αὐτός εἰμι ...], 2.62.1, 2.62.2); ἐμέ (2.60.4, 2.64.1 [twice]); ἐμοί (2.60.2, 2.60.5, 2.64.2); ἐμόν (2.61.2).
15. Griffith, *Sophocles* Antigone, 36.
16. Perhaps an oblique allusion (made with the gift of Thucydidean hindsight) to Alcibiades' responsibility for the Athenians' eventual defeat: Alcibiades had had a garden named after him (Plut. *Alc.* 24.7), and was at times very rich indeed (e.g. Lys. 19.52; Plut. *Alc.* 10.3; Ael. *VH* 3.28; Const. Porph. *De virt. et vit.* 1.232).

his lack of social graces: "Pericles was overbearing and insolent in conversation, and his pride had in it a great deal of contempt for others" (Plut. *Per.* 5.3), which corresponds closely to the Creon of *Antigone*.

More Periclean evocations in Creon's language include the frequent use of the words φρονεῖν (to be resolute), νοῦς (mind), δίκη (justice) and their cognates. These are all marked words closely associated with Pericles. The relevant testimonia are replete with references to Pericles' φρόνημα (his resolve);[17] Νοῦς (Mind) was central to the thought of Pericles' favourite philosopher, Anaxagoras (Plut. *Them.* 2.5); and Pericles' constant concern was for δικαιοσύνη (honesty or incorruptibility; Plut. *Per.* 2.5), given that "he had so much opportunity for gain".[18] Another frequent word in *Antigone* is μηχανή and cognates and compounds (79, 90, 92, 175, 349, 363, 364); if Pericles is in the frame, they would be allusions to his novel skill with siege-engines (μηχαναί), recently seen to good effect at Samos (Plut. *Per.* 27.3).

Another linguistic peculiarity of Pericles' own diction was, judging by speeches in Thucydides, the use of expressions such as περὶ βραχέως (for a small matter), διὰ μικρόν (for a trifle), ἐπὶ βραχείᾳ ... προφάσει (on [no] small plea) and τὸ ... βραχύ (the small matter), all within a few lines of each other in the *Histories* (Thuc. 1.140.4–141.1). Creon seems to use something of the sort, in urging brevity on Antigone at 446: σὺ δ᾽ εἰπέ μοι μὴ μῆκος, ἀλλὰ συντόμως (Tell me, not at length, but briefly) and in his reference to "a little curb" (σμικρῷ χαλινῷ; 477) with which recalcitrant horses might be broken.[19] In addition, the observation of the Chorus at 1327, βράχιστα γὰρ κράτιστα τὰν ποσίν κακά (Briefest is best when trouble is in the way), perhaps marks its members out, polymorphically,[20] as extensions in some way of the Periclean characterization: perhaps to indicate the more reasonable side of Pericles' character. If so, this reinforces the view that the play is principally an evocation of Pericles and that Creon is the main character in it.

Repetition was another well-known feature of Pericles' way of speaking; Thucydides makes his Pericles say: "Face your enemies not just with φρονήματι [confidence] but with καταφρονήματι [a sense of superiority]" (Thuc. 2.62.3), and Aristophanes has his Periclean Aeschylus in *Frogs* say stupid things such as "here I come and hither I return" (*Ra.* 1154), or "I call upon my father to hear, to hearken"

---

17. For example, Plut. *Per.* 5.1, 8.1, 10.7, 17.4, 31.1, 36.8, 39.1; Stadter, *A Commentary on Plutarch's Pericles*, 75; cf. the Periclean Strepsiades' visit to the Phrontistery in *Clouds* (Vickers, *Pericles on Stage*, 22–41).

18. Stadter, *A Commentary on Plutarch's Pericles*, 193.

19. An appropriate image, if the one to be tamed was based on an Alcibiades who was devoted to horses (e.g. Thuc. 6.15.3).

20. On "polymorphic characterization", whereby different dramatic characters might represent different facets of an historical individual's personality, see Chapter 1, pp. 11–12.

(*ibid.*, 1174).[21] Creon is especially prone to repetition after successive disasters have fallen upon him: ἰὼ φρενῶν δυσφρόνων ἁμαρτήματα (woe for the sins of a dispirited spirit; 1261, on seeing the body of his son) neatly combines Periclean φρόνημα with repetition, while φεῦ φεῦ, ἰὼ πόνοι βροτῶν δύσπονοι (woe, woe for the toilsome toils of men; 1276) combines both repetition and allusions to πόνος (toil [= blood, sweat and tears]), which were apparently such a prominent feature of Pericles' oratory that Thucydides artfully packs his last speech with a series of references to πόνος (Thuc. 2.62.1, 2.62.3, 2.63.1, 2.64.3, 2.64.6).[22] ὤμοι μοι (Ah me) at 1317, when Creon is finally aware of the enormities that his unsympathetic attitude has brought about, is followed by thrice ἐγώ (at 1319 and 1320), culminating in the successive ἴτω ἴτω (Let it come, let it come) at 1329 and 1331.

The encounters between Creon and the guard, the "low class citizen soldier",[23] perhaps reveal Sophocles' view of Periclean democracy, in that the guard stands as a representative of the kind of people who formed Pericles' constituency.[24] It is ironic that the guard outwits Creon, but significant that he lives in fear of him. The threat of being crucified alive (ζῶντες κρεμαστοί; 309) must have been a real one if the tales of the recent Samian excesses were true. If the role of Creon somehow, however allusively, resonates with recent actions of Pericles, then the historical statesman's power clearly rested on something more than statesmanship, and Haemon's thoughts on how the citizens were afraid of Creon's very frown (688–99) again illustrate the likely role of fear during Pericles' ascendancy.[25]

Pericles was, moreover, extremely careful with his money. His family "complained at his exact regulation of his daily expenses, which allowed none of the superfluities common in great and wealthy households, but which made debit and credit exactly balance each other" (Plut. *Per.* 16.5, 36.2). He was also very much aware of the pitfalls of corruption, and for the most part managed to avoid them (*ibid.*

---

21. M. Vickers, "Aristophanes *Frogs*: Nothing to do with Literature", *Athenaeum* **89** (2001), 187–201, esp. 191. This is the Aeschylus who says that "one should not nurture a lion's whelp in the state, but if he be fully grown, it were best to humour him" (Ar. *Ra.* 1431–3), a saying elsewhere attributed to Pericles (Val. Max. 7.2.7).

22. Cf. A. Boegehold, "A Dissent at Athens *ca.* 424–421 BC", *Greek, Roman and Byzantine Studies* **23** (1982), 147–56, esp. 154–5; and compare the tautologous ὅσους πονήσας καὶ διεξελθὼν πόνους (how many labours I laboured and passed through; Soph. *Phil.* 1419, discussed p. 78, below).

23. Griffith, *Sophocles* Antigone, 165.

24. For Pericles' democratic affectations, see Plut. *Per.* 7.3, 14, 15.1–2, 17.1, 23.1.

25. Cf. Thuc. 2.65.9, where Pericles could reduce the citizenry to alarm simply by what he said. W. M. Calder III, "The Anti-Periklean Intent of Aeschylus' *Eumenides*", in *Aischylos und Pindar: Studien zu Werk und Nachwirkung*, E. G. Schmidt (ed.), 217–23 (Berlin: Akademie-Verlag, 1981) and *Theatrokratia*, 28, reminds us of the traditions that Pericles arranged the deaths of Ephialtes and the Athenian herald Athenocritus.

15.3–16.9). This probably lies somewhere behind Sophocles' portrayal of Creon as mean-minded and as one who naturally assumes, on several occasions, that his interlocutors are venal and only interested in monetary gain (221–2, 310–12, 1045–7, 1327), which gives a slightly perverse, but perhaps accurate, spin on Pericles' incorruptibility. Then, Creon's "coldness" has been remarked on;[26] we might well compare what has been called the "bleakness" with which Thucydides' Pericles consoled the relatives of the dead in the Funeral Speech.[27] Conversely, some might choose to see Pericles' coolness under fire and the dignity he displayed in moments of acute crisis.

Creon's language "sometimes reminds one of sophistic debates", and "the *Antigone* reflects contemporary political and intellectual language more obviously than any other Sophoclean play".[28] All very true, but the "intellectual fussiness"[29] is easily accountable for in terms of recent philosophical debate at Athens. Tony Long has a revealing passage:

The Guard, ever eager to show his sophistication, tries to locate the source of Creon's anger, asking if it is his ears or his ψυχή which are distressed (317). When Creon angrily retorts, τί δὲ ῥυθμίζεις τὴν ἐμὴν λύπην ὅπου, the Guard calmly distinguishes the anger which he causes in Creon's ears from the anger Creon's φρένες feel towards the perpetrator of the crime (319).[30]

This "pseudo-sophistic analysis of the senses"[31] is all too reminiscent of the kind of distinction made when "some athlete accidentally killed Epitimius of Pharsalus with a javelin ... and Pericles spent the whole day arguing with Protagoras whether in strict accuracy the javelin, or the man who threw it, or the stewards of the games, ought to be considered the authors of the accident" (Plut. *Per.* 36.5). Pericles is again somehow in the frame, and the plotting resonates with allusions to his discussions with philosophers that were common gossip, if only because his fractious son Xanthippus had publicly ridiculed them (*ibid.* 36.5–6).

26. A. Brown (ed.), *Sophocles:* Antigone (Warminster: Aris & Phillips, 1987), 146.
27. A. W. Gomme, A. Andrewes & K. J. Dover, *A Historical Commentary on Thucydides* (Oxford: Clarendon Press, 1948–81), 2.143 (on Thuc. 2.45.2).
28. A. A. Long, *Language and Thought in Sophocles: A Study of Abstract Nouns and Poetic Technique* (London: Athlone, 1968), 53.
29. Brown, *Sophocles:* Antigone, 147.
30. Long, *Language and Thought in Sophocles*, 53.
31. S. Goldhill, "The Thrill of Misplaced Laughter", in *ΚΩΜΩΙΔΟΤΡΑΓΩΙΔΙΑ: intersezioni del tragico e del comico nel teatro del V secolo a.C.*, E. Medda, M. S. Mirto & M. P. Pattoni (eds), 83–102 (Pisa: Edizioni della Normale, 2006), 90.

Next there is what is "perhaps the coarsest line in Greek tragedy"[32] at 569: when Creon tells Ismene who is pleading for Antigone's life "Others have furrows that can be ploughed". If Creon does somehow "come forward" as Pericles, this is highly appropriate, for it aptly, if somewhat invidiously, resonates with the character of one who "was much given to *aphrodisia*" (Clearch. *FHG* 2.314 ap. Ath. 13.589d), and who was called "King of the Satyrs" on the stage (Hermipp. *PCG* 47.1 ap. Plut. *Per.* 33.8). We noted earlier that there might have been some kind of tension between Sophocles and Pericles arising from the former's pederastic tastes. Pericles' inclinations lay in another direction, and Sophocles in effect says "there are plenty more where she came from",[33] thus indirectly drawing cruel and crude attention to the string of women whose company Pericles enjoyed.[34]

If Creon is on the stage for most of the play, there will be long periods when he is silent. He is thus a "silent, menacing presence" at 582–625,[35] and it is likely that he remains silent on stage after the argument with Haemon while the Chorus sing their hymn to Eros and Aphrodite.[36] Creon actually states, "I would not be silent (σιωπήσαιμι) if I saw ruin rather than safety (σωτηρία) coming to the citizens" (185–6). This is another way in which the characterization of Creon will have set up resonances with the public image of Pericles, for whom silence in public was apparently a typical feature; so much so that it was lampooned in *Frogs* when the Periclean Aeschylus is silent when he first appears on stage (σιγᾷς; 832), and when he is criticized for having characters sitting alone, in silence (σιωπῇ; 916).[37] We know in any case that Pericles quietly endured criticism (πρᾴως καὶ σιωπῇ; Plut. *Per.* 34.1) and obloquy (σιωπῇ; *ibid.* 5.2). The description of Creon as στρατηγός in line 8 is moreover in keeping with a Periclean characterization, for Pericles held the position of general more frequently than any other Athenian before or after (indeed in most years since 448/7).[38] Creon's entry from the field at 155, probably in armour,[39] will have presented the opportunity to show him helmeted in the manner familiar from Pericles' portraits.[40]

Together, these various poles, branches and twigs – arguments of varying strength – constitute a "wigwam" of the kind described in the Preface (p. vii). While such

---

32. Brown, *Sophocles: Antigone*, 168.
33. Griffith, *Sophocles Antigone*, 216.
34. For a list of at least ten (not including his wife or his mistress), see my *Pericles on Stage*, 135.
35. Brown 1987.
36. Griffith, *Sophocles Antigone*, 255.
37. Vickers, "Aristophanes *Frogs*", 190.
38. R. Develin, *Athenian Officials 684–321 BC* (Cambridge: Cambridge University Press, 1989), 81–93.
39. Calder, "Sophokles' Political Tragedy, *Antigone*", 393; *Theatrokratia*, 79.
40. G. M. A. Richter, *Portraits of the Greeks* (London: Phaidon, 1965), 1.102–4, figs 429–43.

features as egocentricity, use of striking metaphor, repetitiveness, menace, concern over money, sophistic argument, silence in public and generalship do not individually point to Pericles, when taken together they make up a recognizable portrait of the statesman, even if that portrait is an unsympathetic one.

The Chorus

It was suggested above that the Chorus might be viewed as a polymorphic extension of the Periclean symbolism with which the figure of Creon is imbued, introduced perhaps to give a more nuanced picture of the protagonist. If this is indeed the case (and it would certainly bear out Aristotle's observation that the Chorus should be "part of the whole and take a share in the action ... as in Sophocles" (Arist. *Po.* 1456a), it will account for the rationalism and humanism of what has been called the "highly problematic"[41] First Stasimon (332–75). If it relates "to the intellectual climate in which Sophocles and his audience lived",[42] it will be one largely engendered by Protagoras, who taught in Athens between 454 and 444 BCE.[43] This is doubtless why Pericles "shared the secular views of his teachers and friends. He was free of the common superstitions of his time, and he sought natural, rational explanations for the phenomena he observed in the world around him".[44] The theme of ἄτη that pervades the Second Stasimon (582–625), and which can afflict a family over generations, corresponds well to the Alcmaeonid curse with which Pericles' family was troubled (Thuc. 1.126–7), and will inevitably have brought it to mind. The bold imagery of the language ("earthquake; sea-storm; a plant harvested as it strains towards the light; the glittering residence of never-sleeping Zeus; a foot stepping on hot embers")[45] has much in common with Pericles' frequent use of striking metaphor (see above), not to mention his practice of "adorning his oratory with apt illustrations drawn from physical science" (Plut. 8.1–2), and will again have created suggestive echoes. The Chorus's hymn to Eros and Aphrodite in the Third Stasimon (781–800) is appropriate if oblique (or "emphatic"; see p. 8, above) allusion is made to a Pericles who "was much given to *aphrodisia*", and if Creon remains silently on stage during the song it is indeed likely that "its tenor and significance

41. Brown, *Sophocles:* Antigone.
42. R. W. B. Burton, *The Chorus in Sophocles' Tragedies* (Oxford: Clarendon Press, 1980), 101.
43. J. S. Morrison, "Protagoras in Athenian Public Life", *Classical Quarterly* **35** (1941), 1–16; W. K. C. Guthrie, *A History of Greek Philosophy* (Cambridge: Cambridge University Press, 1969), 3.63–8.
44. Kagan, *Pericles of Athens*, 178.
45. Griffith, *Sophocles* Antigone, 219.

may be crucially affected".[46] The fates that befall Danae, Lycurgus and Cleopatra and her children in the Fourth Stasimon in a crescendo of cruelty (944–87) may well have a "far from obvious" bearing on Antigone's situation,[47] but they are highly pertinent in the context of a tragedy that probably took as its starting-point the stories told about Pericles having "[taken] the trierarchs and marines of the Samians to the agora at Miletus, bound them to planks, and after they had been left for ten days and were in a miserable state, knocked them on the head with clubs and cast out their bodies without burial" (Plut. *Per.* 28.2). Again, a "wigwam" argument, but one that explains, indeed explains away, the difficulties with which the interpretation of the choruses of *Antigone* has been beset.

Haemon

So much for Creon. What about the other characters: Haemon, Creon's son; Eurydice, his wife; and above all Antigone and Ismene? Does their characterization resonate with any historical individuals? If it does, and if Creon "comes forward" as Pericles, we might well guess that the allusions are to other members of Pericles' extended family. That this sort of investigation is supposed to be off-limits to scholars only adds to the interest of the exercise.

Take Haemon first. It is clear that Creon's relationship with his son is not a happy one. Their encounter on stage is an early example of a debate "across the generation gap".[48] Their discussion begins politely enough, with Haemon saying appropriately placatory things in the hope of gaining his father's goodwill. But Creon's refusal to allow Haemon even to consider marrying Antigone after what she has done is met with increasing frustration on the young man's side. Their disagreement culminates with Haemon declaring that his father will never set eyes on him again, and suggesting that he should "Rave, living with those of your loved ones who are willing <to put up with you>" (765).[49] All this closely parallels Pericles' rather public quarrels with his eldest son Xanthippus, who was at least nineteen in 438, and quite possibly older,[50] and as a young man had quarrelled bitterly with his

---

46. *Ibid.*, 255.
47. *Ibid.*, 283.
48. Strauss, *Fathers and Sons in Athens*, 136–48; cf. E. W. Handley, "Aristophanes and the Generation Gap", in *Tragedy, Comedy and the Polis: Papers from the Greek Drama Conference, Nottingham 18–20 July 1990*, A. H. Sommerstein *et al.* (eds), 417–30 (Bari: Levante editori, 1993); Vickers, *Pericles on Stage*, 42–58.
49. Griffith, *Sophocles* Antigone, 252.
50. Stadter, *A Commentary on Plutarch's* Pericles, 326.

father. Their differences were essentially over money, but Xanthippus also spread rumours that Pericles had had an intrigue with his daughter-in-law, Xanthippus' wife. Their quarrel was to be unresolved down to the time of Xanthippus' death in the plague of 430/29 BCE. Xanthippus' wife was "young and spendthrift", and he initially fell out with his father over the latter's stinginess. We hear of Xanthippus being so angry with Pericles over one financial issue that he "was enraged and abused his father, sneering at his way of life and his discussions with the sophists" (Plut. *Per.* 36.4). Plutarch actually tells us who one of the "sophists" was, namely Protagoras, which serves as a possible chronological marker, in as much as Protagoras was in Athens until 444.[51]

When Sir Lawrence Alma-Tadema was composing his *Phidias and the Frieze of the Parthenon, Athens* now in the Birmingham Museum and Art Gallery, he read his Plutarch very carefully, and having noted that Pericles suffered from a congenital malformation of the skull, gave Xanthippus a similarly shaped head.[52] We do not have any direct information concerning the way Xanthippus spoke, but if Haemon's language resembles that of Creon (as it seems to), then allusions may be there that intensify any possible Periclean reference. The metaphors about yielding and unyielding trees at 712–18 are precisely the sort of thing we hear about in the minute corpus of authentic Periclean utterances; at least "holm-oaks battering their limbs against one another" (cf. Arist. *Rh.* 1407a) belong to the same register. Then Haemon's pleonasm at 763–4, where he says "Never will you see, looking with your eyes, my face again", is the kind of Periclean utterance that Aristophanes makes fun of in *Frogs*, and which we have just seen Sophocles exploiting. Then the scandalous stories about Pericles' carrying-on with his daughter-in-law may ultimately lie behind Creon's statement at 571 to the effect that he would not like "evil wives for [his] sons", and Ismene's enquiry at 574, as to whether Creon "will rob [his] son of this woman", is perhaps similarly based on the public image of the Periclean ménage.

Aspasia

But there is probably yet another woman lurking behind what Sophocles makes Creon and Haemon say to each other. Creon warns his son not to "dethrone [his] reason for pleasure's sake" and end up with "an evil woman to share [his] bed and

---

51. Plut. *Per.* 11.5; D.L. 9.50; Morrison, "Protagoras in Athenian Public Life".
52. M. Vickers, "The *Dramatis Personae* of Alma-Tadema's *Phidias and the Frieze of the Parthenon, Athens*", *Assaph: Studies in Art History* **10–11** (2005–6), 235–9.

home" (648–51). This sounds very much like an oblique allusion not so much to Xanthippus' domestic arrangements as to Pericles' own, all the more effective in the mouth of Creon. For it was said of Pericles that "it was thought that he began the war with the Samians in order to please Aspasia", a woman who "possessed so great an influence and ability that the leading politicians of the day were at her feet" (Plut. *Per.* 24.1-2; cf. 25.1). Similarly, Creon's criticism of his son taking second place to a woman (746) and the charge that his son is "a slave to a woman" (756) are probably intended to put a hypocritical slant on the accusations.

If Creon does "comes forward" as a metaphor for Pericles, his wife Eurydice will somehow have evoked Aspasia. Eurydice is not on stage for long, but the way in which she describes her dallying by the doorway of her house at 1185–8 looks like an oblique allusion to Pericles's practice of never having gone in or out of his house without embracing and kissing Aspasia passionately (Plut. *Per.* 24.9; cf. Ath. 13.589e); and if we know this we can be sure that Sophocles did. We may even charge Sophocles with his own act of cruelty in making Eurydice die a gruesome death; but the curse on Creon that Eurydice utters with her dying breath (1304–5) will have been even crueller, in that it was perhaps the most powerful way – all the stronger for being allusive – in which Sophocles could truly hurt the main target of his criticism, who valued his relationship with Aspasia above all else.

Creon has recently been called "an ordinary, self-centred, unimaginative man, invested with more responsibility than he can carry":[53] an immense contrast, but probably a deliberate one, with the hero of Samos who had carried, but left unburied, all before him. To make a character on the stage reproduce Pericles' stock phrases and peculiarities of speech, and to make him interact with recognizable members of his household was a clever, but hardly unparalleled, means of criticism. The mythological veneer enabled the playwright to be if anything more direct in his criticism, while at the same time distancing himself. Or rather, he does not distance himself, but engages in an analysis of what happened that is richer and more evocative (and safer) than any explicit account of Pericles' cruelty might have been. The dramatic stage was very much part of Athenian political life, and once we recall that a dramatic festival was the occasion for the pouring of libations by the generals, for the display of the annual tribute, for the praise of civic benefactors, and the parade in armour of war orphans,[54] then we can understand how plays might have a political resonance, and how the stage – whether tragic or comic – might be the place where things could be said that were impossible to say in other contexts.

---

53. Brown, *Sophocles:* Antigone, 7.
54. Goldhill, "The Great Dionysia and Civic Ideology".

Alcibiades

But there are other family members to consider. Ever since 447 BCE, Pericles had been joint guardian of Alcibiades and Cleinias, the sons of the war hero Cleinias, who had died at Coronea.[55] Both boys were a handful. The single reference we have to Cleinias tells us a lot about both. Pericles, afraid "that Cleinias would be corrupted by Alcibiades, took him away, and placed him in the house of Ariphron – his fellow guardian – to be educated; but before six months had elapsed, Ariphron sent him back, not knowing what to do with him" (Pl. *Prt.* 320a). Relations between Pericles and his delinquent wards can never have been easy. Stories were told about the infant Alcibiades' wilfulness and obduracy: of his having held up a cart driven by a peasant that threatened to disturb a game of knucklebones by lying down in front of it and refusing to budge (Plut. *Alc.* 2.3–4); of his having as a boy (παῖς ὤν) run away from home to the house of an admirer; of his having taken a mistress when under age, "suffering terrible things, but performing worse", and – most significant, this – boasting that "dressed in women's clothes ... he attended symposia undetected" (Lib. *Fr.* 50.2.12–13). Indeed, Alcibiades' "ambiguous sexuality"[56] is a feature of Plutarch's account of his career, from the charge made against the youthful wrestler that he bit his opponent "like a woman" (Plut. *Alc.* 2.3) to Alcibiades having been buried by his mistress Timandra dressed in her own clothes (*ibid.*, 39.7).[57]

It was only with the greatest reluctance that I admitted even to myself that there might somehow be an evocation of Alcibiades in the figure of Antigone. But odd as it sounds at first, the idea not only works, but enables us – as we shall presently see – to explain away the major difficulty with the play, namely the bizarre speech to which Goethe took such exception. Rather than being thoroughly un-Sophoclean, it is part of Sophocles' skilful character-building. The wilful, headstrong, Antigone has much in common with Alcibiades, who will have been fourteen in 438 and presumably already boasting about dressing as a woman.

Just as the character of Creon might be held to incorporate invidious echoes of Pericles, that of Antigone embodies many personality traits peculiar to Alcibiades. For all that he was very young, these will have been well known to the audience. Even as a child he was one of the richest individuals in Athens, was the object of widespread attention from would-be admirers (Plut. *Alc.* 4–6), and was already

---

55. An inscription (Develin, *Athenian Officials 684–321 BC*, 429; *SEG* 41 [1991] 9; 50 [2000] 21–22, no. 45) has Alcibiades proposing legislation in 422/21 BCE, which implies that he was already thirty years old, and thus born in 452/51 BCE.

56. Duff, "Plutarch on the Childhood of Alkibiades", 97.

57. See further, *ibid.*, 96.

an influential arbiter of taste. For example, while still a schoolboy he objected to playing the *aulos*, in that it disfigured the face and inhibited conversation. He gave up the instrument himself, and "induced his friends to do so, and all the youth of Athens soon heard and approved of Alcibiades' derision of the *aulos* and those who learned it. In consequence of this the *aulos* went entirely out of fashion, and was regarded with contempt" (Plut. *Alc.* 2.5–7).[58]

It is not that Alcibiades had a bad teacher; elsewhere, Athenaeus reports Duris of Samos saying that he was taught the *aulos* by the famous Pronomus (Ath. 4. 184d; cf. Paus. 9.12.5). Significantly, Duris includes this information in a book entitled *Euripides and Sophocles*, and it is difficult to explain why such a topic should have been discussed there unless he had a tragedy – perhaps a particular tragedy – in mind. "'Let the children of the Thebans', Alcibiades used to say, 'play the *aulos*, for they know not how to speak'" (Plut. *Alc.* 2.7). How exquisite of Sophocles, there-fore, to evoke Alcibiades in the person of Antigone, who was very much a "child of Thebes", and how very nice of him to make use of Alcibiades' linguistic pecu-liarities as part of his image building. For it might fairly be said that Alcibiades "knew not how to speak", since throughout his life he preserved a childish speech defect whereby he pronounced "r" as "l" (*ibid.* 1.6–8).[59] In addition, he regularly, but unusually for Greek, began sentences with καί (and), since he often spoke in an excited fashion.[60] One does not have to invoke wigwams here, for this is very strong circumstantial evidence. Duris, moreover, reckoned his own descent from Alcibiades (Duris *FGrH* 76 F 76 ap. *Alc.* 32.2), and will doubtless have been aware of his forebear's regular implicit presence in the works of Euripides and Sophocles.

How might things work in practice? If there are to be any echoes of Alcibiades in *Antigone* at all we might expect to be made aware of them in the opening lines. And if Sophocles did have Alcibiades in mind in creating his Antigone he will have made her speak like him, pronouncing *rho* as *lambda*. There is a fine instance where Antigone is explaining the situation to Ismene (and, of course, to the audience), of a pun of a kind that recurs in Alcibiadean contexts throughout the later fifth

---

58. Cf. "The extraordinary effect which Alcibiades' rejection of the *aulos* has on the other boys and on public opinion generally prefigures his later popularity and influence, and demonstrates the effectiveness of his speech and his charisma" (Duff, "Plutarch on the Childhood of Alkibiades", 104).

59. Alcibiades' son was to adopt both his father's gait and mode of speech: κλασαυχενεύεται τε καὶ τραυλίζεται ("he bends his neck in an affected way and pronounces *rho* as *lambda*": Archipp. ap. Plut. *Alc.* 1.8). For a good discussion of the condition of traulism (or lambdacism), see Y. V. O'Neill, *Speech and Speech Disorders in Western Thought before 1600* (Westport, CT: Greenwood, 1980).

60. D. P. Tompkins, "Stylistic Characterization in Thucydides: Nicias and Alcibiades", *Yale Classical Studies* **22** (1972), 181–214.

century. The most graphic example is in Aristophanes' *Thesmophoriazusae* (168), where Philocles, Aeschylus' nephew (who was also a tragedian) is under discussion. It is said of him that αἰσχρὸς ὢν αἰσχρῶς ποιεῖ (being ugly, he writes in an ugly manner), but in the mouth of one who shared Alcibiades' speech defect, this would play on Αἰσχύλειος ὢν Αἰσχυλειῶς ποιεῖ (being Aeschylean, he writes in an Aeschylean manner), which is neat, for a nephew of Aeschylus.[61] Sophocles gives us the first of many examples of such wordplay in line 5, where αἰσχρόν (shameful) will have played on Αἰσχυλόν (Aeschylus), the Aeschylean "bait" having been laid in line 2, where the "evils from Oedipus" will have recalled Aeschylus' trilogy of the House of Laius, which will have been an influential source of knowledge of Theban mythology.[62]

Antigone's third sentence may be translated as "What is this proclamation [κήρυγμα] they say the general [τὸν στρατηγόν] has just published to the whole city?" (7–8). This can be read as an oblique allusion to a story told about Alcibiades' boyhood described by his contemporary Antiphon in these words:

Alcibiades as a boy [παῖς ὤν] ran away from home to the house of one of his admirers Democrates. When Ariphron proposed to have [his disappearance] proclaimed [ἐπικηρύττειν], Pericles [the στρατηγός *par excellence*] forbade it, saying that if he was dead, he would only be found one day sooner because of the proclamation [διὰ τὸ κήρυγμα], while if he was safe, he would be disgraced for the rest of his life. (Antiph. *Fr.* 66 ap. Plut. *Per.* 3.2)

And Plutarch, as often, purports not to believe the story "which [was] written by an enemy with the avowed purpose of defaming his character" (*ibid.*).[63] But if Sophocles did somehow have Alcibiades in mind in composing *Antigone*, he was not in the business of putting his youthful escapades in an especially favourable light. "As a boy" would make Alcibiades very young here: probably younger than fourteen, and if so, the event will have been prior to a performance of *Antigone* in 438 BCE. The notion of "proclamation" is repeated in Plutarch's account of Alcibiades' shameful escapade; the same image is repeated in Antigone's description of how Creon has made a proclamation (κηρύξαντ'; 32, cf. προκηρύξοντα; 34)

---

61. For further examples, see my *Pericles on Stage* (on Ar. *Nu.* 920, *Eq.* 1321); "Aristophanes *Frogs*", 196 (on Ar. *Ra.* 1475); and *Alcibiades on Stage*.

62. Cf. H. Lloyd-Jones on Aeschylus' *Seven against Thebes*, which "Sophocles certainly had in mind when dealing with this cognate subject" ("Notes on Sophocles' *Antigone*", *Classical Quarterly* 7 [1957], 22), and Griffith, *Sophocles* Antigone, 6.

63. A technique that allows Plutarch to "have his cake and eat it" (Duff, "Plutarch on the Childhood of Alkibiades", 109).

directed at "you and me – me, mark you" (31–2), which she adds with what has been called "fierce pride".[64]

There are some indications that Sophocles may have had Alcibiades' brother Cleinias in mind in his portrayal of Ismene. Alcibiades was famous for persuading his contemporaries to use new-fangled words,[65] and Ismene's opening lines contain such an expression when she says to Antigone "You are clearly red in the face with some piece of news" (20). The word for going "red in the face", καλχαίνουσα, is a highly unusual one derived from κάλχη meaning "purple murex" and which is "virtually synonymous with πορφύρα'.[66] The point that Sophocles may be making here is that his impressionable younger brother might have been among those who were influenced by Alcibiades, and a rich Alcibiades at that (purple being a well-known marker of wealth).[67]

"Alcibiadean laughter" was to become a paradigm of inappropriate behaviour,[68] and if Antigone does "come forward" as Alcibiades, Creon's lines at 482–3 are significant. Antigone's crimes are said by Creon there to be twofold: the original act of ὕβρις (insolence, wanton violence) and the fact that she exulted in what she had done, and laughed (cf. γελᾶν) about it afterwards. On the one hand, "Alcibiades ... was of all Athenians, the most notorious for various types of *hybris*",[69] and on the other was inclined to take nothing seriously, and to ridicule everything; in this case the law. The tables are turned by 838–40, where Antigone complains of being laughed at (γελῶμαι), and accuses the Chorus of insulting her (ὑβρίζεις).

Antigone is an orphan, comes from a badly disturbed family and is in the care of a guardian who is not much good at helping her over her past experiences, and totally unsympathetic towards her expressions of family pride. Alcibiades, too, was an insecure orphan in the care of an excessively severe guardian. Antigone's essential irrationality has been generally overlooked,[70] as has Alcibiades' psychological

---

64. Brown, *Sophocles:* Antigone, 139.

65. Ar. *PCG* 205.6–7.

66. Griffith, *Sophocles* Antigone, 125.

67. To look no further afield than Alcibiades himself, he was later to enter the theatre wearing a πορφυρίς (purple garment; Satyr. *FHG* 3.160 ap. Ath. 12.534c) and to swagger in his purple-dyed robe through the Agora (Plut. *Alc.* 16.1).

68. For example, τὸ γὰρ γελᾶν τὸν Ἀλκιβιάδην ἢ δακρύειν τὸν πένητα ἑπόμενον τῷ πλουσίῳ, καὶ τὰ τοιαῦτα (Alcibiades' laughter, or weeping when poverty accompanies wealth, and the like; Sopat. Rh. *Διαίρεσις ζητημάτων* 8.127).

69. N. R. E. Fisher, *Hybris: A Study in the Values of Honour and Shame in Ancient Greece* (Warminster: Aris & Phillips, 1992), 461.

70. N. E. Collinge, "Medical Terms and Clinical Attitudes in the Tragedians", *Bulletin of the Institute of Classical Studies* **9** (1962), 45–53, is a notable exception.

make-up.[71] His problems will have begun in the first year of his life. He was an insecure baby who very early discovered self-coping mechanisms. His wild oscillations in behaviour suggest that he had a disturbed history of attachment, and had problems holding the world together, problems that will have been the more acute when he was a teenager.

This perhaps helps us understand the full force of the exasperated Chorus's verdict on Antigone, "Your self-willed anger [αὐτόγνωτος ... ὀργά] has brought about your ruin" (875), which is a strikingly vivid definition of an impassioned adolescent state of mind. Antigone's unflinching obduracy was probably based on Alcibiades' "constant need to win and come first" (τὸ φιλόνικον ἰσχυρότατον ... καὶ τὸ φιλόπρωτον; Plut. *Alc.* 2.1). Plutarch gives a fine example of this when he tells of the infant Alcibiades refusing to give way to the wagon (*ibid.* 2.3–4), and another of Alcibiades' eccentric sense of personal rectitude when he knocked on a schoolmaster's door and, on discovering that he did not possess a copy of Homer, beat him up (*ibid.* 7.1–3). Yet another example is given in the anecdote of how Alcibiades once bought a very fine hound for a very large sum, and proceeded to cut its tail off, to universal disapproval. When his friends told him how sorry everyone was for the dog, Alcibiades replied, "Then what I want has come about. I want the Athenians to talk about this, rather than that they should say something worse about me" (*ibid.* 9).

We have already had occasion to note Goethe's reservations about lines 904–20; how they were a blemish only waiting for an apt philologist to demonstrate that they are spurious; how Antigone, on the point of death, "brings forward a motive which is quite unworthy, and almost borders upon the comic". Goethe had in fact been anticipated by August Ludwig Wilhelm Jacob in 1821,[72] but other "apt philologists" were not slow to respond, and the lines in question are often deleted (especially by those who wish to see Antigone as heroine and protagonist).[73] They are more frequently defended, however, but often with tortuous logic.[74] But if

---

71. This last-mentioned gap in scholarship is now being filled. Dr Daphne Briggs, a child psychotherapist, and I gave a paper to the Oxford History of Childhood Seminar in the autumn of 2004 ("Juvenile Crime, Aggression and Abuse in Classical Antiquity: A Case Study", in *Children and Sexuality: The Greeks to the Great War*, G. Rousseau [ed.], 41–64 [Basingstoke: Palgrave Macmillan, 2007]) in which between us we investigated the psychological make-up of the infant and pubescent Alcibiades.

72. A. L. W. Jacob, *Sophocleae quaestiones; praemittuntur disputationes de tragoediae origine et De tragicorum cum republica necessitudine* (Warsaw, 1821), 351–68.

73. For example, Müller, *Sophokles, Antigone*, 1967.

74. D. A. Hester, "Sophocles the Unphilosophical", *Mnemosyne* **24** (1971), 11–59, esp. 55–8 for a long bibliography; Brown, *Sophocles: Antigone*, 199–200; Griffith, *Sophocles Antigone*, 277–9.

Alcibiades does somehow lie behind Antigone, the audience will have expected "unworthy motives", and will have known that "the comic" was Alcibiades' special forte. His first public act involved clownishness (when a quail escaped from beneath his cloak and he dealt with any potential loss of dignity by making the crowd laugh: Plut. *Alc.* 10.1–2), and βωμολοχία (horseplay) was a charge justly laid against him in Plutarch's summary of Alcibiades' career (*ibid.* 40.3).

Antigone's narrative bears a close relation to a tale told by Herodotus (Hdt. 3.119), who was given a large sum of money by the Athenians for his readings, perhaps in 445 (Plut. *Mor.* 862b), when Alcibiades would have been six or seven. What we get in Antigone's speech is in part a childish recollection of lectures that Alcibiades had either heard or heard about, and in part an attempt by Sophocles to replicate Alcibiades' manner of speech as well as his thought processes. Even later in life, Alcibiades:

> strove to find not only the proper thing to say, but also the proper words and phrases in which to say it; and since in this last regard he was not a man of large resources he would often stumble in the midst of his speech, come to a stop, and pause a while, a particular phrase eluding him. Then he would resume, and proceed with all the caution in the world.   (Plut. *Alc.* 10.4)

This perhaps accounts for what has been described as the "self-consciously rhetorical" quality of the speech.[75]

It has been said that "the logic" of speeches in tragedy "can be far-fetched, but it ... cannot ... be absent altogether";[76] but this does not allow for the possibility that Sophocles was making Antigone speak like an impassioned teenager. What the Chorus call her "folly in speech and frenzy at the heart" (λόγου τ' ἄνοια καὶ φρενῶν ἐρινύς; 603) has been taken as a sign of one who might be mentally unbalanced,[77] but it could equally well be understood as a brilliant evocation of normal, impassioned adolescent reasoning. For those who had ears to hear (and given the build-up to the characterization), Alcibiades might have come to mind, not to mention their own offspring. Any perceived mental imbalance, however, can be put down to Alcibiades' character, which was described by Plutarch (who had access to far more sources than we do) as full of "many strange inconsistencies and contradictions" (ἀνομοιότητας πρὸς αὑτὸ καὶ μεταβολάς; *Alc.* 2.1). Goethe's analysis was thus essentially correct, but what he did not know is that there were special reasons for

---

75. Brown, *Sophocles: Antigone*, 200.
76. *Ibid.*
77. Collinge, "Medical Terms and Clinical Attitudes", 51.

the "unworthy" and "comic" character of Antigone's speech. It should be clear that there is no room in this analysis for Antigone as a moral agent or even as a "bad woman".[78]

Most critics today, alas, would agree with Dodds' principle that "what is not mentioned in the play does not exist".[79] If the preceding argument has any merit, then it will be clear that the world outside the play, whether at the level of high politics or low gossip, has a major role, indeed is central to a proper understanding of the action. The limitations of the traditional approach can be seen in a recent commentary, where adhesion to Dodds' critical principle leads the reader up a blind alley. For example:

> Distinctively drawn though each of these figures [Creon, Antigone, the Guard, Ismene, Haimon] is, we should acknowledge none the less that their internal psychological states and personalities, i.e. their true "characters" as such behind their dramatic masks remain largely unformulated by the text, and thus beyond our consideration.[80]

Far from it; public knowledge of the activities of the real-life individuals behind the dramatic personalities could be taken for granted and will have greatly enriched understanding and appreciation of the play. Then, it is scarcely the case that Antigone and Creon "embody and articulate the most typical and generalized characteristics of their precisely defined social roles – Ant[igone] as the devoted sister and unmarried daughter, [C]reon as the stern soldier-ruler and father, each of them fiercely determined to resist any threat to the integrity of these roles",[81] for any "fierce determination" is ultimately derived from the intrinsic qualities of two wholly exceptional individuals. It is indeed the case that "we are not encouraged by the text to ponder the inner workings of their minds",[82] but then the fifth-century audience never had to do so, for they knew them already.

If this interpretation is correct, one immediate consequence is that an Antigone based on a disturbed teenager notorious for his irregular way of life will scarcely

---

78. Cf. H. P. Foley, "Antigone as Moral Agent", in *Tragedy and the Tragic: Greek Theatre and Beyond*, M. S. Silk (ed.), 49–73 (Oxford: Clarendon Press, 1996); Tyrrell & Bennett, *Recapturing Sophocles' Antigone*; C. Sourvinou-Inwood, "Assumptions and the Creation of Meaning: Reading Sophocles' *Antigone*", *Journal of Hellenic Studies* **109** (1989), 134–48; A. Markantonatos, *Oedipus at Colonus: Sophocles, Athens, and the World* (Berlin: de Gruyter, 2007), 216–24.

79. Dodds, "On Misunderstanding the *Oedipus Rex*", 40; see p. 4, above.

80. Griffith, *Sophocles* Antigone, 37.

81. *Ibid.* 37–8.

82. *Ibid.* 38.

have moved an Athenian audience to pity. The benefits are considerable. On the one hand we can now enjoy *Antigone sans* Lacan, and on the other dump a dreary pageant of nineteenth-century philosophizing about the play in two words: "Hegel Schmegel".[83] The sight of a Creon broken as the result of his insistence on a zero-tolerant attitude towards the law will, however, have been moving and instructive, not least for the principal κωμῳδούμενος (or whatever the precise term might be for tragedy). Pericles' inhuman activity on Samos had been held up to public scrutiny and was attacked for its cruelty. The results of his indifferent guardianship of Alcibiades (whose education was entrusted to a Thracian slave who was "useless on account of his old age" (Pl. *Alc.* 1.122b; cf. Plut. *Lyc.* 15) are also laid at his door. We can only assume that some of this criticism was effective and that Pericles' policies were less harsh in the future. Sophocles' strictures had less influence on either Alcibiades or the audience, for events of the last quarter of the fifth century BCE were rendered even more chaotic and unpredictable by Alcibiades' fickle and unstable character, and by the ready reception his crazy schemes were given by the Athenian public.[84]

---

83. For rich bibliographies, see M. Leonard, "Antigone, the Political and the Ethics of Psychoanalysis", *Proceedings of the Cambridge Philological Society* 49 (2003), 130–54, and P. A. Miller, "Lacan's Antigone: The Sublime Object and the Ethics of Interpretation", *Phoenix* 61 (2007), 1–14.
84. Cf. Pelling, "Plutarch and Thucydides", 21–4.

3

Oedipus Tyrannus, Alcibiades, Cleon and Aspasia

The basic purpose of this chapter is to revive the idea first expressed in modern times by the eighteenth-century English classical scholar Samuel Musgrave, that we should perhaps see the historical figure of Alcibiades underlying Oedipus in Sophocles' *Oedipus Tyrannus.*[1] Musgrave (who, according to the *Oxford Dictionary of National Biography*, "had few superiors" as a student of Greek)[2] was writing in the 1770s, at a time when classical scholarship had not yet become *Altertumswissenschaft.* If, however, we take Dodds' dictum that "what is not mentioned in the play does not exist" at face value, we could easily observe that Alcibiades is not mentioned by name in *Oedipus Tyrannus* and stop at this point. There is nevertheless consider-able merit in Musgrave's insight as we shall see, and although he did not spell out the reasons for his belief, a case can be made for Alcibiades underlying Oedipus in both *Oedipus Tyrannus* and *Oedipus at Colonus.*

The most famous attribute of Oedipus is, in Tom Lehrer's words, that he "loved his mother": perhaps overmuch, by most standards ancient or modern. Now while "motherlover", or a synonym, might be a common enough epithet in some circles, the actual phenomenon of sexual relations between a mother and a son is unusual. But without – yet at least – fully identifying Alcibiades with Oedipus it is useful to note that according to his contemporary Antisthenes it was said that Alcibiades was so debauched that "he lay with his mother, his sister and his daughter" (Antisth. 29a Caizzi ap. Ath. 5.220a). The charge could well have had its origins in an invention of the stage, but it well encapsulates an extreme view of one whose lawless, perverted, way of life, was according to Thucydides thought by some in 415 to be an indication that

---

1. S. Musgrave (ed.), *Sophoclis tragoediae septem* (Oxford: Clarendon Press, 1800), 1.289; cf. E. Wunder (ed.), *Sophoclis Tragoediae* (Göttingen and Erfurt: W. Hennings, 1831), 94.
2. And see C. Collard, "Musgrave, Samuel", in *Dictionary of British Classicists*, R. B. Todd (ed.), vol. 2, 694–6 (Bristol: Thoemmes Continuum, 2004).

Alcibiades was aiming at tyranny,[3] and of one who, according to Diogenes Laertius, "When he was a young boy ... lured husbands away from their wives, but when he was a young man ... lured wives away from their husbands" (Bion in D.L. 4.49).

Oedipus also famously had a bad leg, and again, without as yet pressing the possible connection very hard, we might note that Alcibiades was severely injured at Potidaea in 432. The circumstances of the battle were such that Alcibiades had fallen and could not get away, and Socrates (who had taken the twenty-year-old under his wing in a fruitless attempt to persuade him to improve his conduct and to inspire him with *sophrosyne*) stood over him and protected him from further attack.[4] His injury may well have contributed to Alcibiades' "funny walk", which, like his speech defect, was so distinctive that his son, Alcibiades Jr, imitated it (Plut. *Alc.* 1.8). While this is a far-from-clinching argument for an equation between Alcibiades and Oedipus, were such an argument to be made, Alcibiades' distinctive gait would, I submit, not be an impediment.

The science of *Altertumswissenschaft* developed as a reaction to a courtly tradition of couching personalities, events and even universal truths in allegory. "Hidden meanings", including political interpretations, came to be disregarded, even derided. In 1962, we thus find H. Friis Johansen declaring that the "practice of reading contemporary allusions into Sophocles' plays ... is now fortunately dying out".[5] There have, however, been a few brave souls who have been open to a political interpretation of *Oedipus Tyrannus*. They have, though, consistently found Pericles in Oedipus. For Grace Macurdy:

> If we accept the usual dating of 429 BC for the appearance of the play, it seems inevitable that the "tyrannus" (v. 873) who falls from his high place into the depths below must refer to the statesman under whom Athens "was nominally a democracy, but in reality was ruled by one man, her first citizen (Thuc. 2.65)," who fell from power in 430–429 BC.[6]

---

3. "Alarmed at the greatness of his license and his perverted way of life, and of the ambition which he showed in whatever he undertook, people set him down as aiming at tyranny, and became his enemies" (Thuc. 6.15.4). Cf. Munn, *The School of History*, 386 n.56.
4. "While yet a lad he served in the campaign of Potidaea, where he shared the tent of Socrates, and took his place next to him in the ranks. In an obstinate engagement they both showed great courage, and when Alcibiades was wounded and fell to the ground, Socrates stood in front of him, defending him, and so saved his life and arms from the enemy" (Plut. *Alc.* 7.3–5).
5. H. Friis Johansen, "Sophocles 1939–1959", *Lustrum* 7 (1962), 94–288, esp. 163.
6. G. H. Macurdy, "References to Thucydides, Son of Milesias, and to Pericles in Sophocles *OT* 863–910", *Classical Philology* 37 (1942), 307–10, esp. 308; cf. M. L. Earle, *The Oedipus Tyrannus* (New York: American Book Company, 1901); Knox, *Oedipus at Thebes*, 63–4 (with reserva-

For Victor Ehrenberg, "the dramatic idea of Oedipus, the man and the king, coincided, as we may assume, with the experience of Pericles' full glory, fall and death";[7] while for Cedric Whitman, "There may ... be a touch of Aspasia about Jocasta, as there may be a touch of Pericles in Oedipus".[8] But while Pericles was, like Oedipus, burdened with an inherited curse (Thuc. 1.126.2.), he never so far as we know "lay with his mother", nor was such an imputation ever made.

Oedipus Tyrannus as a production of 425 BCE

Any association between Pericles and Oedipus is predicated on *Oedipus Tyrannus* having been produced in or shortly after 429, but we owe to Bernard Knox the important insight that the play is much more likely to have been produced in 425.[9] His arguments are careful and compelling: a model of "wigwam" construction. The references to plague in Sophocles' play had misled earlier commentators into believing that the Great Plague of 430 was alone in question, and they overlooked the apparent allusion in *Oedipus Tyrannus* to the resurgence of the pestilence in the winter of 427/6. The reference to a "former" visitation of the pestilence at line 164 provides a new *terminus post quem* of the autumn of 427, and the first possible occasion for the production of the play, assuming it was performed at the Dionysia, would be the spring of 426. Knox, however, finds additional indications in allusions to "the flame of pain" at 166, and "he burns me" at 191, that accounts of the Sophoclean plague were influenced by the terrible summer of 426, when crops failed, and the air was fiery. This would bring the date for *Oedipus Tyrannus* later still, to the spring of 425.

Then, invocations to the "Delian Healer" (155–7) recall the Athenians' attempts to placate Apollo by purifying Delos in the winter of 426/5. Thucydides describes how the tyrant Peisistratus had formerly, but ineffectually, purified the island, and how the tyrant Polycrates had taken an interest in the cult.[10] Knox notes that this

---

tions); J. Henderson, "Drama and Democracy", in *The Age of Pericles*, L. J. Salamons II (ed.), 179–95 (Cambridge: Cambridge University Press, 2007), 188 (ditto).

7. V. Ehrenberg, *Sophocles and Pericles* (Oxford: Blackwell, 1954), 149.

8. Whitman, *Sophocles*, 135.

9. B. M. W. Knox, "The Date of the *Oedipus Tyrannus* of Sophocles", *American Journal of Philology* 77 (1956), 133–47, and *Word and Action: Essays on the Ancient Theater* (Baltimore, MD: Johns Hopkins University Press, 1979).

10. Thucydides also describes the Athenians' restoration of the Delian festival and accompanying games that had over the years fallen into relative neglect, and adds an interesting coda: "they introduced ἱπποδρομίας (chariot-racing), which did not exist before" (3.104). Gomme sees the hand of Nicias behind the purification (*A Historical Commentary on Thucydides*, 2.415), and S.

sequence of events corresponds to the terms of the Sophoclean Chorus, which speaks of "something done again in the revolution of the seasons" (ἢ περιτελλομέναις ὥραις πάλιν; 156).

Knox well observes that:

> If the *Oedipus Tyrannus* was produced at the Greater Dionysia in 425, or even in the next year, all these puzzling expressions are explained; not only that, they can be seen as adding to the effect of the play, when it was first produced, a whole dimension of immediate reference which must have heightened the effectiveness of the performance enormously.[11]

He then goes on to tie the play firmly down to 425 by demonstrating a series (fifteen by my count) of parodic references to, and echoes of, Sophocles' play in Aristophanes' *Knights*, performed in 424.[12] They are cumulatively convincing, and fix the date January 424 as the *terminus ante quem* for *Oedipus Tyrannus*, the first performance of which must therefore have been in the previous year, in 425.

It is only recently that *Knights* has been seen to be an attack not simply on Cleon, in the person of the Paphlagonian slave, but on two targets, as Aristophanes explicitly states at line 511 with the reference to "the Typhoon *and* the Hurricane". The Typhoon is clearly Cleon, while the Hurricane is whoever lies behind the Sausage-seller, and I have argued elsewhere that it is Alcibiades.[13] There are many reasons why we might see the Sausage-seller in this light, perhaps the most striking being the charge that Paphlagon brings against him that he was tainted by the Alcmaeonid curse (445–6). Dismissed as "highly ridiculous" by Knox,[14] or "utterly absurd" by Sommerstein,[15] but never explained, the charge would fit well if it were

---

Hornblower that of Thucydides himself (*A Commentary on Thucydides* 1 [Oxford: Clarendon Press, 1991], 194–5), but it is not too difficult to see the additional influence of Alcibiades, besotted by horses, in the introduction of chariot-racing. Indeed, we may well read the line as an "emphatic" (see p. 8, above) allusion to early tendencies on his part to tyranny, coming as it does after explicit references to the interest of two actual tyrants in the conduct of the cult; we might compare the tyrannicide passage embedded in Thucydides' account of Alcibiades' adventures in 415: M. Vickers, "Thucydides 6.53.3–59: not a 'digression'", *Dialogues d'histoire ancienne* 21 (1995), 193–200; Chapter 10, below.

11. Knox, "The Date of the *Oedipus Tyrannus*", 144; 1979, 120.

12. Knox, "The Date of the *Oedipus Tyrannus*", 144–7; 1979, 122–4, building on an idea of V. Milio ("Per la cronologia dell' Edipo Re", *Bolletino di Filologia Classica* 35 [1928–9], 203–5).

13. My *Pericles on Stage*, 97–120, and *Alcibiades on Stage*.

14. Knox, "The Date of the *Oedipus Tyrannus*", 145; 1979, 121.

15. A. H. Sommerstein (ed.), *The Comedies of Aristophanes* 2: *Knights* (Warminster: Aris & Phillips, 1981), 167.

Alcibiades' attested maternal descent from the Alcmaeonidae that is in question.[16] The plot seems to play on Alcibiades' less than savoury youthful entanglements (for "Sausage-seller" perhaps read "Dick-seller", with the imputation that he had sold his body for profit; if substantiated, a charge of selling one's body for sexual favours led at Athens to disqualification from certain civic privileges)[17] as well as his grandiose military and political ambitions. The slave Demosthenes, whose fawning attitude recalls that of Alcibiades' many flatterers, foresees the Sausage-seller's success in terms that foreshadow Alcibiades' subsequent career: "O blessed one, O wealthy one! O one who is nothing today, but tomorrow immensely great! O commander of fortunate Athens!" (157–9). "The Agora, the Harbours, the Pnyx" (165) will all belong to him, and the world from Caria to Carthage is to be sold for a bribe (176). This can be read on the one hand as a prediction that Alcibiades will inherit Pericles' mantle, and on the other as a likely reference to Alcibiades' recent, if precocious, participation in a reassessment of the tribute when, "by showing himself threatening and influential he made the public revenue a source of private gain", according to a speech that may or may not be by Andocides ([Andoc.] 4.11).[18] The

---

16. Cf. "He was an Alcmaeonid on his mother's side; she was Deinomache, daughter of Megacles" (Plut. *Alc.* 1.1:); Isoc. 16.25.

17. D. Cohen, *Law, Sexuality and Society: The Enforcement of Morals in Classical Athens* (Cambridge: Cambridge University Press, 1991), 171–202; cf. "the Athenians publicly and officially refused to allow those who sold their bodies for sex to participate in city administration" (R. W. Wallace, "Private Lives and Public Enemies: Freedom of Thought in Classical Athens", in *Athenian Identity and Civic Ideology*, A. Scafuro & A. Boegehold [eds], 127–55 [Baltimore, MD: Johns Hopkins University Press, 1993], 152).

18. On Alcibiades' likely participation in the tribute reassessment despite his relative youth, see R. Develin, "Age Qualifications for Athenian Magistrates", *Zeitschrift für Papyrologie und Epigraphik* 61 (1985), 149–59, and *Athenian Officials 684–321 BC*, 131. Scholars differ as to the date of [Andoc.] 4; some preferring 417 (e.g. A. Schroff, "Zur Echtheitsfrage d. vierten Rede des Andokides", inaugural dissertation, University of Erlangen [Erlangen: Hof- und Univ.-Bucherei, 1901]; A. E. Raubitschek, "The Case against Alcibiades (Andocides IV)", *Transactions of the American Philological Society* 79 [1948], 191–210, reprinted in *The School of Hellas: Essays on Greek History, Archaeology, and Literature*, D. Obbink & P. A. Vander Waerdt [eds], 116–31 [New York: Oxford University Press, 1991]; W. D. Furley, "Andokides iv ('Against Alkibiades'): Fact or Fiction?", *Hermes* 117 [1989], 138–56, and *Andokides and the Herms: A Study of Crisis in Fifth-Century Athenian Religion* [London: Institute of Classical Studies, 1996]; and P. Cobetto Ghiggio, *[Andocide] Contro Alcibiade: introduzione, testo critico, traduzione e commento* [Pisa: Edizioni ETS, 1995]), others maintaining that it was composed as a literary exercise in the early fourth century (e.g. K. J. Maidment [ed.], *Minor Attic Orators* 1 [London: Heinemann, 1941]; Andrewes in Gomme *et al.*, *A Historical Commentary on Thucydides*, 4.287–8; M. Edwards [ed.], *Greek Orators 4: Andocides* [Warminster: Aris & Phillips, 1995], 132–5; H. Heftner, "Ps.-Andokides' Rede gegen Alkibiades ([And.] 4) und die politische Diskussion nach dem Sturz der 'Dreissig' in Athen", *Klio* 77 [1995], 75–104, and "Die pseudo-andokideische Rede 'Gegen Alkibiades' ([And.] 4) – ein authentischer Beitrag zu einer Ostrakophoriedebatte des Jahres 415

Sausage-seller is to become an ἀνὴρ μέγιστος (a very great man indeed; 178), an expression that Knox sees as a reflection of Oedipus' description of himself as ἀνὴρ ἀστῶν μέγιστος (the greatest man of the citizens; 775–6).

Sophocles' prophetic vision

If so, and if there really is merit in Musgrave's view that Alcibiades underlies Oedipus, *Knights* will have been Aristophanes' reaction to another playwright's prophetic vision of Alcibiades' career, based on the same premises: Alcibiades' irregular conduct in his private life, and his ambition – what Plutarch calls his youthful μεγαλοπραγμοσύνη (vast projects; Plut. *Alc.* 6.4). We might even see in *Oedipus Tyrannus* the exemplification of the features described by Aristotle (who was very familiar with the play)[19] in the *Poetics*, when he distinguishes between history and poetry. History deals with "particulars", and the specific illustration he chooses is "what Alcibiades actually did, or what was done to him". Poetry, by contrast, deals with "the universal", which was concerned with "describing the kind of things that a person of a certain character would inevitably say or do" (Arist. *Po.* 1451b.6–11). Sophocles appears to describe the kinds of things that he envisages a mature Alcibiades saying or doing at some time in the future, given his proclivities and ambitions. We might even speculate that Sophocles' success in putting this across was the reason why a play that has been universally admired down the centuries did not win the dramatic competition. If the circumstances surrounding the judging of *Clouds* are any guide, when "the circle around Alcibiades" was instrumental in preventing Aristophanes from winning the first prize (Ar. *Nu.* Arg. 5 Coulon), the judges were intimidated.

One immediate benefit of seeing the action of *Oedipus Tyrannus* lying in the future from the vantage point of an audience watching in 425 is that many of the unlikely and unbelievable elements in the plot become much less disconcerting. For Voltaire, the offences against reason in *Oedipus* were enough to deem classical

---

v. Chr.?", *Philologus* **145** [2001], 39–56; D. Gribble, "Rhetoric and History in [Andocides]-4, 'Against Alcibiades'", *Classical Quarterly* **47** [1997], 367–91, and *Alcibiades and Athens: A Study in Literary Presentation* [Oxford: Clarendon Press, 1999], 154–8).

19. M. Ostwald, "Aristotle on Hamartia and Sophocles' Oedipus Tyrannus", in *Festschrift Ernst Kapp zum 70. Geburtstag am 21. Januar 1958 von Freunden und Schülern überreicht*, 93–108 (Hamburg: M. von Schröder, 1958); T. C. W. Stinton, "Hamartia in Aristotle and Greek Tragedy", *Classical Quarterly* **25** (1975), 237–46; A. Zierl, "Erkenntnis und Handlung im Oidipus Tyrannos des Sophokles", *Rheinisches Museum* **142** (1999), 127–48.

simplicity so much clumsiness,[20] and many other critics have been uncomfortable too. Martin Ostwald once listed the improbabilities: "Is it really possible," he asked:

> that in all those years Oedipus did not even once ask his wife whether she had been married before? Can we believe that he never enquired of Iocasta whether she had any children before the birth of the children whom Oedipus fathered, especially since Iocasta must have been at least twelve or fourteen years older than Oedipus? Is it credible that the man whose unrelenting curiosity is one of the essential elements in the play would not have enquired about the fate of Iocasta's previous offspring? And did he never feel impelled to tell Iocasta his own story some long winter evening – why he had left Corinth, what the oracle had told him, how he had successfully defended himself against a band of distinguished travellers on his way from Delphi to Thebes at the place where the three roads meet?[21]

If the model for Oedipus were in reality to be in his mid-twenties, as opposed to the forty-plus of his dramatic analogue, such details would matter little. Knox speaks of the "discovery of the past in the present action of the play", but it was perhaps instead the "discovery of the *future* in the present action of the play" that Sophocles gave his original audience. When we today consider the future, we realize that the best we can do is to broad-brush the possibilities. "Offences against reason" resulting from fine-tuning are not, indeed cannot be, part of the picture. The closing lines of *Ajax* (1418–20) are perhaps pertinent here: "Mortals can understand many things when they have seen them; but before he sees them no one can predict how he will fare in the future".[22]

If the *Oedipus Tyrannus* begins once again to be a play whose resonances are greater than those arising from the inner workings of the plot, it is no longer profitable to discuss it in self-referential terms. It may, for example, be possible – as able scholars have done – to argue that the Chorus's line in the Second Stasimon at 873, ὕβρις φυτεύει τύραννον (hubris begets the tyrant), is an "absurdity" when viewed solely within the terms of what Sophocles gives us, justifying an emendation to ὕβριν

---

20. R. Lattimore, *The Poetry of Greek Tragedy* (Baltimore, MD: Johns Hopkins University Press, 1958), 87, with n.6; A. Cameron, *The Identity of Oedipus the King* (New York: New York University Press, 1968), 74, 90–91.

21. M. Ostwald, "On Interpreting Sophocles' *Oedipus Tyrannus*", in *The Verbal and the Visual: Essays in Honor of William S. Heckscher*, K.-L. Selig & E. Sears (eds), 133–49 (New York: Italica Press, 1990), 135–6.

22. A. F. Garvie (ed.), *Sophocles* Ajax (Warminster: Aris & Phillips, 1998).

φυτεύει τυραννίς (tyranny gives rise to *hubris*) or the like.[23] But once it is realized that Sophocles may on the one hand be reflecting on Alcibiades' youthful *hubrismata* (external to the play, it is true, but hardly unknown to the audience) and on the other be intimating where they all might lead to, it is no longer possible to reject the unanimous testimony of the manuscripts. As we have seen already, information concerning these youthful follies survives in the anecdotal record, and includes tales, for example, of Alcibiades when a child having held up a cart driven by a peasant by lying down in front of it (Plut. *Alc.* 2.3–5), of his having struck a schoolmaster with his fist for not possessing any of Homer's works (Plut. *Alc.* 7.1), or of his having killed one of his servants by striking him with a club (Antiph. ap. Plut. *Alc.* 3.1–2).

We happen to know where Alcibiades' excesses led, and that by 415 his conduct caused many to fear that he was aiming at tyranny (Thuc. 6.15.2–4).[24] If Musgrave's hypothesis has any merit, it was remarkably perspicacious of Sophocles to have forseen with such clarity ten years earlier the way that things were going. Still in the Second Stasimon, he has the Chorus accurately encapsulate a way of life that it is not too difficult to see as resembling that of Alcibiades – "arrogance in word and deed, disrespect towards the shrines of the gods, unjust gain, laying hands on the untouchable" (883–90) – and while these words do indeed, as Chris Carey has noted, "go far beyond any actions imputed rightly or wrongly to any character in the play",[25] this may perhaps be to miss the point. The real purpose was probably self-evident to the audience, who may well have relished Sophocles' skill in intertwining Alcibiadean resonances with the traditional tale of the house of Laius. Oedipus' account of his encounter with the party travelling from Thebes (794–812) is thus told in Alcibiades' breathless paratactic style, with a stream of initial καίς of the kind Thucydides puts in Alcibiades' speeches.[26] The intransigence of both parties when Oedipus' path in the "narrow way" (στενωπός; 1399)

---

23. R. D. Dawe (ed.), *Sophocles* Oedipus Rex (Cambridge: Cambridge University Press, 1982), 18, 182–3; cf. R. P. Winnington-Ingram, "The Second Stasimon of the Oedipus Tyrannus", *Journal of Hellenic Studies* **91** (1971), 124–7; Burton, *The Chorus in Sophocles' Tragedies*, 184.

24. The contemporary paradigm for tyranny was the Persian empire, and Sophocles further besmirches the character of Oedipus with innuendo heavily laden with references to such matters as Achaemenid court intrigue, the role of πιστοί (literally "trusties") in the Persian state, and the overweening conduct of a τύραννος (tyrant) towards his δοῦλοι (slaves); see further E. D. Francis, "Oedipus Achaemenides", *American Journal of Philology* **113** (1992), 333–57; for evidence that Sophocles was fully aware of the full significance of the "scarlet word" τύραννος, which with its cognates occurs fifteen times in the play, see M. Pope, "Addressing Oedipus", *Greece and Rome* **38** (1991), 156–70.

25. C. Carey, "The Second Stasimon of Sophocles' *Oedipus Tyrannus*", *Journal of Hellenic Studies* **106** (1986), 175–9, esp. 177–8.

26. Cf. Tompkins, "Stylistic Characterization in Thucydides".

was blocked by the carriage (804–5) certainly bears a more than superficial resemblance to that of the infant Alcibiades and the driver when a cart was blocked in the "narrow street" (ἐν τῷ στενωπῷ; Plut. *Alc.* 2.3). Oedipus' angry blow (807) parallels Alcibiades' habitual belligerence, and the "swift blow from his staff" that put paid to the principal traveller (810–12) recalls the fatal outcome of one of the tales with which the anecdotal tradition is replete. Plutarch declared that it was perhaps best to disbelieve the story of the death of Alcibiades' servant felled by a club, for all its circumstantial detail (the murder spot is given), since it was "written by an enemy with the avowed purpose of defaming his character" (καὶ ὅτι τῶν ἀλλὰ τούτοις μὲν οὐκ ἄξιον ἴσως πιστεύειν, ἅ γε λοιδορεῖσθαί τις αὐτῷ δι' ἔχθραν ὁμολογῶν εἶπεν; Plut. *Alc.* 3.2). It is, however, true that the story was told at an early date, and it is also the case that if Sophocles did have Alcibiades in mind in *Oedipus Tyrannus*, he was not in the business of putting his youthful escapades in an especially rosy light.

The expression "where three paths meet" (1399; cf. 800–801) is one that recurs in Plato's *Gorgias* (discussed in Chapter 12), where Socrates tells the Alcibiadean Callicles of how Minos, Rhadamanthys and Aeacus judge the dead in a meadow "at the cross-roads from which lead on the one hand the road to the islands of the blessed, and on the other to Tartarus" (Pl. *Grg.* 524a). The concept of cross-roads being somehow traditionally associated with death (through Hecate, goddess of the Underworld) has been well brought out in this connection by Stephen Halliwell.[27] Plato, *pace* Dodds,[28] was making a knowing allusion to the occasion when Alcibiades was famously represented at a fork in the road, when he was at an age still to change his ways.[29]

Creon and Cleon

Support for the case made so far might be found in the character of Creon. He is first mentioned by Oedipus at 69–70, as παῖδα Μενοικέως Κρέοντα (son of Menoecus, Creon). In the mouth of an Oedipus who employed Alcibiades' habitual speech defect, this will have sounded as Κλέοντα (Cleon). If so, there will have been a certain contemporary relevance, for it would appear that by 425 the historical Cleon was Alcibiades' principal political adversary. Rivalry between Cleon and Alcibiades is actually attested in late sources for the middle of 425. Such rivalry

27. S. Halliwell, "Where Three Roads Meet: A Neglected Detail in the *Oedipus Tyrannus*", *Journal of Hellenic Studies* **106** (1986), 187–90.
28. E. R. Dodds (ed.), *Plato: Gorgias* (Oxford: Clarendon Press, 1959), 375.
29. See further, Chapter 12 below.

probably provides the basis for the arguments between the Paphlagonian and the Sausage-seller in *Knights* of 424, and it also seems to inform the interaction of Oedipus and Creon in *Oedipus Tyrannus*. Nowhere is this more apparent than at 1422, where Oedipus has just blinded himself, and is standing with his eye-balls adrift and blood running down his cheeks. Creon's first remark on seeing this harrowing scene is οὐχ ὡς γελαστής ... ἐλήλυθα (I have not come to laugh), which is not simply perhaps a heartless response to Oedipus' distressing condition, but meant to be a Cleonian reaction to Alcibiadean ridicule of a kind that apparently came to a head a few months after *Oedipus Tyrannus* was performed in March of 425.

An anecdote concerning Alcibiades and Cleon was still being told centuries later. In its simplest form, the story went that "When Cleon undertook the business at Pylos, Alcibiades laughed and was found guilty of hubris" (Anon. in Hermog. *Comment. in Stat.* 7.199). In other versions, it is apparent that the prosecution took place after Cleon's victorious return in mid-summer 425.[30] It is not too difficult, however, to envisage Alcibiades having laughed at Cleon a few months earlier, and for his claque being behind the taunts when Cleon was having second thoughts about his involvement in events at Pylos ("His vain words moved the Athenians to laughter"; Thuc. 4.28.5). Such ridicule may well have rankled; hence perhaps Creon's unsympathetic reaction to Oedipus' plight. We have in any case already seen Sophocles exploiting the young Alcibiades' propensity to inappropriate laughter in *Antigone* (see p. 29, above).

Much of the groundwork for an equation between Creon and Cleon has already been laid by Frederick Ahl.[31] He observes that Oedipus describes Creon as a προστάτης (303), as does Teiresias (411) and notes that the word also carried the meaning of "the political leader of the people", in particular a demagogue. Cleon, judging by his later reputation, was the *prostatēs* par excellence. Furthermore, Ahl notes that "the names Cleon and Creon are not far apart upon the aristocratic Athenian tongue", but he does not make the crucial link between Oedipus and Alcibiades, nor is he "trying to suggest that Sophocles' Creon *is* Cleon, but rather that Sophocles uses the suggestive resonances of Cleon in the play to color his presenta-tion of Creon". Ahl is perhaps too cautious here, for Sophocles' Creon possesses many arguably Cleonian features. Thus, Creon's "brusque tones" at 1425–8 and a

---

30. For example, "Alcibiades laughed on hearing of Cleon's activities at Pylos, and when the latter returned he charged him with *hybris*" (Aps. *Rh.* 348); "Alcibiades laughed when Cleon's achieve-ments at Pylos were announced, and when Cleon returned he charged him with an offence" (Syrianus, Sopatrus and Marcellinus, *Schol. Hermog.* 1.587). See page 29 above for "Alcibiadean laughter" as a paradigm of inappropriate behaviour.

31. Ahl, *Sophocles' Oedipus*, 93–7; cf. *Two Faces of Oedipus*, 100–101.

remark that to R. D. Dawe sounds "unsympathetic, and not justified by anything we have seen in the play",[32] are very much in keeping with the rough personality of the historical Cleon, and the tone of the rancorous debate between Oedipus and Creon at 532–677 has much in common with that of the dialogue between the Cleonian Paphlagon and the Alcibiadean Sausage-seller in *Knights*. The character of Cleon was all too well known to Sophocles' audience, and the playwright had no need to elucidate or elaborate it. If this was indeed the case, then it can surely no longer be argued that "what is not mentioned in the play does not exist".

The Sausage-seller's victory over Paphlagon in *Knights* will have been a reversal of Oedipus' abject humiliation before Creon. Not only does Sophocles indicate how he thinks Alcibiades' career on present showing will turn out, but he compounds the insult by making him absolutely dependent on the whim of his arch-enemy, Cleon. It is a very cleverly crafted, and very pointed, barb. What is certainly not the case is that the figure of Creon left Sophocles with "problems of characterization which he could not easily resolve, or problems upon which he did not feel it worthwhile to expend excessive effort [*sic*], the end of the play being already in sight",[33] nor should we see Creon as "the character with no fate, the character alien to fate … the unchanging standard against which all the changes are measured";[34] rather, the character of the historical analogue was no mystery to Sophocles' audience.[35]

Jocasta and Aspasia

Still on the subject of Creon, one of the supposed oddities in *Oedipus Tyrannus* is that he "expends no word of any kind on the recent suicide of his own sister" Jocasta.[36] If the real-life model for Jocasta was Aspasia, however, we would hardly expect Creon to be concerned at her fate. Cedric Whitman, following Max Pohlenz, once saw "a touch of Aspasia about Jocasta",[37] seeing in her rejection of divination (707–10) something of the "intelligent piety" of the circle around

---

32. Dawe, *Sophocles* Oedipus Rex, 237, 239.
33. Dawe, *Sophocles* Oedipus Rex, 239 (the "end of a commentary" no doubt being in sight?).
34. K. Reinhardt, *Sophocles* (Oxford: Blackwell, 1979), 132.
35. On Cleon in general, see for example A. G. Woodhead, "Thucydides' Portrait of Cleon", *Mnemosyne* 13 (1960), 289–317; M. Ostwald, *From Popular Sovereignty to the Sovereignty of Law: Law, Society and Politics in Fifth-Century Athens* (Berkeley, CA: University of California Press, 1986), 205–24; Hornblower, *A Commentary on Thucydides*, 423; Vickers, *Pericles on Stage*, ch. 6.
36. Dawe, *Sophocles* Oedipus Rex, 237.
37. M. Pohlenz, *Die griechische Tragödie* (Leipzig: B. G. Teubner, 1930), 225; Whitman, *Sophocles*, 135.

Pericles. Sophocles shows by light touches that Aspasia is indeed his model; at least, we can construct a respectable wigwam. Jocasta enjoins Oedipus to tell her what has been happening in terms that recall Aspasia's renown as a teacher (she is called διδάσκαλος in the *Menexenus*; Pl. *Mx.* 235e; cf. Ath. 5.219b; Aesch. Socr. *Fr.* 17 [Dittmar]): δίδαξον κἄμ' (teach me too), she says at 697.[38] Oedipus agrees, adding that he holds her in greater honour than the members of the Chorus. σέβω (I respect) is the word he employs (700), but it is one that may have reminded the audience of the charge of ἀσεβεία (impiety) that had been brought against Aspasia either in court[39] or on the comic stage.[40] Then, Sophocles' use of σιωπῆς (silence) at 1075 has been misunderstood in the past: for example, "Sophocles can only by special pleading be acquitted of the charge of using here a piece of dramatic technique not appropriate to the situation",[41] for there is so much noise on and off stage that we can scarcely think in terms of silence. If, however, we take this reference to Jocasta's last moments as a delicate and respectful nod in the direction of Pericles, who (as we had occasion to note in the previous chapter; p. 21, above) met criticism of his policies πρᾴως καὶ σιωπῇ (with quiet endurance; Plut. *Per.* 34.1), then the problem disappears.

Whether Alcibiades ever did "lie with" his *de facto* stepmother is open to question, but the notion that he did so must have been widespread if, as Barry Strauss has persuasively argued, Euripides' Hippolytus shares many characteristics with Alcibiades.[42] In such a ménage, the plump Cretan Phaedra is likely to be the Ionian Aspasia from Miletus, itself founded from Crete.[43] And while we are still concerned with women, we might take note of Judith Butler's question as to whether psychoanalysis would have been different if it had taken Antigone rather than Oedipus as its point of departure.[44] This is not now quite so bold a postulate as it perhaps first

---

38. On Aspasia in general, see for example H. Maehly, "De Aspasia Milesia", *Philologus* 9 (1853), 213–30; M. M. Henry, *Prisoner of History: Aspasia of Miletus and her Biographical Tradition* (Oxford: Oxford University Press, 1995); Podlecki, *Perikles and his Circle*, 109–17; M. Vickers, "Aspasia on Stage: Aristophanes' *Ecclesiazusae*", *Athenaeum* 92 (2004), 431–50. On the *Menexenus*, see, for preference, E. F. Bloedow, "Aspasia and the Mystery of the Menexenos", *Wiener Studien* (new series) 9 (1975), 32–48.

39. Ostwald, *From Popular Sovereignty*, 195.

40. Wallace, "Private Lives and Public Enemies", 131, 148 n.16.

41. Dawe, *Sophocles* Oedipus Rex, 203.

42. Strauss, *Fathers and Sons in Athens*, 166–75.

43. Vickers, "Alcibiades and Aspasia" and *Alcibiades on Stage*.

44. J. Butler, *Antigone's Claim: Kinship between Life and Death* (New York: Columbia University Press, 2000), 58.

appeared to be; for in either case the troubled character of Alcibiades would have lain behind Freudians' misapprehension and error.[45]

***

There is much more to be said and there are many more analogies to be found between the accursed houses of Alcmaeon and Laius. From ὁ πᾶσι κλεινὸς Οἰδίπους (Oedipus famous to all; 8) to τὰ κλείν' αἰνίγματ' (the famous riddle; 1525) Sophocles' audience will have been diverted, disturbed and dismayed by "the kind of things" that the famous son of Cleinias (ὁ Κλεινίου, as Alcibiades was usually called)[46] "would inevitably say or do" should his tragic flaws be given full rein, and they will have watched in awe as such "things'" were made manifest by means of a slow realization on the part of the protagonist that – in Dawe's words – "his whole φύσις [nature] has been κακή [evil] from the moment of his birth".[47] And if the last lines of the play, including τὰ κλείν' αἰνίγματ', are, as has been claimed, an interpolation by someone editing *Oedipus Tyrannus* for a later performance together with *Oedipus at Colonus*,[48] they will probably have been added when there was still an awareness of Alcibiades' likely involvement in both plays, as we shall see in Chapter 7.

---

45. On which see, for example, Knox, *Oedipus at Thebes*, 197–8; H. Ellenberger, *The Discovery of the Unconscious: The History and Evolution of Dynamic Psychiatry* (New York: Basic Books, 1970); F. J. Sulloway, *Freud, Biologist of the Mind: Beyond the Psychoanalytic Legend* (New York: Basic Books, 1979); A. Grunbaum, *The Foundations of Psychoanalysis: A Philosophical Critique* (Berkeley, CA: University of California Press, 1984); M. B. Macmillan, *Freud Evaluated: The Completed Arc* (Amsterdam: North Holland, 1991); R. Webster, *Why Freud was Wrong: Sin, Science and Psychoanalysis* (London: HarperCollins, 1996), esp. xi–xvii; F. C. Crews, *Unauthorized Freud: Doubters Confront a Legend* (New York: Viking, 1998). If the present argument has any merit at all, Jonathan Lear's analysis is improbable: "What was Sophocles's message to the Athenian citizens who flocked to the theater? You ignore the realm of unconscious meaning at your peril. Do so, and Oedipus's fate will be yours" ("A Counterblast in the War on Freud: The Shrink is In", *New Republic* [25 December 1995], 24).

46. Cf. 'ὦ παῖ Κλεινίου' ἀντὶ τοῦ 'ὦ Ἀλκιβιάδη' ("O son of Cleinias" instead of "O Alcibiades"; Tib. *Fig.* 35.10).

47. Dawe, *Sophocles* Oedipus Rex, 176, on line 822. Alcibiades' φύσις was a major element in the fourth-century "cult" of Alcibiades: I. Bruns, *Das literarische Porträt der Griechen im fünften und vierten Jahrhundert vor Christi Geburt* (Berlin: W. Hertz, 1896), 512; cf. Gribble, *Alcibiades and Athens*, 139.

48. F. Ritter, "Sieben unechten Schlussstellen in den Tragödien des Sophokles", *Philologus* 17 (1861), 422–36, esp. 424–8; Knox, *Oedipus at Thebes*, 265; R. D. Dawe, *Studies on the Text of Sophocles* (Leiden: Brill, 1974–78), 1.266–73. For arguments in favour of authenticity, see W. M. Calder III, "The Staging of the Exodus: Oedipus Tyrannus 1515–30", *Classical Philology* 57 (1962), 219–29; *Theatrokratia*, 143–5.

4

Ajax, Alcibiades and Andocides

Mention was made above (p. vii) to the role of pity and fear in Athenian tragedy. There can have been few plays in which such notions were engendered to a greater extent than in Sophocles' *Ajax*. But before we can indulge in any micro-political analysis of the play, we need to know when it was first performed.

Today, "general opinion among scholars ... favours a date in the later 440's" for *Ajax*.[1] This assertion is becoming gradually more muted – "all we can say in the present state of the evidence is that nothing contradicts a date in the 440s, but that certainty is impossible",[2] or "the dating of Sophocles' play to the early 440s – if correct"[3] – but it is the brave critic who disregards the consensus that *Ajax* is relatively early and who rejects the scholarship that has been devoted to a study of supposed Sophoclean stylistic development. The study of style, it should be said, is not always helpful; indeed it can be positively misleading. That it plays such a prominent role at all is due to misplaced respect for J. J. Winckelmann, concerning whose contribution to science Wilamowitz unwittingly gave the game away in stating:

> In producing a history of style such as no scholar had ever dreamed of in the domain of either poetry or prose, Winckelmann set an example which all succeeding ages should look up to with admiration. It is the source of the sap that has made almost every branch of our science grow and put forth leaves.[4]

---

1. W. B. Stanford (ed.), *Sophocles* Ajax (London: Macmillan, 1963), 296; cf. "some time in the 440s?" (J. Hesk, *Sophocles* Ajax [London: Duckworth, 2003], 14).
2. Garvie, *Sophocles* Ajax, 8.
3. R. Scodel, "The Politics of Sophocles' *Ajax*", *Scripta Classica Israelica* **22** (2003), 31–42, esp. 35; Lloyd-Jones, *Sophocles*, 9, argues for a date in the 30s or 20s.
4. U. von Wilamowitz-Moellendorff, *History of Classical Scholarship* (London: Duckworth, 1982), 96–7.

Leaves yes, but precious little in the way of fruit. In the context of the date of *Ajax*, it has recently been admitted that "most of the criteria are subjective. None is conclusive in itself, and even cumulatively the evidence does not amount to a great deal".[5] As the sage once put it, "forty zeros still add up to zero"; or, in other words, stylometry in Sophocles' *Ajax* ain't worth a hill of beans.

Since "there is no certain date for *Ajax*",[6] all bets for the 440s are off. In principle, the play could have been written any time between 468, when Sophocles won his first victory, and 406 BCE, when he died. It is unlikely, though, that it dates to the very end of his life, for he will then have been occupied with *Oedipus Coloneus*. We also know that he wrote the trilogy of which *Philoctetes* formed part in the months before the spring of 409 BCE. It will be argued on the basis of historical evidence in what follows that the likely date for *Ajax* is the spring of 410 BCE, which would make it fit comfortably into the framework of his oeuvre. Sophocles had been a *proboulos* since 412 BCE, but will have had the time to write once the Four Hundred took over in the early summer of 411 BCE. There was, moreover, a time when it seemed natural to group *Ajax* and *Philoctetes* together on the not unreasonable grounds that Odysseus "appears as the leading instrument in the development of the plot".[7]

Alcibiades and Ajax

One argument in favour of an early date was the quasi-Homeric character of the play. Not for nothing was Homer described in antiquity as the epic Sophocles and Sophocles as the tragic Homer.[8] The parallels between *Ajax* and the *Iliad* are often very close, but "whether this has any bearing on the dating" is, quite rightly, "quite another matter".[9] It will be argued presently that the situation of Alcibiades in 410 BCE lies behind Sophocles' plotting; if so, the Homeric theme may well have something to do with Alcibiades' attested devotion to Homer, a devotion that informed much of his conduct, and of which we specifically hear when, as we have

5. Garvie, *Sophocles* Ajax, 8.
6. R. F. Kennedy, "Athena/Athens on Stage: Athena in the Tragedies of Aeschylus and Sophocles". PhD dissertation, Department of Classics, Ohio State University (2003), 113.
7. Donaldson, *Theatre of the Greeks*, 125.
8. D.L. 4.20; G. M. Kirkwood, "Homer and Sophocles' Ajax", in *Classical Drama and its Influence; Essays Presented to H. D. F. Kitto*, M. J. Anderson (ed.), 51–70 (London: Methuen, 1965); B. Zimmermann, "Der tragische Homer: Zum Aias des Sophokles", in *Epea pteroenta: Beiträge zur Homerforschung. Festschrift W. Kullmann*, M. Reichel & A. Rengakos (eds), 239–46 (Stuttgart: Steiner, 2002).
9. Garvie, *Sophocles* Ajax, 8.

seen, he knocked on a schoolmaster's door and, when he discovered that he did not possess a copy of Homer, beat him up (Plut. *Alc.* 7.1–3). Alcibiades was inspired by Homeric values, so much so that he could be described as "not the son of Achilles, but Achilles himself" (Plut. *Alc.* 23.6).

More to the point, perhaps, in the context of *Ajax*, illogical belligerence, arrogance and obstinacy were Alcibiades' special hallmarks. His "constant need to win and come first" (τὸ φιλόνικον ἰσχυρότατον ... καὶ τὸ φιλόπρωτον; Plut. *Alc.* 2.1) were always in evidence, as we frequently have had occasion to note, and judging by the anecdotal tradition this had been the case from his earliest youth. We have noted that as a child he was so intent on playing a game in the street that he refused to budge when a carter threatened to run him over (Plut. *Alc.* 2.3–4). Still young, he is said to have "killed one of his servants by striking him with a club, at the gymnasium of Sibyrtus" (Antiph. ap. Plut. *Alc.* 3.1–2). Other stories include his having beaten up a rival *choregus* "before the audience and judges" ([Andoc.] 4.20–21), his having prevented Aristophanes from winning first prize for *Clouds* in 423 BCE by intimidating the judges (Ar. *Nu.* Arg. 5 Coulon), and his having gone to the Record Office and "expunged with his wetted finger" an indictment against the comic poet Hegemon of Thasos (the officials were afraid to renew the charge "for fear of Alcibiades"; Ath. 9.407c). He held a painter prisoner in his house until a commission was finished (Plut. *Alc.* 16.5; [Andoc.] 4.17), and struck the richest man in Athens on the chin with his fist "as a joke" (Plut. *Alc.* 8.5). He was also bold in battle, to the extent that in the fourth century BCE the Romans erected a statue to him as "the bravest of the Greeks" (Plin. *HN* 34.12).

Early official recognition of Alcibiades' prowess in the field came his way when he served at Potidaea aged about 20. He was badly injured in battle and won the ἀριστεῖον or prize for valour (Plut. *Alc.* 7.5; Isoc. 16.29). By rights the prize should have gone to Socrates, but Alcibiades' ἀξίωμα (worth, fame, reputation, or social clout due to the status of his family, perhaps)[10] was such that "the generals seemed anxious to bestow [the prize]" on Alcibiades instead. There had been a family tradition of winning ἀριστεῖα: one of Alcibiades' forebears, a certain Cleinias son of Alcibiades, had been granted such a prize at Artemisium in 480 BCE (Hdt. 8.17),[11] and it might appear that the honour at Potidaea, which consisted of a suit of armour, came to him almost by hereditary right. Thucydides, on formally introducing Alcibiades in the *Histories*, speaks of how he was influential on account of the reputation of his ancestors (5.43.2). Many years later, in 397 BCE, Isocrates

---

10. See Chapter 10, below.
11. J. Hatzfeld, *Alcibiade: étude sur l'histoire d'Athènes à la fin du Ve siècle*, 2nd edn (Paris: Presses Universitaires de France, 1951), 12.

was to make Alcibiades Jr say that when his father won the hand of Hipparate daughter of Hipponicus he won another ἀριστεῖον (Isoc. 16.31), an achievement that was in keeping with the noble lineage to which he alludes at 16.25. Alcibiades himself elsewhere elaborates on his ancestry: from Zeus himself, via Eurysaces and the latter's father Ajax (Pl. *Alc.* 1.121a). The only other family in fact or fiction in which the ἀριστεῖον was regarded as somehow hereditary was the mythical one of Ajax in Sophocles' play. His father Telamon had won the ἀριστεῖον when he fought against Troy under Heracles, and Ajax's distress is in large part the result of frustrated expectation that he would be awarded Achilles' armour as though by right.

This was all cogently argued by H. Grégoire in the 1950s,[12] but all he got for his pains was ridicule: "embarrassing",[13] "bizarre",[14] "very far-fetched".[15] It is customary these days to ignore the substantial achievements of what we might call the Belgian school of tragic criticism. It is true that the conclusions of Grégoire, Roger Goossens and their colleagues were often "hit and miss", but at least they were shooting in the right direction, and they have much to teach us. Grégoire rightly saw Alcibiades lying behind Ajax, and rightly saw Menelaus and Agamemnon – antipathetic towards Ajax – as somehow personifying Spartan and Argive antipathy towards Alcibiades. Ever since Welcker, Menelaus' adverse comments on archery have often been taken as a reflection of fifth-century Spartans' low opinion of archery.[16] Where Grégoire faltered was in assuming that since Alcibiades himself had brought about a treaty between Athens and Argos in 420 BCE, Sophocles' *Ajax* must be earlier than that date, concluding that the play was performed between Sphacteria and Delium. There is, however, another, later, context that may prove to be more acceptable.

This is the period in 412–410, when Alcibiades' loyalties (if one can use the word in connection with him) had changed yet again. His position at Sparta had become increasingly insecure, not least because of the personal enmity of Agis, the king whose wife he was suspected of having seduced when Agis was fortifying Decelea (a policy that had been proposed by Alcibiades). He therefore left Sparta and crossed to Ionia, where, still acting in the Spartan interest in collaboration with

---

12. H. Grégoire & P. Orgels, "L'*Ajax* de Sophocle, Alcibiades et Sparte", *Annuaire de l'Institut de Philologie et d'histoire orientales et slaves* **13** (1953), 653–63; H. Grégoire, "La Date de l'*Ajax* de Sophocle", *Academie Royale de Belgique, Bulletin de la Classe des Lettres* **41** (1955), 187–98.
13. Friis Johansen, "Sophocles 1939–1959", 171.
14. Rose, "Historicizing Sophocles' *Ajax*", 80.
15. Scodel, "The Politics of Sophocles' *Ajax*", 31, citing Friis Johansen's acerbic summary and not the articles themselves.
16. F. G. Welcker, "Über den Aias des Sophokles", *Rheinisches Museum* **3** (1829), 43–92, 229–364, reprinted in *Kleine Schriften 2*, 264–340 (Bonn: E. Weber, 1845); Grégoire & Orgels, "L'*Ajax* de Sophocle", 655; Scodel, "The Politics of Sophocles' *Ajax*".

Astyochus and Tissaphernes, he induced Chios, Erythrae, Clazomenae, Teos and Miletus to revolt from Athens (Thuc. 8.14–17).

The significant event so far as *Ajax* is concerned is an engagement before Miletus in which Alcibiades participated (although Thucydides adds the information almost as an afterthought: "for [Alcibiades] had been present, and had fought on the side of the Milesians and Tissaphernes"; Thuc. 8.26.3). The Athenians in Samos had received reinforcements "towards the end of the summer" of 412 in the form of "a thousand Athenian hoplites and fifteen hundred Argives, of whom five hundred were originally light-armed, but the Athenians gave them heavy arms". Together with another thousand allied troops, they crossed over to Miletus and took up a position outside the city. The engagement was indecisive, the Athenians on one wing putting to flight the Peloponnesians and Tissaphernes' cavalry, but the Argives on the other wing falling before the Milesian onslaught. The Argives had made the mistake of underestimating their Ionian enemy: "The Argives on their own wing dashed forward, and made a disorderly attack upon the troops opposed to them, whom they despised; they thought that being Ionians, they would be sure to run away". They had not reckoned with the presence of Alcibiades, who presumably had put backbone into the troops under his command, so that the Argives "were defeated by the Milesians, and nearly three hundred of them perished" (Thuc. 8.25.3). The outcome being inconclusive, the Athenians pulled out, and "the Argives hurrying away ... after their disaster, went home in a rage" (Thuc. 8.27.6). It was not long before Alcibiades deserted the Spartan cause (the fact that the Spartans had condemned him to death did not encourage loyalty here) and threw his lot in, for the moment, with Tissaphernes (Thuc. 8.45). By the time of the likely performance of *Ajax*, he was on the Athenian side again, but based on Samos.

A jealous king and hostile Spartans on the one hand, and Argives disgruntled at an Alcibiades-induced slaughter of many of their soldiery on the other, might well lie behind the plotting of an *Ajax* performed in the spring of 410 BCE. The three hundred dead Argives were only Alcibiades' most recent victims, however. Otherwise, he was noted for the delight he took in animal cruelty and animal butchery. As noted, an anecdote relates how Alcibiades once bought a very fine hound for a very large sum, and proceeded to cut its tail off, to universal disapproval. When his friends told him how sorry everyone was for the dog, Alcibiades replied "Then what I want has come about. I want the Athenians to talk about this, rather than that they should say something worse about me" (Plut. *Alc.* 9). There is a tale about the young Alcibiades strolling into "the fields of his admirers, and having selected the most beautiful bulls, sacrific[ing] them" (Schol. Luc. 20.16). Not many years before the likely performance of *Ajax*, he had single-handedly slaughtered "a great number of sacrificial animals" at the Altar of Zeus in the precinct at Olympia after his Olympic victory in 416 BCE.

These had been given to him by the Chians and there were enough beasts to feed the whole crowd (Plut. *Alc.* 12.1; cf. [Andoc.] 4.30; Thuc. 6.16.2; Ath. 1.3e). Alcibiades' enthusiasm for sacrificing is further attested by his having successfully proposed a decree providing for monthly sacrifices at the Temple of Heracles at Cynosarges near Athens (Ath. 6.234d). Violence of any kind was very much part of Alcibiades' make-up, as we have seen, just as βία (violence) was part of his name, and this was a coincidence of which Athenian writers made much.[17]

At about the same time as Alcibiades' Olympic triumph and its attendant slaughter of animals, there was another massacre being conducted, this time of the inhabitants of the island of Melos. It is clear from the sources that this was the direct result of Alcibiadean policy, and that Alcibiades would have participated in person had he not considered his presence at the Olympic games to be more important.[18] The cities that had provided the furnishings and victuals for the celebrations surrounding Alcibiades' Olympic victory were, according to Satyrus, regularly used "as so many handmaidens" whenever Alcibiades travelled abroad (Ath. 12.534d), and two of them, the Chians and the Lesbians, supplied ships to assist the Athenians at Melos. Thucydides' account of the Melian campaign (5.84–116) follows the briefest of references to an attack on Argos, but one in which Alcibiades is specifically named. In the summer of 416, Alcibiades, who was one of the generals for that year,[19] "sailed to Argos with twenty ships" and took three hundred captives from among the anti-democratic party there. The "Athenians" – by implication not including Alcibiades but presumably acting on his orders – deposited these individuals on nearby islands. Again not including Alcibiades, the "Athenians" then "attacked the island of Melos" (5.84.1). Alcibiades had already returned to Athens (Diod. 12.81.3), leaving the Melian campaign in the hands of others (Thuc. 5.85.3), one of whom supplied a team of horses that Alcibiades entered in his own name at Olympia (Isocr. 16).

It is not that Thucydides is silent about Alcibiades' involvement at Melos, but he puts the idea of his insidious presence across in an oblique, but nonetheless effective, fashion, by making "the Athenians" in the famous dialogue with the Melians speak with his voice (Thuc. 5.85–11).[20] We learn most about Alcibiades' direct concern with Melos from a speech attributed to Andocides: Alcibiades is said to have presented a motion that the islanders be enslaved ([Andoc.] 4.22). Plutarch adds the information that Alcibiades supported the motion that men of military

---

17. See p. 158, below.
18. M. Vickers, "Alcibiades and Melos: Thucydides 5.84–116", *Historia* **48** (1999), 265–81; Chapter 9, below.
19. Develin, *Athenian Officials 684–321 BC*, 148.
20. Vickers, "Alcibiades and Melos"; Chapter 9, below.

age should be put to the sword (Plut. *Alc.* 16.5–6); Thucydides simply records the bloody consequence, without directly mentioning Alcibiades' involvement: "The Athenians put to death all who were of military age, and made slaves of the women and children" (Thuc. 5.116.4). We learn from the Andocidean speech that Alcibiades "bought a woman from among the captives and has had a son by her, a child whose birth was more unnatural than that of Aegisthus, since he is sprung from parents who are each other's deadliest enemies" ([Andoc.] 4.22). The speaker continues, "When you are shown things of this kind on the tragic stage, you regard them with horror; but when you see them taking place in Athens, you remain unmoved – and yet you are uncertain whether the tales of tragedy are founded on the truth or spring merely from the imagination of poets" (*ibid.*).

This uncertainty, as to whether the tales told by tragedians are based on the truth or are poets' inventions, should be at the heart of modern, as well as ancient, criticism of Athenian tragedy. The choice of plot will have been governed by whatever was in the news. In 410 BCE, Alcibiades' problems will have been at the forefront of everyone's minds, and a veteran politician like Sophocles will have been alert to the fact. In *Ajax*, many aspects of the plot resonate with what we know Alcibiades' experiences to have been, whether his ancestral ἀριστεῖον, his enmity with the Spartan Agis, his responsibility for the deaths of 300 Argives, his sacrificing hundreds of animals at Olympia,[21] his involvement in the massacre of the menfolk of Melos or his having taken a prisoner of war as his mistress and having a child by her. There is not of course a one-to-one relationship between recent history and Sophocles' plotting, but there is a sufficient overlap to justify seeing the playwright as a shrewd commentator on current affairs, and a perceptive judge of the characters of prominent contemporaries.

We shall examine another of these presently, but first let us look for further support for the case made so far: that it is Alcibiades who lies behind Ajax. The examples that follow are of uneven merit, it is true, and they are only a sample (it is not necessary to taste all the sea to know that it is salty), but they cumulatively turn on its head the position that in his plays Sophocles stood aloof from the world of politics. They also remove many of the problems with which current criticism of the play is beset; they constitute not so much a "wigwam", but rather a "big top", if not a "three-ring circus". Ajax's madness and mutability alone, for example, raise

---

21. Cf. "Sacrificial priest and victim are here the same" (M. Sicherl, "The Tragic Issue in Sophocles' *Ajax*", *Yale Classical Studies* 25 (1977), 67–98, esp. 97), and "Ajax, forgetting his trouble, has performed a complete sacrifice with all due rites, in perfection of loyal worship" (*Aj.* 710–13). On tragedy and ritual sacrifice, see W. Burkert, "Greek Tragedy and Sacrificial Ritual", *Greek, Roman and Byzantine Studies* 7 (1966), 87–121, esp. 112.

many questions, but the answers fall easily into place when viewed against the background of an Alcibiades whose character was full of "many strange inconsistencies and contradictions" (ἀνομοιότητας πρὸς αὐτὸ καὶ μεταβολάς; Plut. *Alc.* 2.1), and any apparent flaws in the tragic hero would have been intentional.[22] Sophocles is indeed "reaching after effects of irony which can only be described as bizarre",[23] for such was the nature of his principal model. The nature of Ajax's regard for the truth, or the lack of it,[24] is related to his madness, but again, when we reflect that the likely model was one who had once fooled Spartan envoys by means of "deceit and oaths" (Plut. *Nic.* 10.4), who had betrayed his city, and who was epitomized as πανοῦργος ἐν τῇ πολιτείᾳ καὶ ἀναλήθης (a tricky politician and deceitful; Plut. *Alc.* 41.1), problems recede, and there is thus no incompatibility between any apparent deceit and the supposed character of Ajax. Nor will there be any need to explain away any impieties on Ajax's part, for they will all have been part of Sophocles' skilful character building, and Alcibiades' impiety needs no gloss; ditto, Alcibiades' hubris and his μεγαλοπραγμοσύνη (grandiose schemes; Plut. *Alc.* 6.4), which also seem to have informed the picture that Sophocles creates.[25] The "unsettled problem"[26] of Ajax's claim ἐθηλύνθην (I was made female; 651) might be resolved by reference to Alcibiades' sometime effeminacy, of which Sophocles makes much in Antigone and which was to be a constant feature of Alcibiadean characterization.[27] Even the apparent Themistoclean references in *Ajax*[28] are at home in a play based on one who had in 412 been resident in Themistocles' place of exile, and who was very much aware of the reputation of his predecessor.[29]

---

22. Cf. E. Vandvik, "Ajax the Insane", *Symbolae Osloenses, Supplement* **11** (1942), 169–75.

23. J. Moore, "The Dissembling Speech of Ajax", *Yale Classical Studies* **25** (1977), 47–66, esp. 55.

24. For example, Welcker, "Über den Aias des Sophokles"; C. M. Bowra, *Sophoclean Tragedy* (Oxford: Clarendon Press, 1944), 39ff.; K. Reinhardt, Sophokles (Frankfurt: V. Klostermann, 1947), 31; Sicherl, "The Tragic Issue in Sophocles' *Ajax*"; G. Crane, "Ajax, the Unexpected and the Deception Speech", *Classical Philology* **85** (1990), 89–101.

25. On *hubris* in *Ajax* see, for example, Garvie, *Sophocles* Ajax, 12–16; μέγας and its cognates occur far more frequently in *Ajax* than in any other Sophoclean tragedy. Cf. Them. *APo.* 5.1.56, who gives a short list of famous μεγαλοψύχοι, that consists of "Alcibiades, Ajax and Achilles".

26. O. Taplin, "Yielding to Forethought: Sophocles' Ajax", in *Arktouros: Hellenic Studies, presented to Bernard M. W. Knox*, G. W. Bowersock *et al.* (eds), 122–9 (Berlin: de Gruyter, 1979), 128; cf. R. A. S. Seaford, "Sophokles and the Mysteries", *Hermes* **122** (1994), 282.

27. Cf. Duff, "Plutarch on the Childhood of Alkibiades", 96–7; and the discussions of Eur. *Hel.* and Ar. *Lys.* in Vickers, *Alcibiades on Stage*.

28. E. Okell, "Does Themistocles 'Hero of Salamis' Lie behind Sophocles' *Ajax*?", Paper delivered to the joint Classical Association and Classical Association of Scotland conference, 4–7 April 2002, University of Edinburgh.

29. Plutarch was very conscious of the similarity between both men's careers. Some parallels are mentioned by A. J. Podlecki, *The Life of Themistocles: A Critical Survey of the Literary and*

A feature of *Ajax* that is usually passed over with little comment, if any, is the title of the play in Greek: Αἴας μαστιγοφόρος or *Ajax the Whip-carrier*. The whip is alluded to from time to time: Ajax threatens to attack Odysseus with it at 110, and at 242 the imaginary scourging is described – Odysseus is tied to a pillar and whipped with a piece of harness. What is perhaps relevant here is the tale that Alcibiades himself had undergone just such a whipping at an uncertain date at the hands of the Eleians. He had just won an Olympic victory, and was asked by the Eleians where he came from. "The best city", he replied, and so they whipped him (ἐμαστίγωσαν αὐτόν). Alcibiades was outraged at this and tried to bring pressure to bear at Athens to make war on the Eleians because they had insulted Athens (τὴν πόλιν ὑβρίζοντες). The tale is preserved in two versions by Hermogenes the rhetorician (*Inv.* 2.4.37). The victory must have been before 416, for in that year there could have been no doubt as where Alcibiades came from (and the fact that as quoted by Plutarch, Euripides' encomium of 416 BCE implies a previous victory,[30] adds credence to the tale).

Odysseus and Andocides

We can safely associate Menelaus and Agamemnon with contemporary Sparta and Argos, and presumably with figures recognizable to the audience, if not to us. Menelaus' gruffness in any case has much in common with the popular image of Spartans, who were surly creatures: "anger" and "sour looks" being the normal reaction even to one's neighbour at Sparta (Thuc. 2.37.2). Menelaus' lines are also distinguished by a certain laconism of expression.[31] But what of Odysseus, who plays such a prominent role in the play? He is characterized as Ajax's mortal enemy, and if we were to look around for a contemporary of Alcibiades who might have played a similar role in 410, we need look no further than Andocides. And just as Alcibiades was reckoned to be a descendent of Ajax, Andocides was thought

---

Archaeological Evidence (Montreal: McGill-Queen's University Press, 1975), 139 n.9, and W. J. Schneider, "Eine Polemik Polemons in den Propyläen: Ein Votivgemälde des Alkibiades – Kontext und Rezeption", *Klio* **81** (1999), 18–44, esp. 23 n.40. See too Chapter 11, below.

30. Plutarch wrote δὶς στεφθέντ' (*Alc.* 11.3), cleverly misquoting the Διὸς στεφθέντ' that Euripides presumably wrote, as G. Hermann saw (Eur. 755.5 Page).

31. On which see E. D. Francis, "Brachylogia Laconica: Spartan Speeches in Thucydides", *Bulletin of the Institute of Classical Studies* **38** (1991–3), 198–212; D. P. Tompkins, "Archidamus and the Question of Characterization in Thucydides", in *Nomodeiktes: Greek Studies in Honor of Martin Ostwald*, R. Rosen & J. Farrell (eds), 99–111 (Ann Arbor, MI: University of Michigan Press, 1993).

to be descended from Odysseus (Hellanic. *FGrH* 4 F 170b ap. Plut. *Alc.* 21.1). Andocides' denunciations on turning state's evidence in 415 had contributed to the deaths of some of Alcibiades' circle,[32] and it has even been suggested that he was involved in a conspiracy to have Alcibiades expelled.[33] Precise details of the events of 415 BCE are still shrouded in mystery, but Andocides managed to stay in Athens if only for a short period, while Alcibiades was condemned to death *in absentia*. This discrepancy must have rankled with Alcibiades.

In the event, Andocides was soon to be in exile himself, having fallen foul of a decree proposed by the otherwise unknown Isotimides that those who had been guilty of impiety should be excluded from all the sacred places of Attica. Andocides was the only person still in Athens to whom this applied, for all the rest had gone into exile (and might we perhaps detect the hand of Alcibiades in this legislation?). Andocides went into voluntary exile and in 410 BCE was active in trade. In particular, in September 411, after the fall of the Four Hundred at Athens, he had begun to supply materiel – specifically oar-spars, corn and bronze – to the Athenian fleet at Samos (Andoc. 2.11–12), supplies that led to an immediate improvement in the Athenians' fortunes. Samos, however, was where Alcibiades had been stationed ever since Thrasybulus had won an amnesty for him during the summer of 411 BCE. For supplies to arrive and be utilized on Samos there must have been some kind of understanding between Alcibiades and Andocides. The real puzzle of *Ajax* is why Odysseus, Ajax's implacable enemy, should have weakened and allowed the burial of the hero's corpse towards the end of the play. In the language of myth that Sophocles employs, it is an action that echoes the short-lived collaboration in the interests of Athens between two individuals who had every reason otherwise to dislike each other. Andocides' fear, and Alcibiades' loathing, are well expressed at the beginning of the play when Odysseus is afraid to confront Ajax (74–88), and when Tecmessa describes the cruel, if imaginary, treatment of Odysseus (239–44). The rehabilitation of the dead hero is Sophocles' gloss on contemporary events.

Teucer, Alcibiades and Andocides

There is a school of thought that holds that there is a lack of dramatic unity in *Ajax*; at its extreme, that the last 555 lines are so much padding.[34] Not everyone shares

---

32. Ostwald, *From Popular Sovereignty*, 537–50.
33. W. Ellis, *Alcibiades* (London: Routledge, 1989), 61.
34. A. J. A. Waldock, *Sophocles the Dramatist* (Cambridge: Cambridge University Press, 1951), 49–75.

this view of course,[35] and A. F. Garvie's note on Teucer, "from now until the end of the play Teucer will, in a sense, represent Ajax",[36] more closely reflects ancient dramatic practice. For ancient dramatists would often represent different aspects of an individual's personality by means of different characters on the stage, and by invoking such "polymorphic characterization" supposedly "broken-backed" plays can be seen instead to possess a highly effective dramatic unity. Thus, for example, in Aristophanes' *Clouds* Strepsiades "comes forward" as an exaggerated version of Pericles, while Pheidippides embodies many characteristics of Alcibiades; later in the same play the scene between the Stronger and the Weaker Arguments is not an uncomfortable disruption, but keeps the κωμῳδούμενοι on stage all the time.[37] Teucer's "harmony with his brother"[38] is in keeping with this principle, so that if Ajax "comes forward" as Alcibiades, so too does Teucer, thus preserving a continuity that might otherwise be missing. Teucer's "overwhelming rhetorical victory" over Agamemnon in a "devastating speech",[39] for example, matches Alcibiades' reputation as one who was δεινότατος εἰπεῖν (an extremely clever speaker; D.L. 12.84.1, 13.68.5).

But Teucer is a more complex figure than this, and in contrast to Ajax reveals himself to be rather more flexible, in the manner of Odysseus. "Teucer's qualities ... emerge as neither fully Odyssean nor completely Ajaxian".[40] Such a conflation of historical figures in a single fictional one is not unparalleled. To return to *Clouds* once more: the views attributed to "Socrates" are made up from a bundle of philosophers in the circle of Pericles (e.g. Damon, Zeno, Protagoras, Anaxagoras), while Pheidippides incorporates features of Xanthippus, Pericles' physical son, as well as of Alcibiades.[41] The choice of the name Teucer for another portmanteau figure is not only significant but clever, for a historical Teucer was among those who had denounced those, including Alcibiades, who had profaned the Mysteries (Plut. *Alc.* 20.6). He was a metic who only gave evidence under immunity from prosecution.

35. Cf. M. Heath, *The Poetics of Greek Tragedy* (Palo Alto, CA: Stanford University Press, 1987); C. Eucken, "Die thematische Einheit des Sophokleischen Aias", *Würzburger Jahrbücher für die Altertumswissenschaft* (new series) **17** (1991), 119–33.
36. Garvie, *Sophocles* Ajax, 216.
37. M. Vickers, "Alcibiades in Cloudedoverland", in *Nomodeiktes*, Rosen & Farrell (eds), 603–18; *Pericles on Stage*, 22–58; *Alcibiades on Stage*.
38. Garvie, *Sophocles* Ajax, 218.
39. Heath, *The Poetics of Greek Tragedy*, 202.
40. Hesk, *Sophocles* Ajax, 125.
41. Vickers, *Pericles on Stage*, 29–33. And see further on such "Arcimboldesque" characterization, Chapter 11, below.

"No sooner had Teucer denounced [the conspirators] than they fled the country" (Andoc. 1.15).[42]

The conflation of elements of Alcibiades and Andocides in the characterization of Teucer explains why "the *rapprochement* between Odysseus and Teucer is so warm ... because they are both, in their own ways, admirable exponents of the same traditional set of values; they have the same ideals, admire the same kind of action and person, and so understand each other perfectly".[43] Teucer is neither a "goody"[44] nor a "baddie",[45] but he does effectively reinforce the Athenian audience's prejudices against their Spartan enemies and their own Argive allies (who must have been asking embarrassing questions after the events at Miletus of 412). He also stands for common sense in testing times. Things are so bad, Sophocles seems to be saying, that sworn enemies should put their excesses behind them and unite in the face of adversity.

The final lines of the Chorus – "Mortals can understand many things when they have seen them; but before he sees them no one can predict how he will fare in the future" (1418–20)[46] – are often dismissed as banal, but they are not. They are full of foreboding tinged with hope. The Athenians were playing for high stakes in 410, and Sophocles was well placed to know how very high those stakes were. "The miserable condition of the Chorus on campaign"[47] well encapsulates (and will have brought home to the audience in Athens) the current state of those Athenians encamped by the sea not far from Troy in the spring of 410, unsure of how matters will develop under the command of an unpredictable Alcibiades. To paraphrase Garvie on Aeschylus' *Supplices*,[48] the conclusion of this chapter is that *Ajax* fits very well among the surviving works of Sophocles' maturity, as well as into the political situation in 411/10 BCE. If so, it is to be hoped that Friis Johansen's embarrassing scholarship[49] can be set aside, and that the many historical riches still to be mined from Sophocles' plays can be brought to light.

42. O. Aurenche, *Les Groupes d'Alcibiade, de Léogoras et de Teucros: remarques sur la vie politique athénienne en 415 avant J.C.* (Paris: Belles Lettres, 1974), 113.
43. Heath, *The Poetics of Greek Tragedy*, 203.
44. *Ibid.*
45. Nearly everyone else.
46. Translated by Garvie, *Sophocles* Ajax.
47. Heath, *The Poetics of Greek Tragedy*, 201.
48. A. F. Garvie, *Aeschylus'* Supplices: *Play and Trilogy* (Cambridge: Cambridge University Press, 1969), vi.
49. Friis Johansen, "Sophocles 1939–1959", 171.

5

Philoctetes, Alcibiades, Andocides and Pericles

Sophocles' *Philoctetes* dwells on the plight of the homonymous Greek hero who has been abandoned on the island of Lemnos by his countrymen on account of a repugnant wound in his foot. Years later, Odysseus, accompanied by Neoptolemus, the son of Achilles, returns to Lemnos to acquire the bow that Philoctetes had been granted by Heracles, without which the Greeks would never take Troy. In his *The Cure at Troy* (1990) Seamus Heaney reshaped Sophocles' play in order to make it fit the contemporary political picture (he identifies Philoctetes with Unionism, Neoptolemus with the Southern Irish, and Odysseus with the Provisional IRA).[1] In similar fashion, I believe that the poets of antiquity would reshape old tales in order to fit a contemporary situation (which would go a long way to explain the discrepancies with which ancient mythology is replete). Heaney's veiled political analogue is thus in principle identical with Sophocles' treatment of events of his own day, in which reconciliation was again much to the fore, in this case centred on the terms on which Alcibiades might be allowed to return from exile.

But to make such a connection between Heaney and Sophocles is tantamount to heresy to those who believe in Dodds' "essential critical principle" that "what is not mentioned in the play does not exist",[2] and who share Wilamowitz's position that politics never intrude on Sophoclean drama.[3] It is boring to hear this trotted

---

1. C. Meir, "Classical and Political Analogues in Heaney's *The Cure at Troy*", in *The Classical World and the Mediterranean*, G. Serpillo & D. Badin (eds), 256–60 (Cagliari: Tema, 1996), 256-7.
2. Dodds, "On Misunderstanding the *Oedipus Rex*", 40; *The Ancient Concept of Progress*, 68; *Oxford Readings in Greek Tragedy*, 180.
3. Wilamowitz, "Excurse zum Oedipus des Sophokles", 59, quoted p. 1, above. He made a similar point in the specific context of *Philoctetes*: "Kein Vers weist aus dem Drama heraus auf irgend etwas in der Gegenwart des Dichters ... Ein gelungenes zeitloses Kunstwerk" (*Die dramatische Technik des Sophokles* [Berlin: Weidmannsche Buchhandlung, 1917], 316–17). Cf. W. M. Calder III, "Sophoclean Apologia: *Philoctetes*", *Greek, Roman and Byzantine Studies* **12**

out again, but while lip service is paid to the view that surviving Greek tragedies "have a strongly contemporary application to the problems of the Athenian *polis*",[4] the degree to which this may actually have occurred is a matter of scholarly dispute, and it is still the modern orthodoxy that "clear contemporary references seem to be limited to a few exceptional events".[5] Some have been bolder, and in the context of *Philoctetes*, A. M. Bowie sees the play as a means of filtering "Alcibiades and the political world of Athens ... through the myth" of the Homeric hero;[6] G. Ugolini finds it "difficult to free [him]self from the idea that Sophocles wished to allude to Alcibiades and to his return when he chose the theme of the *Philoctetes* for the Dionysia of 409 BC";[7] and in the general context of the later fifth century BCE at Athens, Mark Munn has written that "the public conscience was both entertained and at the same time informed about underlying meanings and ironies within contemporary events through the allegories of tragedy and the farces of comedy".[8]

It will be argued here that recent political events were at the forefront of the minds of both Sophocles and his audience in 409 BCE, and that *Philoctetes* can be shown to reflect in close detail one of the deepest concerns of the Athenians, namely, whether or not Alcibiades would return to Athens and on what terms. We saw in Chapter 4 how Alcibiades had been placed in 410. Much had changed since 425, when he was a rival of Cleon and already a potential tyrant in Sophocles' eyes. He had been elected one of the three generals for the Sicilian expedition in 415 BCE (a campaign he had done much to promote); he had been suspected of involvement in various acts of impiety on the eve of the fleet's departure, had been condemned to

(1971) 153–74, esp. 153; *Theatrokratia*, 193–4. Recent studies of *Philoctetes* in this mode thus include: M. W. Blundell, *Helping Friends and Harming Enemies: A Study in Sophocles and Greek Ethics* (Cambridge: Cambridge University Press, 1989), 184–225; R. G. Ussher (ed.), *Sophocles Philoctetes* (Warminster: Aris & Phillips, 1990); J. C. Gibert, *Change of Mind in Greek Tragedy* (Göttingen: Vandenhoek & Ruprecht. 1995); H. M. Roisman, "The Appropriation of a Son: Sophocles' *Philoctetes*", *Greek, Roman and Byzantine Studies* 38 (1997), 127–71; T. Visser, *Untersuchungen zum Sophokleischen Philoktet: Das auslösende Ereignis in der Stückgestaltung* (Stuttgart: B. G. Teubner, 1998); E. Lefèvre, *Die Unfähigkeit, sich zu erkennen: Sophokles' Tragödien* (Leiden: Brill, 2001); M. Altmeyer, *Unzeitgemässes Denken bei Sophokles* (Stuttgart: Franz Steiner, 2001). For earlier bibliography, see Calder, *Theatrokratia*, 215.

4. Easterling, "Tragedy, Greek", 1541; cf. Griffin, *Sophocles Revisited*, 73–6.
5. Pelling, *Greek Tragedy and the Historian*, 216.
6. A. M. Bowie, "Tragic Filters for History: Euripides' *Supplices* and Sophocles' *Philoctetes*", in *Greek Tragedy and the Historian*, Pelling (ed.), 39–61, apparently unaware of my "Alcibiades on Stage: *Philoctetes* and *Cyclops*", *Historia* 36 (1987), 171–97, on which this chapter is partly based.
7. G. Ugolini, *Sofocle e Atene: Vita politica e attività teatrale nella Grecia classica* (Rome: Carocci, 2000), 210.
8. Munn, *The School of History*, 2.

death *in absentia* and had had his property confiscated and sold at public auction; in exile in Sparta, he had advised the Spartans on the most effective ways to defeat Athens. He was currently still in exile, but acting apparently in the Athenian cause in Ionia. We know from many contemporary sources that in 409 BCE the deepest concerns of most Athenians were embodied in the person of Alcibiades, in the part he had played in bringing his city almost to its knees, and in the hope that he might still rescue it from its misfortunes.

We know for certain that Sophocles' *Philoctetes* was performed in the archonship of Glaucippus, in 409 BCE, when it won first prize (Arg. *Phil.*). The reading that follows is predicated on the possibility that tragic poets might allude to Alcibiades, and that if they did their audience would be alert to such allusions; and that they would recognize every subtlety the playwright might introduce as part of his exploration of contemporary political realities (and if the case made for political readings of *Antigone, Oedipus Tyrannus* and *Ajax* in earlier chapters holds good, there should be little difficulty in viewing *Philoctetes* in the same fashion). It will be argued here that both Philoctetes and Neoptolemus stand, polymorphically, for Alcibiades; Odysseus and the Merchant for Andocides; and Heracles for Pericles. The reasons will be spelled out in detail later on.

The view that Philoctetes was intended to represent Alcibiades is in fact not new, and goes back to the eighteenth century.[9] "Able critics", in the words of R. C. Jebb, "have favoured the view that [Sophocles'] choice of subject was in some way connected with the return of Alcibiades", although Jebb himself considered that to read political allegory into Sophocles' play "is surely to wrong him grievously as a poet".[10] One problem with reading allegorical meanings into Greek drama, however, is that once permitted there is no end to the ideas that might be put forward. Charles Lenormant saw Philoctetes as an idealization of the sufferings of the Athenian people,[11] and others have seen in him the aged Sophocles.[12] Faced

---

9. M. Lebeau le cadet, "Mémoires sur les tragiques grecs", *Mémoires de littérature; tirés des registres de l'Académie des Inscriptions* 35 (1770), 432–74, esp. 447. For other versions of this theory, see A. Schöll, *Sophokles, sein Leben und Wirken* (Frankfurt: Hermann, 1842), as reported by R. C. Jebb (ed.), *Sophocles, the Plays and Fragments* 4: *The Philoctetes* (Cambridge: Cambridge University Press, 1898), xli; S. Piazza, *La politica in Sofocle* (Padua: Tipografia del Seminario, 1896), 107ff.; H. Patin, *Études sur les tragiques grecs: Sophocle*, 9th edn (Paris: Hachette, 1913), 125–6; Ugolini, *Sofocle e Atene*, 188 n.17, 203–4 n.86.

10. Jebb, *Sophocles, the Plays and Fragments*, xl–xli (the next sentence reads: "at the same time it must be recognised that the coincidence of date is really remarkable").

11. C. Lenormant, "Du Philoctète de Sophocle: á propos de la représentation de cette tragédie à Orléans", *Le Correspondant* (25 July) (1855), 6.

12. E. Turolla, *Saggio sulla poesia di Sofocle* (Bari: G. Laterza, 1948), 174–9; cf. Calder, "Sophoclean Apologia: *Philoctetes*"; *Theatrokratia*.

with such a range of views, for the most part incompatible with one another, it is hardly surprising that many scholars have been reluctant to read contemporary allusions into Sophocles' plays.[13]

The dramatis personae

Philoctetes and Neoptolemus

There are many reasons why Alcibiades should have been on the minds of Sophocles and his Athenian audience in 409 BCE.[14] His association with the Spartans had come to an end in 412 BCE and he spent the next few months at the court of Tissaphernes in Caria. In 411 BCE he was invited to join the Athenian forces at Samos and assisted them to defeat Peloponnesian fleets at Cynossema and Cyzicus. Between these events he spent a month imprisoned at Sardis, but managed to escape. At Athens, some had protested at the possibility of Alcibiades' return, while others thought that he should be restored, being "the only man capable of saving us" (Thuc. 8.53–4). Alcibiades was not in fact to return until 407 BCE, as a direct result of the debate of which both *Ajax* and *Philoctetes* form a significant part. In 409 BCE Alcibiades was in the Hellespont, having blockaded Chalcedon at the end of 410 BCE.[15] The hesitation shown by Philoctetes to undertake the task he is asked to do has been well compared by Ugolini to Alcibiades' own hesitation and well-founded doubts as to whether it would be wise to return (and even when he did, he took care that he was guarded "by an escort of trusted men who would defend him in the event of any attack"; Xen. *Hell.* 1.4.19).[16]

In the *Little Iliad* it is Diomedes who rescues Philoctetes from Lemnos, while Odysseus brings Neoptolemus from Scyros. Diomedes has been dropped altogether from the story as told by Sophocles, and we might well ask why. The replacement of Diomedes by Neoptolemus is another implicit reference to the career of Alcibiades, for it was a certain Diomedes whom Alcibiades is said to have deprived of a valuable chariot team (Diod. 13.74.3) at Olympia in 416 BCE to race it himself ([Andoc.] 4.26–9; Plut. *Alc.* 12.3–5),[17] and the case was still being argued more than a couple of decades later (Isoc. 16). Diomedes would not have been appropriate; the plot had to be altered if it was to refer to Alcibiades without jarring.

---

13. For example, Friis Johansen, "Sophocles 1939–1959", 163; Ussher, *Sophocles Philoctetes*, 19; Lefèvre, *Die Unfähigkeit, sich zu erkennen*, 273 n.177.

14. See Ugolini, *Sofocle e Atene*, ch. 11: "Il ritorno di Alcibiade".

15. Hatzfeld, *Alcibiade*, 277; Munn, *The School of History*, 163.

16. Ugolini, *Sofocle e Atene*, 206–8.

17. Vickers, "Alcibiades and Melos"; Chapter 9, below.

Neoptolemus takes Diomedes' place in the *Philoctetes*, just as Alcibiades apparently usurped the historical Diomedes' place at Olympia. He does not, as has been thought in the past, represent Thrasybulus or even Pericles the younger;[18] rather, Sophocles seems again to employ the device of "polymorphic characterization", this time to make Neoptolemus reflect features of Alcibiades' history and Protean character that would be out of place in the figure of Philoctetes. In the main, these are Alcibiades' more positive qualities; but "almost every detail of [his] behaviour can be variously interpreted",[19] greatly in keeping with the character of the Alcibiadean model.[20] Sometimes Neoptolemus is in danger of being led astray by Odysseus, at other times there is a chance that he will recover a sense of honour and truth. The ephebic quality of the character of Neoptolemus was noted by Pierre Vidal-Naquet.[21] The *ephebeia* was an institution in which Alcibiades was deeply interested, to the extent that he distorted the oath for his own ends (Plut. *Alc.* 15.7–8);[22] it is nevertheless probably relevant that the priestess of Agraulos (the deity to whom the ephebic oath was sworn; *ibid.*; cf. Dem. 19.303) was the only religious official not to have condemned Alcibiades in 415 (Plut. *Alc.* 22.5). It may be significant too that Alcibiades was likened to both Neoptolemus and Achilles. Plutarch speaks of him at Sparta: "if you saw only his outside, you would say 'this is not the son of Achilles, but Achilles himself'" (*ibid.*, 23.6).

Neoptolemus is the personification of a young Alcibiades, an image that he retained into early middle age, if not beyond.[23] His naive attitude towards the use of deception is due in the first instance to the Iliadic Neoptolemus, who significantly declares his hatred of duplicity in addressing "none other than Odysseus" (Hom. *Il.* 9.312).[24] Malcolm Heath sees him as a "young man" lacking "experience and judgement" and draws a telling analogy with Hippolytus in Euripides' extant play where

18. Cf. Jebb, *Sophocles, the Plays and Fragments*, xli (Thrasybulus); M. H. Jameson, "Politics and the Philoctetes", *Classical Philology* **51** (1956), 217–27, esp. 221–7 (Pericles the younger).

19. Easterling, "*Philoctetes* and Modern Criticism", 29; *Oxford Readings in Greek Tragedy*, 218; cf. Gibert, *Change of Mind in Greek Tragedy*, 143–58.

20. Cf. Munn, *The School of History*, 95–126.

21. P. Vidal-Naquet, "Le *Philoctète* de Sophocle et l'Éphébie", in *Mythe et Tragédie en Grèce Ancienne*, J. P. Vernant & P. Vidal-Naquet (eds), 161–84 (Paris: F. Maspero, 1972); note, however, Gibert's important corrections: *Change of Mind in Greek Tragedy*, 154.

22. P. Siewert, "The Ephebic Oath in Fifth-Century Athens", *Journal of Hellenic Studies* **97** (1977), 102–11, esp. 108.

23. Cf. Nicias' adverse comments on Alcibiades' "youth" in 415 BCE, when he was more than thirty-five years old (Thuc. 6.12.2).

24. M. W. Blundell, "The *phusis* of Neoptolemus in Sophocles' *Philoctetes*", in *Greek Tragedy*, I. McAuslan & P. Walcot (eds), 104–15 (Oxford: Oxford University Press, 1993), 104.

Hippolytus' servant considers his master to be a "young man comparably extreme and foolish in his attitude to sex" (Eur. *Hipp.* 114–20).[25] Hippolytus, it is becoming clear, is another stage manifestation of Alcibiades.[26] His vices become virtues on the stage: Alcibiades' notorious promiscuity becomes Hippolytus' absolute chastity. In similar fashion, Alcibiades' less than strict regard for truth (cf. Plutarch's ἀναλήθης [a liar]: Plut. *Alc.* 41.1) becomes "emphatically" stronger when shown as an "exaggerated aversion to guile".[27] Alternatively, we can accept William Calder III's view that Neoptolemus is lying through his teeth,[28] in which case the parallel with Alcibiades becomes even closer.

The stress laid on Neoptolemus' φύσις (inherited human qualities or capacities)[29] also carries strong Alcibiadean overtones. The subtitle of the Platonic dialogue *Alcibiades* is περὶ ἀνθρώπου φύσεως (Concerning the nature of man: D.L. 3.59; Olymp. *in Alc.* 3); indeed the magnificence of his φύσις was a major element in the fourth-century "cult" of Alcibiades,[30] and many believe too that the philosophical φύσις in the *Republic* (489d–502c) was modelled on Alcibiades.[31] Callicles in Plato's *Gorgias* insistently puts forward views concerning νόμος and φύσις (482c–486), and a case can be made for him too probably being a mask for Alcibiades.[32] Then "the Athenians" in the Melian Dialogue who again "come forward" as Alcibiades[33]

25. M. Heath, "Sophocles' *Philoctetes*: A Problem Play?", in *Sophocles Revisited*, Griffin (ed.), 137–60, esp. 144.

26. Strauss, *Fathers and Sons in Athens*, 166–75; Vickers, "Alcibiades and Aspasia" and *Alcibiades on Stage*.

27. Heath, "Sophocles' *Philoctetes*", 144. On "*emphasis*", see p. 8, above.

28. Calder usefully notes: "Neoptolemos is the young opportunist, attractive, clever, a realist through and through, like Alcibiades unencumbered by conscience" ("Sophoclean Apologia: *Philoctetes*", 168–9). Cf. Calder, *Theatrokratia*, 16, 213. For Mary Whitby, not only does "Philoctetes [have] obvious affinities with the longed for but awesome exile [Alcibiades]", but "elements of Alcibiades can also be recognised ... in the the youthful, aristocratic and wilful Neoptolemus, who is ambivalent in his allegiance" ("The Origins of Neoptolemus in *Philoctetes*", *Greece and Rome* 43 [1996], 31–42, esp. 41 n.37).

29. K. Alt, "Schicksal und φύσις in Sophokles' Philoktet", *Hermes* 89 (1961), 141–79; Blundell, "The *phusis* of Neoptolemus", 104.

30. Bruns, *Das literarische Porträt der Griechen*, 512; cf. Gribble, *Alcibiades and Athens*, 139; N. Denyer (ed.), *Plato Alcibiades* (Cambridge: Cambridge University Press, 2001), 3.

31. For example, "it has long been admitted that this picture is drawn chiefly from Alcibiades" (J. Adam, *The Republic of Plato*, 2nd edn [Cambridge: Cambridge University Press, 1963], 2.25); "a clear allusion to Alcibiades" (C. C. W. Taylor, *Plato Protagoras* [Oxford: Clarendon Press, 1976], 64). See too Gribble, *Alcibiades and Athens*, 219–22.

32. M. Vickers, "Alcibiades and Critias in the *Gorgias*: Plato's 'Fine Satire'", *Dialogues d'histoire ancienne* 20 (1994), 85–112; Chapter 12, below.

33. Vickers, "Alcibiades and Melos"; Chapter 9, below.

observe that both gods and men exercise power by the sanction of superior natural strength, ὑπὸ φύσεως ἀναγκαίας (Thuc. 5.105.2).

Odysseus and the Merchant

Hellanicus of Lesbos thought that Andocides, whose denunciations in 415 BCE had been largely responsible for Alcibiades' fall from power, was descended from Odysseus (*FGrH* 4 F 170b ap. Plut. *Alc.* 21.1), and there are many grounds for believing that Andocides underlies the character of Odysseus in *Philoctetes* as well as in the *Ajax* of the previous year. Philoctetes and Odysseus are at odds throughout, as were Alcibiades and Andocides in real life.[34] Philoctetes and Odysseus only meet face to face at 974. Until then, Odysseus makes his presence felt through the deceits that he persuades Neoptolemus to practise and, polymorphically, through the slippery character of the Merchant (and Hellanicus is again our source for the tradition that Andocides was also descended from Hermes, the god of merchants; *FGrH* 4 F 170b in Plut. *Alc.* 21.1).[35] Against a background of enmity between Alcibiades and Andocides, we can well understand why Odysseus is reluctant to be seen by Philoctetes without warning, and why he says that he is the person Philoctetes would prefer above all the Greeks to capture (46–7; cf. 70–74). The characters of Odysseus, a wanderer away from home, and of the Merchant, well suited that of Andocides, an aristocrat in exile – and in trade – from 415 to 403 BCE. Andocides was so eager to get back to his native city that he wrote an unsuccessful appeal, *On his Return*. The exact date is disputed,[36] but if we can associate the fourteen grain ships that Andocides claimed to have in the Piraeus (Andoc. 2.21) with the "many grain ships running into the Piraeus" that King Agis saw from Decelea (Xen. *Hell.* 1.1.35) then

---

34. The origin of their enmity may not be unconnected with the fact that Taureas, the rival *choregus* whom Alcibiades once struck during a dramatic competition (which Alcibiades went on to win; [Andoc.] 4.20–21; Dem. 21.147) was a kinsman of Andocides (Munn, *The School of History*, 59, 367–8 n.30).

35. On the similarities between Odysseus and the Merchant, see, for example, M. W. Blundell, "The Moral Character of Odysseus in *Philoctetes*", *Greek, Roman and Byzantine Studies* 28 (1987), 307–49, esp. 324; on Andocides' ancestry see R. Thomas, *Oral Tradition and Written Record in Classical Athens* (Cambridge: Cambridge University Press, 1989), 159–60; Furley, *Andokides and the Herms*, 49–52.

36. "[E]ither … September 411 to April 410 … [or] … approximately January 409 to September 408" (Maidment, *Minor Attic Orators*, 454–5); "the date of this speech must be between 410 and 405" (D. M. MacDowell, *On the Mysteries* [Oxford: Clarendon Press, 1962], 4–5 n.9); "shortly after 410" (Thomas, *Oral Tradition and Written Record*, 139); "the speech may fall within the period between early 409 … and the autumn of 408" (Edwards, *Greek Orators 4*, 89); "c. 409" (Furley, *Andokides and the Herms*, 53 n.20).

a date in 409 BCE is possible, and it is possible too that Andocides and the food he brought were also among the deepest concerns of the Athenians in that year.

A problem in the usual interpretation of *Philoctetes* is the way in which Odysseus appears "needlessly [to] advertise [the] amorality ... of his one attempt at persuasion" and how he "load[s] the moral case against himself", by the language he uses.[37] Odysseus' deceitfulness and cynicism have been read as Sophocles' negative reaction to the claims of the sophistic notions that flourished in Athens at the end of the fifth century BCE.[38] Rather, the "individualism, utilitarianism and cynicism" that are certainly present can probably be read as Sophocles' reaction to Andocides' machinations in the months preceding *Philoctetes*. This may well repel those who, unfathomably, only ever discuss Sophocles in purely literary terms, but it is an explanation that meets the facts, and one that also removes the problem. For, like Odysseus, Andocides appears to have been somewhat economical with the truth. His "remarkable version of Athenian history during the Pentekontaëtia [Andoc. 3.3–9]" is "understandably quite neglected as evidence of the actual events" and is a "scrambled series of half-truths". "Each section is complemented with puzzling and wildly inaccurate details." He "inverts" and "upgrades" events so as to enhance his family's historical role;[39] so much so indeed that the passage has "won Andocides the most notorious reputation for historical inaccuracy".[40] But this is in a speech delivered in 391/0 BCE. More germane to the present discussion is what was said in his speech *On his Return*, where, it has been noted, he loads the case against himself with an "arrogant aristocratic tone".[41] He also, by means of a "rhetorical trick", manages to transform "a genuine but embarrassing memory into a fine democratic past".[42] In short, "antiquity remembered [Andocides] as a notable orator, but an untrustworthy man",[43] and "the Athenian Assembly rejected his plea because they were not convinced that [he] was concerned with anything but his personal interest".[44] We may justifiably speculate that Andocides' assertion that "it is not possible for me to deceive the older ones among you in lying" (Andoc. 2.26)[45] did not go down well

---

37. Heath, "Sophocles' *Philoctetes*", 147.
38. P. W. Rose, "Sophocles' *Philoctetes* and the Teachings of the Sophists", *Harvard Studies in Classical Philology* **80** (1976), 49–105, esp. 92; cf. Ugolino, *Sofocle e Atene*, 201–2.
39. Thomas, *Oral Tradition and Written Record*, 119–21.
40. Edwards, *Greek Orators 4*, 194.
41. A. Missiou, *The Subversive Oratory of Andokides: Politics, Ideology and Decision-making in Democratic Athens* (Cambridge: Cambridge University Press, 1992), 27; Edwards, *Greek Orators 4*, 191, cf. 90.
42. Thomas, *Oral Tradition and Written Record*, 142.
43. Furley, *Andokides and the Herms*, 69.
44. Missiou, *The Subversive Oratory of Andokides*, 48.
45. Translated by Edwards, *Greek Orators 4*.

with the aged Sophocles, and that Odysseus' self-condemnatory "insidious persua-sion in the cause of deceit"[46] is the playwright's reaction to Andocides in particular and sophistry in general.[47]

The Chorus of Sailors

The role of the Chorus in the *Philoctetes*, who deliver "only one purely choral ode of the traditional type",[48] has long been a puzzle to those who have tried to place them within the context of an imagined development of Sophoclean choruses. If, however, we see Neoptolemus' sailors as representing the thetic class at Athens – the backbone of the democracy, but sympathetic to Alcibiades' attempts at rehabilitation – we can understand why they are shown as simple men speaking simple language, loyal to Neoptolemus but ready to listen to Philoctetes. They are at first taken in by Odysseus,[49] but eventually approve of the return of the hero. Alcibiades was popular with both Athenian soldiers and sailors (Plut. *Alc.* 19.4); some of them had recently been enriched by Alcibiades' distribution of booty from Halicarnassus and Cos (Diod. 13.41.2–3), and they were largely responsible for his eventual return.

Heracles

It has been rightly said that "the ghost of Pericles haunts the last quarter of the fifth century".[50] His is the voice "familiar to, but long unheard" by the Alcibiadean Philoctetes at 1445–6, when Heracles suddenly comes on the scene. We have already seen how Pericles' habit of repeating himself was ridiculed by Sophocles,[51] and how Thucydides gives a "toned down" version at 2.62.3. Sophocles uses the same linguistic peculiarity to mark Heracles as Periclean at the beginning of his main speech in making him say somewhat tautologically ὅσους πονήσας καὶ διεξελθὼν πόνους (how many labours I laboured and passed through; 1419, cf. Creon at *Antigone* 1276). There is also some indirect evidence that Pericles was represented elsewhere on the Athenian stage as Heracles. Aspasia was called Omphale by either Cratinus or Eupolis (Schol. Pl. *Mx.* 235e); "Pericles", as Philip Stadter quite properly

---

46. Blundell, "The Moral Character of Odysseus", 327.
47. On Sophocles and sophistry, see, for example, Rose, "Sophocles' *Philoctetes* and the Teachings"; Blundell, "The Moral Character of Odysseus", 326–7.
48. O. Taplin, "Sophocles in his Theatre", in *Sophocle*, 155–74 (Geneva: Fondation Hart, 1983), 73.
49. Cf. Blundell, "The Moral Character of Odysseus", 325; S. L. Schein, "The Chorus in Sophocles' *Philoctetes*", *Studi italiani di filologia classica* **81** (1988), 196–204.
50. Jameson, "Politics and the Philoctetes", 222.
51. At, for example, *Ant.* 1261, 1276; p. 16 above.

states, "would have been Heracles".[52] There are, however, rather more reasons than this for an identification between Heracles and Pericles, and they will be discussed below.

The profaner of the Mysteries; the Hermocopid

Philoctetes does not appear on the stage until 220, but Sophocles indicates that he represents Alcibiades long before. He uses various means towards this end, alluding to Alcibiades' history, his personal characteristics and his well-known tastes by employing devices that are not far removed from caricature. Alcibiades' speech patterns[53] are later employed to good effect. Moreover, Sophocles uses Alcibiades' well-known speech impediment to generate deliberate ambiguities that frequently make it possible for two – or more – things to be said simultaneously. Even Philoctetes' name, with its overtones of covetousness, fits well with the accusations of greed brought against Alcibiades ([Andoc.] 4.32; cf. Thuc. 6.12).

We are to meet a man whose diseased foot made him unwelcome company at festivals and who "filled the camp with wild cries of ill omen" (7–10). These indications of religious pollution, which are repeated throughout, lay stress on Alcibiades' status as an undischarged profaner of the Mysteries ever since 415 BCE (Plut. *Alc.* 22.4–5; cf. Thuc. 8.53). There is much intentional irony here too, for Alcibiades was greatly admired for his personal beauty (Pl. *Prt.* 309a; *Alc.* 1.113b, 123a; *Smp.* 216c–219e; Plut. *Alc.* 4.1, 16.4; Ath. 12.534c, etc.) and as noted his gait was so distinctive that it was imitated by his son (Plut. *Alc.* 1.8); to represent him on the stage as a cripple was unkind, but no worse perhaps than showing him in 425 BCE as Oedipus, who was similarly disabled. The serious wound that Alcibiades had received at Potidaea (Plut. *Alc.* 7.4) probably lies behind both characterizations. The references to a δίστομος πέτρα (two-mouthed cave; 16) and an ἀμφιτρῆτος αὐλίου (cave with a double entrance; 18, cf. 159 and 952) are perhaps intended to recall Alcibiades' tendency towards double-dealing and general untrustworthiness (cf. ἐπαμφοτερίζοντα τὸν Ἀλκιβιάδην; Plut. *Alc.* 25.7).

The brief but grim descriptions of (i) Philoctetes' sleeping arrangements (a "hard straw mattress for someone to sleep on"; 33), (ii) his treasury ("a cup made from a single piece of wood, a work of some poor craftsman, and some firewood"; 35–6) and (iii) his washing line, hung with pus-laden rags (39) make for consistent contrasts with accounts of the way in which Alcibiades actually lived. Thus,

---

52. Stadter, *A Commentary on Plutarch's* Pericles, 240.
53. Cf. Tompkins, "Stylistic Characterization in Thucydides".

(i) details of Alcibiades' "beds" were inscribed on a stele set up near the Eleusinion in the Athenian Agora in *c.*414 where the confiscated property of those who had been found guilty of impiety was listed. Among the goods mentioned were: a χαμεύνη παράκολλος (a low bed with only one end to it) and a κλίνη ἀμφικνέφαλλος (or more properly ἀμφικέφαλος [a bed with cushions at both ends; LSJ]), as well as leather, linen and woollen pillows, all "belonging to Alcibiades" (Poll. 10.36–38) – information still freely available in the second century CE, and doubtless known to Sophocles' audience in 409 BCE. At sea, Alcibiades "had the planks of his trireme cut away so that he should sleep more softly ... on leather thongs" (Plut. *Alc.* 16.1). The Alcibiadean reality will have been luxurious. (ii) Likewise Alcibiades' love of real treasure was well-known. He had stolen half of the plate belonging to his lover Anytus in a raid on his dining-room (Plut. *Alc.* 4.5) and in order to add lustre to his celebration of his Olympic victory in 416, he had commandeered gold vessels belonging to the official Athenian delegation ([Andoc.] 4.29; Plut. *Alc.* 13.3, cf. 45). A "wooden manger", however, figured prominently among his property sold in 414.[54] (iii) As for his clothing, it was as far removed from pus-laden rags as it was possible to get: purple robes figured large (Plut. *Alc.* 16.1), and there were the twenty-two *himatia* listed among the goods that had recently been put up for auction[55] – and strung up on a line perhaps? In short, Alcibiades' way of life was characterized by "luxury, drunkenness and debauchery" (Plut. *Alc.* 1.8; cf. *Mor.* 800d),[56] although he also gained a reputation for being able, chameleon-like (Plut. *Alc.* 23.4), to adopt whatever way of life was called for. Sophocles was pushing this ability to extremes in the way he represented Philoctetes' circumstances.

At 54–5, Odysseus asks Neoptolemus to "deceive the soul of Philoctetes with words". For Odysseus, "words, not deeds, succeed among men" (98–9). It was with good reason that a scholiast said of these lines that "[Sophocles] attacks the *rhetores* of his time". Lying is justified if it brings safety (109), and it is not shameful to do something for gain (111). This reliance on rhetoric recalls Andocides' oratorical skills, which were probably being employed, although ineffectually, at Athens in *c.*409 BCE. Andocides was μισόδημος καὶ ὀλιγαρχικός (Plut. *Alc.* 21.2), and the deceits practised by Athenian oligarchs in the troubled times at the end of the fifth century are well known.[57] "Gain" recalls Andocides' current mercantile role. The invocation to Hermes that Odysseus makes on his exit (133) is ironic, given

---

54. W. K. Pritchett, "The Attic Stelai", *Hesperia* **22** (1953), 225–99, esp. 265.
55. W. K. Pritchett, "Attic Stelai, Part II", *Hesperia* **25** (1956), 167, 190–210; "Five New Fragments of the Attic Stelai", *Hesperia* **30** (1961), 23–9, esp. 23.
56. Gribble, *Alcibiades and Athens*, 69–79.
57. Jameson, "Politics and the *Philoctetes*", 224 n.16; Ostwald, *From Popular Sovereignty*; Munn, *The School of History*.

(i) Andocides' likely participation in the mutilation of the Herms (Andoc. 2.15),[58] (ii) the presence of an important image of Hermes outside his family's ancestral home in Athens (Andoc. 1.62), and (iii) Andocides' supposed descent from the god. The irony is redoubled by the prayer to Athena Polias, "who always protects me" (134), since in 409 BCE Andocides was struggling, albeit vainly, to return beneath Athena's protection.

Philoctetes on stage

In the dialogue between the Chorus and Neoptolemus, we learn of the unhappy lot of the exile, and of the Sailors' pity for the exile we are about to meet (169–89). Their speculation that he may have been well-born (180–81) is well founded if the reference is intended to be to Alcibiades, although the description of his physical circumstances is exaggerated. Neoptolemus' assertion that it was Chryse (194; the name means "Goldie") who brought Philoctetes to such a low point well suits Alcibiades: he was not only eager to acquire gold whenever possible, but he was said actually to have carried a golden shield, which doubtless attracted as much criticism as the ivory thunderbolt-wielding Eros inlaid on it (Plut. *Alc.* 16.1–2; cf. Ath. 12.534e).[59] The need for Philoctetes to take part in the fall of Troy (196–9) was analogous to the feeling widespread in 409 BCE that if Alcibiades could be restored to power, then Athens would be victorious on both land and sea (cf. Plut. *Alc.* 27.1, 32.4).

At 200, we get the first indication of Philoctetes' approach. The Chorus hear the footstep of a man in pain, of a man crawling along (201, 207). In Alcibiadean terms, we are reminded of religious pollution. Sophocles characterizes his hero by alluding "emphatically" to the thunderbolt-bearing Eros on the shield Alcibiades is supposed to have carried. It probably lies behind the image at 295–7, where we hear how Philoctetes extracted a spark, an ἄφαντον φῶς, literally an "obscure light", which "always protected [him]", by rubbing stones together. This would have constituted the meanest imaginable natural analogue for Alcibiades' thunderbolt; Sophocles again makes his point with extravagant hyperbole. "Which always protected me" (297) is both an allusion to the emblem of Alcibiades' shield,

---

58. Cf. Ostwald, *From Popular Sovereignty*, 327; Furley, *Andokides and the Herms*, 60; Munn, *The School of History*, 116.

59. We might also note that in R. Stupperich's reconstruction of the programmatic arrangement of statues in the Baths of Chrysippus at Constantinople ("Das Statuenprogramm in den Zeuxippos-Thermen", *Istanbuler Mitteilungen* **32** [1982], 210–35), Alcibiades stands between Aphrodite and Chryse.

which presumably "always protected him", and to Odysseus/Andocides' words at 134 referring to Athena Polias, his protective deity, more real in hope than in fact. Philoctetes' primitive living conditions recall Alcibiades' gift for survival whatever the environment, and contrast with the luxury for which he was famous.

A constant theme is the enmity of the sons of Atreus towards Philoctetes (e.g. 263ff., 321ff., 455, 510, 586, 592, 794, 872, 1355, 1384, 1390). If Menelaus represents Sparta and Agamemnon Argos, we can understand why the point is made so insistently. In 415 BCE Alcibiades had taken refuge first in Argos then in Sparta, but by 409 BCE he was at odds with both states, as we saw in the discussion of *Ajax* in the previous chapter. Alcibiades did not stay long in Argos in 415 BCE before moving to Sparta (Plut. *Alc.* 23.1). He had also been responsible for the deaths of nearly three hundred Argive hoplites before Miletus in 412 BCE (Thuc. 8.26.3). Despite the help he had given to Sparta, Alcibiades was also unwelcome in Lacedaemon because it was widely believed that he had cuckolded King Agis (Plut. *Alc.* 23.7; cf. Thuc. 8.45), because Agis knew that he was carrying out Alcibiades' policies (Plut. *Alc.* 24.3), and not least because Alcibiades had been responsible for recent defeats of the Peloponnesian fleet. Not surprisingly, Neoptolemus shares Philoctetes' aversion to "the sons of Atreus" (320–21); he also speaks of having experienced "Odysseus' violence" (321). In mythical terms this will have referred to Neoptolemus' loss of his father's arms to Odysseus; in contemporary political terms to the disruption to Alcibiades' career as a consequence of the activities of Odysseus' supposed descendant Andocides and his co-conspirators.[60]

When Neoptolemus comes to tell his own story (343–90), Sophocles puts more of Alcibiades' own history into his mouth. The "elaborately decorated ship" (343) sent to collect Neoptolemus is presumably a reference to the *Salaminia*, a vessel used by the Athenians for official business, which was sent in 415 BCE to fetch Alcibiades back to Athens (Plut. *Alc.* 21.7). Neoptolemus' voyage is set in the east, Alcibiades' took place in the west; but Neoptolemus' port of call – Sigeum – is an eastern analogue for Thurii, where Alcibiades jumped ship (and was close to where Alcibiades was now serving). Both had close links with Athens: Sigeum came under Athenian control in the sixth century, and Thurii was founded in 444 BCE with a strong Athenian element. "A short time later" Neoptolemus went to the sons of Atreus (360–61), as Alcibiades had gone to Argos and Sparta. Neoptolemus is rebuffed, as Alcibiades eventually was, and Odysseus is to blame for Neoptolemus' misfortunes, as Andocides almost certainly was for those of Alcibiades.

The Alcibiadean theme is then taken up by the Chorus (391–402), who speak of the Pactolus rich in gold. This river flows by Sardis, the capital of the western-

---

60. Cf. Furley, *Andokides and the Herms*, 60, and pp. 55–6, above.

71

most satrapy of the Persian empire. This is no accidental reference to the Persians, as the allusion at 400–401 to bull-slaying lions, the most characteristic of all Persian motifs,[61] makes clear. Alcibiades, of course, was no stranger to Sardis, having been imprisoned there in 411 BCE (Plut. *Alc.* 27.5, 28.1). Philoctetes' extreme dislike of Odysseus' evil, lying and perjurious tongue (407–9) reflects Alcibiades' probable view of his enemy. Philoctetes is neatly made to conclude the same speech by enquiring about Ajax, from whom Alcibiades claimed descent (Plut. *Alc.* 1.1), as we saw in Chapter 4.

Line 438 attracts attention for several reasons. Philoctetes' words, ξυμμαρτυρῶ σοι (I bear witness with you), are interesting, not simply on account of the political implications of words beginning in συν-[62] but because Alcibiades is the subject of the same verb in its only occurrence in Thucydides (Thuc. 8.51). The sentence in the second half of the line begins with καί. It is a fact that Alcibiades' language in Thucydides' speeches is characterized by the frequent use of initial καί,[63] and we saw how Sophocles made conspicuous use of the mannerism in Oedipus' account of his adventure in the "narrow way". Philoctetes and Neoptolemus use initial καί nineteen times each,[64] occasionally in clusters of two or three. One such cluster occurs at 451–2, where the hesitant language reflects another feature of the way in which Alcibiades is said to have often delivered speeches (Plut. *Alc.* 10.4).[65]

Impiety and *hubris*

The lines spoken by Philoctetes at 446–52, in which he denounces the gods, are regarded as among the most impious that Sophocles ever puts into the mouth of one of his characters. Such a declaration in a tragedy might well have generated a shock of disapproval among the more pious members of the audience,[66] but for the fact that Philoctetes' hardening of his heart against the gods, his *hubris*,[67] is part of

---

61. Cf. E. F. Schmidt, *Persepolis*, vol. 2 (Chicago, IL: Oriental Institute, 1957), pl. 19; M. C. Root, *The King and Kingship in Achaemenid Art* (Leiden: Brill, 1979), 236; M. Roaf, "Sculpture and Sculptors at Persepolis", *Iran* **21** (1983), 1–164.

62. Aurenche, *Les Groupes d'Alcibiade*, 40–41.

63. Tompkins, "Stylistic Characterization in Thucydides".

64. Contrast the Chorus' single example (1121); the relatively high scores of Odysseus and the Merchant – seven and three respectively – can be accounted for by the fact that Andocides is one of the few other orators regularly to employ a paratactic style (*ibid.*: 204 n.45).

65. For other examples of hesitation, see 239–41, 660–61.

66. Bowra, *Sophoclean Tragedy*, 295.

67. Lefèvre, *Die Unfähigkeit, sich zu erkennen*, 192–4; cf. Fisher, *Hybris*, 461 on Alcibiades' excessive *hubris*.

the characterization of a religious outcast, which was still Alcibiades' official status; the curses that had been cast against him in 414 BCE would not be lifted until after his return to Athens in 407 BCE.

At 453 Philoctetes is first addressed as a native of Oeta. Oeta was not only the traditional site of Heracles' funeral pyre (cf. 1430–32), but also the scene of a highly significant event. In 480 BCE, the Spartan king Leonidas had obstructed the advance of Xerxes' army near Mount Oeta until certain treacherous Greeks showed the Persians an alternative route: "The Persians took this path, and ... continued their march through the whole of the night, having the mountains of Oeta on their right hand, and on their left those of Trachis" (Hdt. 7.217). In making Philoctetes follow the Persians' route, Sophocles perhaps alludes not only to Alcibiades' close relations with the representatives of the Great King, but to a hope that he will be in a position to entrap and defeat the Spartans.

Philoctetes says that if Neoptolemus will agree to take him, he will be content to occupy quarters in any part of the ship – "in the bilge, in the prow or in the stern" (482) – ironic in that Alcibiades altered the deck of his own ship so that he could sleep more comfortably (Plut. *Alc.* 16.1). Rather than alienating Alcibiades from his men such behaviour seems to have endeared him to them. This is probably why Neoptolemus' sailors, the spokesmen for the crews of Athens' fleet, are made to plead Philoctetes' cause (507–18). Neoptolemus cautions them (519–21), but then agrees to carry his polluted passenger. Philoctetes is extremely grateful, and expresses his thanks to his "dear sailors" (531). The act of *proskynesis* that he proposes to make to his place of exile (533–4) is probably to be read as an allusion to Alcibiades' ongoing conversations with the local representatives of the Great King (e.g Thuc. 8.108; Plut. *Alc.* 27.6–7), a monarch before whom *proskynesis* (kow-tow) was the customary form of obeisance (e.g. Hdt. 1.134; Arr. 4.10–11).[68]

Earlier, Neoptolemus carried along the story of Alcibiades' adventures; similarly the Merchant who approaches at 539ff. represents Andocides much as does Odysseus. Just as Neoptolemus' *boyscoutisme* reflects Alcibiades' interest in the *ephebeia*, the trader reflects the mercantile side of Andocides' career (cf. Andoc. 1.137). He introduces himself at 542, together with his fellow merchant, his ξυνέμπορον.[69] "Not to keep silent" (551) came easily to Andocides, and the news that "the sons of Theseus" had sent a fleet for Philoctetes will not have told an Athenian audience anything they did not know already about contemporary events, although the passing reference to Phoenix (562) may have brought back memories of Alcibiades'

---

68. Cf. P. Briant, *From Cyrus to Alexander: A History of the Persian Empire* (Winona Lake, IN: Eisenbrauns, 2002), 222–4.
69. On the oligarchic resonance of συν- compounds, see p. 72, above.

undertaking in 411 BCE to bring in the Phoenician fleet on Athens' side (Thuc. 8.81, 88, 108).

Some of the exchanges that follow between Neoptolemus, Philoctetes and the Merchant help to carry forward the mythical plot; others dwell pointedly on Andocides' role in recent Athenian history. Between them, they constitute a respectable wigwam. Philoctetes asks Neoptolemus why the Merchant bargains secretly (579–9); in the speech *On his Return*, Andocides speaks of secret proposals he had placed before the Athenian Boule (Andoc. 2.3.19–22). Neoptolemus insists that Odysseus should speak openly (580–81); the speech *On his Return* may well have been the product of some such demand made of Andocides. The Merchant begs Neoptolemus not to discredit him with the army by making him say what he should not, for he has a mutually beneficial trading relationship with them, from which, however, he has scarcely enriched himself (582–4); Andocides had supplied oar-spars, corn and bronze to the Athenian forces in Samos in 411 BCE,[70] but insisted that he had provided the oar-spars at cost and thus did not make the profit he might have done (Andoc. 2.12). Later, at 624, Philoctetes refers to the way in which Odysseus' father had "come to the light from Hades", and the Merchant replies, "I don't know about that" before retreating to his ship (624–7). This is probably another dig at Andocides and, if so, a cruel one. For "Odysseus' father" we are to read Andocides' own: the Leogoras who had been denounced for his participation in the profanation of the Mysteries,[71] and whose innocence Andocides vociferously asserted (Andoc. 2.7) in a speech that must surely have been delivered before rather than after the performance of the *Philoctetes*. We might even guess that the failure of Andocides' appeal was due to awkward questions being asked about the events of 415 BCE.

When Neoptolemus is offered the bow by Philoctetes (658–9), he is at pains to state that although he badly wants it he will only accept it if it is lawful (θέμις) to do so (660–61). θέμις is usually employed "with reference to institutions and customs subject to some form of divine regulation".[72] In other words, Alcibiades will only be allowed back to Athens, vital as his presence is for the success of the war effort, when he has been purified of his pollution. As early as 411 BCE, his friends had been making public efforts to ensure his return (Thuc. 8.97; Plut. *Alc.* 33.1), but it was only in 407 BCE that he actually arrived back in Athens. An important

---

70. Furley, *Andokides and the Herms*, 60.
71. *Ibid.*, 66–8.
72. N. J. Richardson, *The Homeric Hymn to Demeter* (Oxford: Clarendon Press, 1974), 224, *ad v.* θεμιτόν.

element in Alcibiades' rehabilitation was the lifting of the curses cast against him in 414 BCE (Plut. *Alc.* 33.3).

The hub of the play

The chorus sung by the Sailors at 676ff. comes at the hub of the play, and serves both to recapitulate the plot so far, and to reinforce the likely Alcibiadean reference of *Philoctetes*. The Sailors make every allowance for Philoctetes/Alcibiades, although their account is not without irony. The adulterous Ixion's fate may be likened to that of Alcibiades after he had fallen foul of Agis of Sparta, whose wife he had allegedly seduced and got with child. The reference to Philoctetes' enforced abstinence from "grain sown in holy ground" at 706 probably alludes to Alcibiades' poor standing with Eleusis, whose sacred cult was intimately associated with cereals. Even to suggest that Alcibiades, recorded by Pliny in a list of famous topers of antiquity (Plin. *HN* 14.144), might have gone without wine for ten years, and that he made do with standing water (715–16) would have raised a smile from his contemporaries. The χάλκασπις ἀνήρ at 726 is Heracles, who will eventually arrive and resolve all problems. There is an interesting expression employed by Philoctetes when, after his terrible attack of pain (737ff.), he hands Heracles' bow to Neoptolemus for safekeeping, and warns him to φθόνον ... πρόσκυσον (respect Envy; 776). One of the reasons why Alcibiades had had to beat a hasty retreat from Sparta was διὰ φθόνον (on account of the envy) of the "most powerful and ambitious of the Spartiates" (Plut. *Alc.* 24.3), and soon after his return to Athens Alcibiades made a speech in which he blamed his misfortunes on "bad luck and a φθονερός δαίμων [an envious spirit]" (*ibid.*, 33.2). The role of envy in Alcibiades' fate was already, presumably, a commonplace in 409 BCE.

Throughout most of the next scene (730–914) Neoptolemus is addressed by Philoctetes as τέκνον (child) or ὦ παῖ (boy): terms of endearment, but also allusions to Alcibiades' perennially controversial youth.[73] Once, however, Philoctetes learns that Neoptolemus proposes to take him to Troy, rather than to take him home, he addresses him as ὦ ξένε (stranger; 923) as though to distance himself. At 927–8, Philoctetes denounces Neoptolemus as a πανουργίας ... τέχνημα (an exemplar of villainy), appropriate in that when Plutarch summed up Alcibiades' lifetime achievement, it was to describe him as "a πανοῦργος [villain] and a liar" (Plut. *Alc.* 41.1). Then (927–62) Philoctetes bewails the fact that Neoptolemus has betrayed him; in Alcibiadean terms this is extremely ironic since Alcibiades had spent the

---

73. Cf. Develin, "Age Qualifications for Athenian Magistrates".

previous few years betraying his country in the most effective way possible. Mention of Philoctetes' two-doored house in line 952 probably again alludes "emphatically" to Alcibiades' propensity for double-dealing. While Neoptolemus is not, in Philoctetes' view, κακός (bad), he has been misled by bad men: κακῶν δ' ἀνδρῶν (971). This prepares us for the reintroduction of Odysseus/Andocides, whom it is not difficult to envisage being branded as κακός (and the word occurs not infrequently in Andocides' extant works).

Rivalry between exiles

At all events, once Odysseus' identity is discovered by Philoctetes (976ff.) he is described as ὦ κακῶν κάκιστε (O worst of evil men; 984). Philoctetes then elaborates on this characterization in the speech that follows, accusing Odysseus/Andocides of having encouraged Neoptolemus to indulge in deceit (1012–15). He lays a curse on Odysseus, as often before (1019), and recalls that his own absence was enforced because his presence at religious functions was unwelcome (1031–9). This was precisely the position in which Alcibiades still found himself in 409 BCE; his pollution was not lifted until after his return to Athens in 407 BCE. There was, however, as we saw above, a movement in favour of allowing Alcibiades to return, which is why Philoctetes can dream of release from his affliction (1044). We might even speculate that one of the conditions that Alcibiades demanded before he would come back (and he was surely in a position to lay down terms) was that Andocides' own plea should be refused. Andocides did not in fact return to Athens until 403 BCE, the year after Alcibiades' death.

The ensuing dialogue between Odysseus and Philoctetes closely reflects the positions of Andocides and Alcibiades in 409 BCE. Odysseus' shameless – and self-condemnatory – cynical pose (1050–52) says outright what a sceptical observer (such as Sophocles) might have seen lurking between the lines in Andocides' speech *On his Return*. The hangdog approach is identical; Odysseus and Andocides both know that they are up against a greater force that requires appeasement, and yet their arrogance slips out. Odysseus mentions (1056–8) Teucer as a possible substitute for Philoctetes in the archery stakes, and describes himself as being in no way inferior. As we saw in the discussion of *Ajax*, Teucer was the name of one of those who had, together with Andocides, volunteered information concerning the profanation of the Mysteries (Andoc. 1.15).[74] Neoptolemus and Odysseus leave Philoctetes alone singing of his lot (1081–94) in terms that recall both Alcibiades'

---

74. Aurenche, *Les Groupes d'Alcibiade*, 113.

tendency to blow hot and cold (cf. 1082) and his ability to withstand extreme circumstances. Philoctetes is reminded (1095–100) that his misfortunes have come about through his own fault: true if these words apply to Alcibiades. The sailors also refer to their friendship for Philoctetes (1122); Alcibiades was, as we have seen, always popular with the ranks of the navy.

Philoctetes/Alcibiades again recalls (1136–9) the machinations of Odysseus/Andocides, but the Chorus persuade him (1140–45) to change tack. He does so in a song that includes references to his philandering as well as serious criticism of Alcibiades' career. The word for the weapons (βελέων; 1151) that Philoctetes grieves to have lost can also mean "thunderbolt" (on which see above, p. 70). Porson's clever emendation of the unanimous reading of the manuscripts of χῶρος (place) at 1153 to χολός (limping) is unnecessary, for the actor will have made the change in any case. The thunderbolts of Alcibiades' blazon are alluded to again, more fully, at 1198–9: even if Zeus himself were to attack with his characteristic weapons, Philoctetes/Alcibiades will not come away with the Sailors. At 1201–2 he recalls his pollution. He wishes to amputate his diseased limb and to die (1207–8) in order to see his father in Hades (1210–13). For Alcibiades to visit the Underworld to see either his physical father Cleinias or his guardian Pericles, he would have to purge his pollution, which is why Philoctetes is anxious to sever the offending limb that throughout has served as a symbol of religious guilt.

The next scene between Odysseus and Neoptolemus well reflects the real-life relationship between Andocides and an Alcibiades whose star in 409 BCE was again on the ascendant. Odysseus' blustering closely recalls the veiled threats in Andocides' speech *On his Return*. Neoptolemus begins by regretting his deceit and his Odysseus-like behaviour. His proposal to return Philoctetes' bow to its owner is a mythical analogue of a fear lest Alcibiades should decide not to throw in his lot with the Athenians again; Odysseus' objections, an analogue of Andocides' reluctance to see Alcibiades back at Athens at all. Odysseus' claim that the whole assembly of the Greeks, himself included (1243; ἐν δὲ τοῖς ἐγώ), will prevent Neoptolemus' plan from being put into action reflects Andocides' belief that he would soon be an active member of the Athenian assembly. Neoptolemus/Alcibiades (and Sophocles) know better, for it is by no means certain that Andocides will be back. Justice, not cleverness, will win the day. Odysseus' threat against Neoptolemus evokes the fact that Andocides' grain ships did not have to call at Athens (cf. Andoc. 2.21), and Odysseus' words (1255) when he reaches for his sword confirm this. He speaks of the κώπη (handle) of his weapon, a word that recalls the κωπέας (oar-spars) that Andocides claimed to have supplied to the Athenians at cost (Andoc. 2.11). Neoptolemus reminds Odysseus that he too can reach for his sword; Andocides could quite easily be put to death had Alcibiades so wished. Neoptolemus' final warning (1259–60) to Odysseus to be prudent doubtless echoed the Athenians' reaction to Andocides' advances.

The touching scene where Neoptolemus hands back the bow to Philoctetes is briefly interrupted by Odysseus: Andocides is so desperate to ensure success that he will put the survival of the young democracy at risk (1298). Sophocles here makes an implicit warning not to place too much trust in Andocides. Philoctetes, however, is prevented from sending his βέλος (weapon [or thunderbolt]; 1299, 1300) against his personal enemy. He has to be content with a jibe against Odysseus: a coward when it comes to arms, for all his talk (1307), Andocides had not exactly covered himself with glory during the war. Neoptolemus then reminds Philoctetes of his sickness in terms that are unmistakably those of religious pollution (1326–8), but tells him that if he returns to Troy with him, a cure will be found; in other words, Alcibiades is being formally invited back and told that he will be cleansed of his pollution. With Alcibiades back in the fold, Athenian victory over the Spartans will be quick (the prophecy of Helenus, 1336–42). Lines 1344–7 neatly summarize the position: once back and healed, Philoctetes will win fame for taking Troy; once back and his position regularized, Alcibiades will win fame for defeating the Spartan enemy. Philoctetes doubts the wisdom of returning (1348–72) and Neoptolemus repeats the offer to cure his disease (1379–80), adding (1381) that the outcome would be best for both parties: the reference is to Athens' hoped-for victory and Alcibiades' glorious part in it. Philoctetes, however, is not persuaded to go to Troy, but holds Neoptolemus to his promise to take him home. Quite what, if any, is the contemporary political reference of this twist in the plot is unclear, but Philoctetes' reluctance to fight disappears with the appearance of Heracles.

Heracles and Pericles

The arrival on stage (or above it) of Heracles (1409) marks the turning point of the play. Heracles is but a lightly disguised Pericles, and the points of resemblance are cumulatively compelling; between them, an excellent wigwam. At first, Philoctetes and Neoptolemus only hear Heracles' voice (1411); Pericles' voice was distinctive, like that of Peisistratus, according to those who had heard both (Plut. *Per.* 7.1). He has come from the heavenly regions to tell them of Zeus' plans for them: a reflection of Pericles' role as "the Olympian". He begins by repetitively describing his labours (πονήσας ... πόνους; 1419) in terms that recall Pericles' last speech in Thucydides, where there are five references to πόνοι, in the context of the hard work that the Athenians would need to undertake in order to succeed in the war (2.62–4) (and if Creon's vocabulary in *Antigone* is any guide, Pericles had been urging Athenians at the siege of Samos in similar terms; see p. 19, above). Philoctetes has had troubles too (1422; cf. 760); out of them he will make a εὐκλεᾶ (illustrious) ... βίον (life) – with wordplay on elements of both Pericles' and Alcibiades' names.[75] Heracles enjoins Philoctetes to go with a newly mature Neoptolemus (cf. the force of ἀνδρί; 1423),[76] get cured of his disease and, "having been chosen from the army as first in valour", perform their allotted Homeric military tasks. Alcibiades was to have the religious curses lifted a year or so later, and the likelihood of that will already have been discussed, ever since the prospect of his return was raised. Sophocles, who had his finger on the political pulse at Athens, will have been aware of such discussions. And the whole point of bringing Alcibiades ("the bravest of the Greeks": Plin. HN 34.12) back to favour was so that he would lead Athens to victory. Having performed these tasks, he will be granted the ἀριστεῖ (prize of valour; 1429), just as Alcibiades had been granted the ἀριστεῖον at Potidaea in 432 BCE (Plut. Alc. 7.5). The booty is to be brought back home, to Oeta/Athens, to be placed beside Heracles'/Pericles' funeral pyre; Pericles' funeral must have been quite a memorable occasion. (And did Alcibiades perform the rite of kindling the pyre [cf. 670, 727–8, 801–3]? It is difficult to think who else might have done so.)

The advice that Heracles gives to Neoptolemus is to join forces with Philoctetes; if the nobler side of Alcibiades' nature could be revived, things would go well. The image that Heracles uses is a telling one in the context of Alcibiades. His comparison of Philoctetes and Neoptolemus to "twin lions" probably rests on the same basis as Aeschylus' remark in the Frogs, in the context of Alcibiades, about rearing lions in the state (1431): "It were best not to raise a lion cub in the city, but having done so, to indulge his ways" (Ar. Ra. 1431–2; Plut. Alc. 16.3). The line is attributed to Pericles by Valerius Maximus (7.2.7), and there is no reason to doubt the fact.[77] Heracles' most important injunction, however, is that Philoctetes and Neoptolemus should εὐσεβεῖν τὰ πρὸς θέους (be reverent towards the things of the gods; 1441, cf. 1443). This is highly appropriate in the case of a revenant Alcibiades, for it was a formal charge of ἀσεβεία (impiety) that had been the start of

---

75. Cf. Sophocles' wordplay elsewhere on βιός (bow) and βίος (life) at, for example, 931 and 1416–17: D. Robinson, "Topics in Sophocles' Philoctetes", Classical Quarterly (new series) **19** (1969), 34–56, esp. 43–4; A. S. Henry, "Bios in Sophocles' Philoctetes", Classical Review (new series) **24** (1974), 3–4; Vickers, "Alcibiades on Stage".

76. Ussher, Sophocles Philoctetes, 161.

77. Cf. Vickers, "Aristophanes Frogs". On Alcibiades' leonine characteristics, see E. F. Bloedow, "On Nurturing Lions in the State: Alcibiades' Entry on the Political Stage in Athens", Klio **73** (1991), 49–65; Munn, The School of History, 193–4; Duff, "Plutarch on the Childhood of Alkibiades", 98–9.

his troubles (Plut. *Alc.* 19.3).⁷⁸ All this has the approval of πατὴρ Ζεύς (father Zeus; 1442–3), for whom the Heraclean analogue of "the Olympian" is the spokesman.

It is not too difficult to see why Philoctetes falls in with Heracles' proposals (and it is worth noting in passing that any other explanation is fraught with problems).⁷⁹ His "change of mind", like so many innovations in Greek drama, can be ultimately laid at the door of Alcibiades.⁸⁰ Alcibiades had been struggling to gain the mantle of Pericles – in *Philoctetes* represented by the bow⁸¹ – ever since the mid-420s BCE.⁸² Here at last, if only on the stage, was the kind of sanction he had craved for so long. No wonder too that Neoptolemus readily falls in with the plans (and note the initial καί in κἀγώ; 1448). Philoctetes' final song is not without further pointed references to Alcibiades. Notable among these are the "Nymphs of the marshy λειμωνιάδες [meadows]", doubtless an allusion to Tissaphernes' Carian paradise "full of meadows", which was called "Alcibiades" (Plut. *Alc.* 24.7); and the "mountain of Hermes" to a deity naturally interested in Alcibiades (sculptors used his features for those of Hermes [Clem. Al. *Protr.* 4.53.6]). The Sailors' final prayer (1469–71) is both poignant and pertinent in 409: the homecoming for which they pray is that of Alcibiades.

***

There are many more contemporary references in the *Philoctetes*, but this selection ought to be sufficient to restore to favour the view once held by "able critics". The reading presented here is, moreover, once again in harmony with Aristotle's view of tragedy, which describes the kind of things that "a person of a certain character would inevitably say or do" (Arist. *Po.* 1451b). Sophocles' play allows for a searching exploration of all the political options available to the Athenians in the spring of 409 BCE: "events ... such as might happen, and of things possible", expressed moreover by "describing the kind of things" that Alcibiades, Andocides,

---

78. The view cited, but rejected, by Jebb that "the closing words of Heracles ... convey a lesson to the suspected profaner of the Mysteries" (*Sophocles, the Plays and Fragments*, xli) has much to recommend it. Ugolini is very sound: "This reference to *pietas* and moderation can also refer to the case of Alcibiades, celebrated in Athens for his free-thinking and impiety" (*Sofocle e Atene*, 212).

79. "The great difficulty in the play is found in the reversal of decision which Heracles as *deus ex machina* orders and which is accepted readily by the previously adamant Philoctetes" (P. W. Harsh, "The Role of the Bow in the Philoctetes of Sophocles", *American Journal of Philology* **81** [1960], 408–14, esp. 408). For a detailed account of many of the proposed solutions, see Visser, *Untersuchungen zum Sophokleischen Philoktet*, 241–64.

80. See Gibert, *Change of Mind in Greek Tragedy*, 143–58 for another view.

81. Hence, no doubt, Philoctetes' warning to Neoptolemus at 775–7 lest his weapons cause grief to him "as they did to me and to the one who possessed them before me".

82. Cf. Vickers, *Pericles on Stage*, 98–9; Munn, *The School of History*, 75.

or representatives of Athens' fleet "would inevitably say or do" (*ibid.*, 1449b.26). Such an exploration was couched in mythical terms and, thanks to the universality thereby introduced, could be conducted in a considerably freer manner than was possible on most other public occasions. Athens' history thus provided the material for its citizens' "deepest concerns" as it unfolded day by day.

6
Alcibiades in exile: Euripides' *Cyclops*

The role of Alcibiades in Athenian comedy was a commonplace in antiquity. Plutarch cites "the comic dramatists" as evidence for Alcibiades' powerful oratory (Plut. *Alc.* 10.4), and Libanius usefully poses the rhetorical question: "What play did not include [Alcibiades] among the cast of characters? Eupolis, Aristophanes, did they not show him on the stage? It is to him that comedy owed its success" (Lib. *Fr.* 50.2.21). I have discussed Alcibiades' role in Aristophanes' extant plays elsewhere;[1] this book is concerned with his equally prominent role in the tragedies of his day. Indeed, we might well ask, "What tragedy of Sophocles did not include Alcibiades?" (Of the surviving plays, only *Trachiniae* and *Electra*, in fact, did not.)

Each tragic trilogy performed at a dramatic festival was rounded off by a satyric drama, the precise purpose of which is still obscure. It may have harked back to more traditional festival fare, of a kind performed before tragedy turned away from purely Dionysiac stories; it may have been intended to provide comic relief after the serious business of tragedy. But whatever its specific role, it can be shown – sometimes at least, for the evidence is extremely scanty – to have been no less political than tragedy. Euripides' *Cyclops* is no less imbued with Alcibiadean allusion than the Sophoclean plays we have discussed so far, and is of special interest because it reveals how another playwright who was somewhat more sympathetic towards Alcibiades dealt with the same situation, namely, issues arising from the debate surrounding Alcibiades' return from exile. Sophocles was sceptical at best of Alcibiades' ambitions, while Euripides, having been employed like Pindar or Bacchylides to sing Alcibiades' praises after his Olympic triumphs (Ath. 1.3e; Plut. *Alc.* 11.1–3; cf. Isocr. 16.34), tended to put a rosier spin on his activities.

---

1. Vickers, *Pericles on Stage* and *Alcibiades on Stage*.

For all that arguments have been put forward for a performance of *Cyclops* in 424,[2] it is more reasonable to see the play as having been performed in 408, in the year after *Philoctetes*. Milman Parry had already demonstrated in 1930 that Polyphemus' early line: ἔα· τίν' ὄχλον τόνδ' ὁρῶ ... (Lo! What crowd is this ...?; 222) is a self-parodying response to Aristophanes' repetition at *Thesmophoriazusae* 1105 of *Andromeda Fr.* 124, ἔα· τίν' ὄχθον τόνδ' ὁρῶ (Lo! What crag is this ...?),[3] and that the play must thus postdate a *Thesmophoriazusae* performed in 411 or 410. A. M. Dale then noted the coincidence of the expressions δι' ἀμφιτρῆτος τῆσδε (*Cyc.* 707) and δι' ἀμφιτρῆτος αὐλίου (Soph. *Phil.* 19) to refer to the cave-dwellings of the Cyclops and of Philoctetes respectively,[4] which would indicate that the play was performed after 409 BCE. Richard Seaford has now shown beyond reasonable doubt that the play was indeed most probably performed in 408 BCE,[5] and there are, as we shall see, additional internal arguments for placing *Cyclops* in that year.

Alcibiades, Odysseus and Silenus

Like *Philoctetes*, *Cyclops* again seems to examine the Alcibiades question, and in much the same way by evoking his ambition, treachery, greed, lusts, religious pollution and speech impediment. The seaward side of Mt Etna was, after all, an appropriate place in which to set a play concerned with Alcibiades, for it was there, at Catana, that he was invited in 415 BCE to return to Athens to face charges of impiety (Plut. *Alc.* 21.7). Alcibiades, moreover, more than anyone else had pushed for the Sicilian expedition (Plut. *Alc.* 17.2).[6]

---

2. D. F. Sutton, *The Greek Satyr Play* (Meisenheim am Glan: Hain, 1980), 114–20, finds similarities with Euripides' *Hecuba*.
3. M. Parry, "Studies in the Epic Technique of Oral Verse-Making, I: Homer and Homeric Style", *Harvard Studies in Classical Philology* 41 (1930), 73–147, esp. 140–41, reprinted in *The Making of Homeric Verse: The Collected Papers of Milman Parry*, A. Parry (ed.), 266–324 (Oxford: Clarendon Press, 1971), 319.
4. A. M. Dale, "Seen and Unseen on the Greek Stage: A Study in Scenic Conventions", *Wiener Studien* 69 (1956), 96–106, esp. 106, reprinted in his *Collected Papers*, 119–29 (Cambridge: Cambridge University Press, 1969), 129.
5. R. A. Seaford, "The Date of Euripides' Cyclops", *Journal of Hellenic Studies* 102 (1982), 161–72, and Seaford (ed.), *Euripides Cyclops* (Oxford: Clarendon Press, 1984), 48–51.
6. Cf. "it is tempting to see an allusion to [the Athenian Sicilian] expedition or its aftermath in Odysseus' encounter with the monster who resides beneath Mount Aetna, but," D. Konstan adds, "there is little in the play that suggests political allegory" ("Introduction", in *Euripides Cyclops*, H. McHugh [trans.] [Oxford: Oxford University Press, 2001], 17).

Although Odysseus had been used in both *Ajax* and *Philoctetes* to represent Andocides, the popular image of the hero contained sufficient elements to enable Euripides to employ him for Alcibiades in *Cyclops*. Odysseus and Alcibiades were aristocrats in exile, articulate and eager to return home. The careers of Andocides and Alcibiades since 415 BCE in any case had enough in common for Odysseus to stand for the one as easily as the other. If it was wrong to think that since Heracles was one the plot of an Heracleid should also be one (Arist. *Po.* 1451a), then there should be no difficulty in seeing mythical characters as raw material to be used by a playwright to reflect whatever political realities he wished to explore. The mythical character of Odysseus is as fluid as that of Creon, who "comes forward" in Sophocles as three different historical characters.

Athenians were still very much aware of Alcibiades early in 408 BCE. He had not yet returned from exile but was besieging Byzantium and Chalcedon on the Bosphorus on their behalf. As we have already seen, he had since 415 BCE spent time at Argos, Sparta and in Ionia, at first working against Athens' interests but more recently working on her behalf. He had advised the Spartans on how best to harm Athens, and Tissaphernes on how to exercise an even-handed policy towards both Sparta and the Athenians. He assisted Tissaphernes in negotiations with Athens in 412 BCE, one likely consequence of which was to demonstrate to the Spartans that they were not indispensable. Relations between Tissaphernes and his supposed allies went from bad to worse and the suspicion grew that Alcibiades was responsible.[7]

Alcibiades, understandably, turned these events to his own advantage. In 411 BCE, he "magnified to excess his present influence over Tissaphernes" and "announced that he had prevented the Phoenician fleet from coming to the assistance of the enemy, and that he had made Tissaphernes a greater friend of the Athenians than ever" (Thuc. 8.81). Whatever the precise truth of these statements, the wedge that had been driven between Tissaphernes and the Peloponnesians could easily, to an audience in 408 BCE, have been regarded as "one in the eye" for the Spartans.

Euripides' *Cyclops* is a dramatic expression of a shift of political alliances ostensibly achieved by Alcibiades. There may also be resonances of Alcibiades' thirty days' imprisonment at Sardis towards the end of 411 BCE and of his escape with the alleged connivance of Tissaphernes (Plut. *Alc.* 27.5–28.1). Moreover, if we today are in a position to know that Lycurgus the Spartan lawgiver (whoever, or what, he may in reality have been)[8] was poked in the eye with a stick by a certain Alcander

---

7. D. M. Lewis, *Sparta and Persia* (Leiden: Brill, 1977), 102, 110.
8. P. A. Cartledge, *The Spartans: The World of the Warrior-heroes of Ancient Greece, from Utopia to Crisis and Collapse* (Woodstock, NY: Overlook, 2003), 57–9.

(Plut. *Lyc.* 11), we can be sure that the story was well known to Athenians towards the end of the fifth century. Since it is less familiar today, it might bear re-telling. The rich at Sparta were aggrieved with Lycurgus that they would have to eat in common mess-halls. They attacked him, but he took sanctuary in a temple. It was here that "one Alcander", a youth who was otherwise not without natural talent, but was "hasty and headstrong" came up to him and "hit him in the face with a stick and put his eye out". The rest of the story is concerned with the way in which a merciful (but calculating) Lycurgus turned a "wicked and wilful young man" into a civilized human being. The moralizing tale is one that clearly appealed to Plutarch, and the outlines would also appear to have appealed to Euripides (who, as we have seen, was at present essentially friendly towards Alcibiades), with their implicit expectation that the hero comes right in the end (and it will also have chimed with the story of Alcibiades' having somewhat recklessly hit his future father-in-law in the face; Plut. *Alc.* 8.1). The story of *Cyclops* was thus an appropriate vehicle for anti-Spartan propaganda and the coincidence of the names of Alcander and Alcibiades (both Spartan names in any case [cf. Thuc. 8.6]) was too good an opportunity to pass up.

The Cyclops' loss of vision is the main burden of the plot of Euripides' play. Odysseus/Alcibiades drives a stake into the eye of a figure who, as we shall see, is represented as a gross caricature of a Spartan. The Cyclops' eye, however, will also have recalled the world of Achaemenid Persia. The King's Eye was a functionary who was very much a part of the Greeks' perception of their powerful eastern neighbour (e.g. Xen. *Cyr.* 8.2.10–12).[9] The Great King's ambassador Pseudartobas was described as ὁ βασιλέως ὀφθαλμός (the King's Eye; Ar. *Ach.* 95, cf. 92), and we might speculate that both Pseudartobas and Polyphemus were equipped with prominent optical organs. The Cyclops' eye is here the King's Eye, and its loss to the Cyclops is analogous to Spartan loss of Tissaphernes' support in the war. These assertions are supported in detail throughout the play.

The Spartan setting

Silenus (and later the Chorus of satyrs) stress their enslavement (δοῦλοι [24]; δοῦλος [79]) and they describe their tasks. Silenus fills Polyphemus' troughs and cleans his house; satyrs graze the Cyclops' sheep. Their vocabulary has a distinctly Laconian ring: πίστρα (trough) (29, cf. 47) is, as Strabo informs us (8.3.31), a shortened

---

9. Cf. Francis, "Oedipus Achaemenides", 334–5; Briant, *From Cyrus to Alexander*, 343–4.

version of ποτίστρα; *apocope* was a well known characteristic of Laconian speech.[10] The word for clean, σαίρειν (29, 33), also sounds Laconian: καθαιρεῖν (cf. 35) shortened and with *theta* changed to *sigma* (cf. σιώ for θεώ [Ar. *Lys.* 142, 148, 174]). διάκονος (servant) at 31 recalls the service of helots (διακονία; Plut. *Num.* 24.7; cf. κἀδιακόνουν at 406). The image of enslavement to a Spartan master, a situation in which it was said a slave was most a slave (Plut. *Lyc.* 28.5), is enhanced when we learn that the cleansing of the Cyclops' cave is to be done with a σιδηρᾷ ... ἁρπάγῃ (iron rake). This can also mean "iron booty" (Thuc. 8.62), and the Spartans were notorious for keeping their money in the form of iron (e.g. Plut. *Lyc.* 9.2; *Lys.* 17.3ff.; *Mor.* 226c). The implication for Alcibiades is perhaps that he only got "iron booty" from Sparta. The Chorus too use Laconian expressions: πίστραις (49, cf. 29); χαίταν (hair [75]; cf. χαίτας [with the same Doric accentuation] Tyrt. 1.39 Diehl). They end their song at 81 with a series of Spartan-sounding *sigmas*. Silenus and company are represented as helots, doing their Spartan master's housework and running his farm.

Alcibiades' son was said to have imitated his father: κλαυσαυχενεύεται τε καὶ τραυλίζεται (he bends his neck and doesn't know his r's from his l's; Plut. *Alc.* 1.7). Silenus speaks of the advent of oarsmen and an admiral carrying empty vessels around their necks, ἀμφὶ δ᾽ αὐχέσιν (87), vessels whose weight gave them good reason to "bend their necks" like Alcibiades. Silenus speculates that "They are coming in search of βορᾶς [food; 88]". On his lips (for he too, polymorphically, "comes forward" as Alcibiades), this will have been heard as βολάς (thunderbolts), and will thus have conjured up the thunderbolt imagery on Alcibiades' shield, of which Sophocles had made great play in *Philoctetes* the year before. Likewise, when the word is spoken by Odysseus/Alcibiades, the first time he utters a word with an isolated *rho* in it at 98, it will have engendered the same meaning (as will βορᾶς at Soph. *Phil.* 274, spoken by Philoctetes). Euripides is employing a by now hoary pun. Odysseus' next lambdacism is the standard one: εἰσολῶ for εἰσορῶ (see; cf. Ar. *Vesp.* 45; Soph. *Phil.* 249, 411, 501, 929, 935). At 117 there is a pun that not only alludes to Alcibiades' notorious womanizing, but also makes it clear that Sophocles was making the same point when Philoctetes/Alcibiades spoke similar words (cf. *Phil.* 1145 ff.). "Who does live in this land?" asks Odysseus: "a race of wild beasts?" (ἡ θηρῶν γένος; 117). In Alcibiades-talk this would sound like ἡ θηλέων γένος (a race of females). Alcibiades chose Eros as his shield emblem with good reason. The full catalogue of his amours – did we know them – would be immensely long. Many

---

10. A. Thumb & E. Kieckers, *Handbuch der griechischen Dialekte*, pt. 1, 2nd edn (Heidelberg: C. Winter, 1932), 89; cf. Colvin, *Dialect in Aristophanes*, 203–6.

of his affairs were the cause of scandal, hence no doubt the allusions made to them by playwrights.

The themes of womanizing and drunkenness are pursued in the ensuing dialogue. Silenus appropriately represents the side of Alcibiades' nature that was prone to heavy drinking. He states that drunkenness brings on desires that have to be satisfied, by groping for a breast and "fondling a titivated λειμῶνος [meadow; 171]". The erotic note will have been even more emphatic if Silenus pronounced χεροῖν (hands) as χελοῖν (lips), that is, "nuzzling a titivated meadow". Sophocles too had used meadow imagery towards the end of *Philoctetes* (1454), and with good reason. There was a meadow belonging to Tissaphernes in Caria of which Plutarch says: "For of all his gardens, that which was the finest in respect of its meadows [λειμώνων] and the salubrity of its streams, and which possessed kiosks and regally equipped pleasure resorts, he called 'Alcibiades'; and everyone continued to call it that and so describe it" (Plut. *Alc.* 24.7).[11] Euripides then tells us, although indirectly, what Alcibiades got up to in Tissaphernes' satrapal retreats. For this is one of the purposes of the Chorus's question, "Did you have a go at Helen when you took Troy?" (177), as Odysseus/Alcibiades' reply shows: "We sacked [ἐπέρσαμεν] the whole of the house of the sons of Priam" (178). ἐπέρσαμεν must surely carry the secondary meaning "we played the Persian" and "the sons of Priam" must be a reference to contemporary orientals. Line 178 thus means in effect, "We made ourselves thoroughly at home in Caria". As we have already noted, Alcibiades was famous for making himself thoroughly at home anywhere (cf. Plut. *Alc.* 23.4–5). The Chorus's allegation that unfaithful Helen could not resist anyone with "coloured pants on his legs" (182) or "wearing a gold torc around his neck" (μέσον τὸν αὐχένα; 184) both alludes to Alcibiades' supposed appearance in Ionia and provides yet another excuse for making fun of his bent neck. The other reason why Euripides brings up the subject of Helen's unfaithfulness is to recall Alcibiades' alleged adulterous relationship with the wife of Agis, who, like Menelaus (mentioned at 185), was a King of Sparta.

Silenus offers Odysseus refuge in one of the many καταφυγαί (refuges) in the cave (197); the same word, καταφυγὰς ἠσκημένας (delightful resorts) is used by Plutarch to describe the pleasure-domes in the Carian garden known as "Alcibiades" (Plut. *Alc.* 24.7). Odysseus refuses and prefers to stand his ground. His shield (200) will

---

11. This garden was probably the piece of land referred to in the so-called Letter to Gadatas (ML 12); cf. P. Briant, "Histoire et archéologie d'un texte: la *Lettre de Darius à Gadates* entre Perses, Grecs et Romains", in *Licia e Lidia prima dell'ellenizzazione. Atti del Convegno internazionale, Roma 11–12 ottobre 1999*, M. Gorgieri, M. Salvini, M.-C. Trémouille, P. Vannicelli (eds) (Rome: Consiglio Nazionale delle Ricerche, forthcoming) (www.achemenet.com/ressources/souspresse [accessed Feb. 2008]).

protect him just as it had against a myriad host of Phrygians (μυρίον δ' ὄχλον), the terminology applied to contemporary Persians. If Odysseus is to die, he will die nobly (201). Alcibiades was renowned for bravery; the Romans regarded him as the bravest of all the Greeks (Plin. *HN* 34.12).

When the Cyclops finally appears (203), he is immediately characterized as a Spartan, for there are no fewer than four sentences in the first line he speaks. Laconic brevity of speech was proverbial (e.g. Plut. *Lyc.* 20),[12] but this is extreme even by Spartan standards. The last of the Cyclops' sentences, τίς ἡ ῥᾳθυμία (what is all this idleness about?; 203), recalls an Ionian practice which Plutarch carefully contrasts with the Spartan way of life (Plut. *Alc.* 23.5). Polyphemus enquires about his flocks (206–10) and threatens his slaves with beating; we might compare the Spartan practice of giving helots a certain number of blows once a year lest they forget their servile status (Ath. 16.657d). His first speech ends with four sentences in two lines; still exaggerated, but evidently laconic – and Laconian. He goes on to ask (214) whether his meal is ready, and does so in words that recall the meadow through which the Chorus – and by extension Alcibiades – liked to run their fingers (or their lips) (170). Silenus' description of the visitors' actions and threats is untrue in terms of the action, but contains more allusions to contemporary life and politics. To show Silenus/Alcibiades more than ready to betray Odysseus/Alcibiades to his master is an amusing reflection on Alcibiades' own conduct. To be bound beneath a three-cubit torc (235) is a patent analogy for living beneath the Persian yoke, a fate that the freedom-loving Spartans would have taken amiss. The eye through which the Cyclops guts were to be squeezed is the King's Eye, Tissaphernes, the whip is a reference to the helots' annual drubbing, and quarry work and turning millstones (240) references to the fate of prisoners of war.

The speech in which Polyphemus decides to eat his visitors (241–9) ends in βορᾶς (food). Euripides is setting up another thunderbolt pun near the beginning of Odysseus' speech at 254. Odysseus, like the Cyclops earlier, is laconic: he uses short, clipped expressions, especially σῶν ἆσσον ἄντρων (nearer your cave) at 255 and πωλῶν τὰ σά at the conclusion of the speech (260). Like Silenus, Odysseus is playing the Alcibiadean chameleon, speaking in the language of the locals: "When [Alcibiades] was at Lacedaemon ... you would say ... this man has surely been brought up by Lycurgus" (Plut. *Alc.* 23.5–6).

When Polyphemus asks Odysseus whence he has come, he replies, Ἰλίου δ' ἄπο πέρσαντες ἄστυ (having sacked Troy [we came here]; 277–8). Again, there is a wordplay on πέρσαντες; not only does it mean "sacked", but as at 178 must refer to Alcibiades' sojourn at Sardis. For the laconizing Polyphemus not to have any time

---

12. Cf. Francis, "Brachylogia Laconica".

for Helen (280–81) is natural, but for Odysseus, given that Helen has already been set up as an analogue for Timaea, for Agis' wife to reply that it was terribly "hard going" and that those involved in Helen's recapture are "shagged out" (ἐξηντληκότες [drained]; 282), is not diplomatic. Polyphemus' scorn for an army that sailed to Phrygia for the sake of a single woman is probably a jibe directed against both Alcibiades and Agis of Sparta. It was said of Alcibiades at Sparta that "if you looked more closely at his feelings and actions you would say 'this is still the woman of old'" (Plut. *Alc.* 23.6). In 413 BCE, the jealous Agis had spoken of himself taking direction of Spartan operations in Ionia with a view, we may be sure, of eliminating Alcibiades (Thuc. 8.8–9).[13]

Odysseus' reply (285) is again laconic: θεοῦ τὸ πρᾶγμα (a god was responsible); μηδέν' αἰτιῶ βροτῶν (don't blame men). His prayer to Poseidon (286ff.) is also laced with Spartan references. He addresses Poseidon ἐλευθέρως (in the spirit of freedom; 287). The freedom of Greece was something that Sparta in particular was proud to have fought for.[14] This spirit underlies the next few lines (290–96) where Greek shrines of Poseidon are said to have been protected against Phrygians, for whom we may now read Persians. The language of 294 is mock archaic, intended to sound Laconian: δίας Ἀθάνας σῶς (and might we perhaps assume Odysseus to have been pronouncing *thetas* as *sigmas* ever since he began addressing Polyphemus?). The slaughter at Troy (305) was brought about with spears (δοριπετῆ), or perhaps by guile (if δορι- [spear] played on δόλι- [guile]): the usual Spartan view of archery (cf. Thuc. 4.40). Odysseus' appeal is so eloquent that Silenus warns Polyphemus (313–15) that if he eats any of his intended victim's tongue he will become extraordinarily glib: an apt description of Alcibiades, but ironic coming from such a source.

The Cyclops does not reply directly but breaks into a speech in which he makes statements that are wholly, but consistently, opposed to traditional Spartan values: an example of the comic technique described by Gilbert Murray, in which "a man from Aberdeen was represented as wildly scattering his money" in a twentieth century farce.[15] "Wealth is god for wise men", he begins (316). How very different from Lycurgus' teachings (Plut. *Lyc.* 8–10). The Spartans were an exceedingly religious people, anxious lest they do anything contrary to ritual precedent; blasphemy against Poseidon and Zeus would have been unthinkable. Polyphemus' spurning Zeus' thunderbolt is, of course, a reference to Alcibiades and the wordplay with which this play is laden. Polyphemus' solitary gluttony is very much against the

13. Cf. Hatzfeld, *Alcibiade*, 219.
14. Cf. R. Seager & C. Tuplin, "The Freedom of the Greeks of Asia: On the Origins of a Concept and the Creation of a Slogan", *Journal of Hellenic Studies* **100** (1980), 141–54.
15. G. Murray, *Aristophanes, a Study* (Oxford: Clarendon Press, 1933), 86.

Spartan code; Spartans were trained from their earliest youth to be abstemious (Plut. *Mor.* 237e–f) and were supposed to eat in communal dining halls (Plut. *Lyc.* 10, 12). His reluctance to move camp (324) is most un-Laconian; Spartans were required to move camp frequently (Xen. *Lac.* 12.5; Plut. *Mor.* 228d). To describe lawmakers as ever-changing (338–9) was to strike at the very roots of Spartan life, for Lycurgus' legislation was considered immutable (Plut. *Lyc.* 13). This, however, was clearly Euripides' aim: to make the Cyclops attack everything a good Spartan should stand for and to do so in a way that would amuse an Athenian audience. Whatever the precise reference of the Cyclops' invitation to Odysseus and his men to worship him (346), he is blaspheming in a way no real Spartan would, which makes the caricature all the more telling.

Pylos, Delos and Caria

Blasphemy leads quickly to Odysseus' prayer to Athena and Zeus (350–55), a prayer that occurs at the very centre of the play. Then comes a choral ode (356–74), followed by Odysseus' account of what transpired in the cave. This not only tells of the Cyclops' cruel treatment of Odysseus' shipmates, but also dwells on Alcibiades' role in recent history. Lines 387, 392, 393 and 403 all end with apparent references to the ever-increasing heat of the fire: πυρὸς φλογί (the flame of the fire; 387); ἐπέζεσεν πυρί (heated in the fire; 392); ἐγκεκαυμένους πυρί (burnt in the fire; 393); ἐξώπτα πυρί (done to a turn in the fire; 403). In Odysseus' mouth πυρός will have sounded like Πύλος: an apparent reference to Pylos and the Spartan defeat in 425 BCE. This defeat was brought about in large part by the burning of woodland on Sphacteria; hence, no doubt, the logs and pine needles mentioned at 383–4 and 385. Odysseus then says how "bravely, with tears streaming down my face I went close to the Cyclops and served him" (405–6). Not only is κἀδιακόνουν (serve) used for the service of helots (cf. 31), but we should note that in 415 BCE Alcibiades claimed to have helped the Spartans especially after Pylos (Thuc. 6.89). This claim was made in a speech at Sparta, one consequence of which was that the Spartans "determined to send immediate assistance to the Syracusans" (Thuc. 6.93). This led to the Athenians' defeat and the imprisonment of the survivors in the stone quarries at Syracuse. Odysseus seems to allude to this when he describes his companions as "crouching with fear like birds in the hollows of rocks, the blood gone from their faces" (407–8). As Seaford has implied,[16] this well evokes the atmosphere of Thucydides' account of the Athenian captives' awful fate in the Syracusan quarry

---

16. Seaford, "The Date of Euripides' Cyclops", 172 (but oddly not in *Euripides Cyclops*).

(Thuc. 7.87). Meanwhile, Odysseus plies Polyphemus with wine, to which he is unaccustomed. Spartans, indeed, were generally supposed to drink wine sparingly (e.g. Plut. *Mor.* 224d). Odysseus slips away, leaving his shipmates behind (425–6): a typically Alcibiadean ploy. He then declares that he would like to save the satyrs and himself. In effect, Euripides is making Alcibiades stir up a helot revolt; compare Alcibiades' proposal to station helots at Pylos (Thuc. 5.56). When Odysseus tells the satyrs of his plan for revenge, he explains how he will blind the Cyclops with a piece of olive wood he has found in the cave, which he will heat in the fire. The satyrs pretend to be eager to join in lifting the weapon, described henceforth as a δαλός (471, 472, 484, 593, 630, 647). δαλός is un-Homeric in this context and plays on Δᾶλος, Δῆλος (Delos), the centre of the Delian League. The instrument with which our laconizing Cyclops will be blinded is the Athenian Empire, manipulated by Alcibiades.

The lovemaking and carousing of which the Chorus sing at 487–510 recall Alcibiades' favourite activities, and Odysseus/Alcibiades is the ideal person to recommend the pleasures of wine (519ff.). The wine has the same effect on Polyphemus as that described earlier by Silenus (169ff.): it makes him feel lustful. There is an important difference, however, in that it makes him behave like a popular Athenian image of Spartans. Apologists for the Spartan way of life went out of their way to explain that Lacedaemonians did not give way to temptations of the flesh, especially homoerotic temptations, but "such a state of affairs [was] disbelieved by some" (Xen. *Lac.* 2.12–14), and λακωνίζειν was an Athenian synonym for παιδεραστεῖν (Ar. *PCG* 398; Eup. *PCG* 385.1).[17] Hence Polyphemus' preference for boys (584) and the disgusting things he does to Silenus (585–9). Even an off-stage Alcibiades sodomized by a Spartan must have been very funny indeed.

Does the Chorus's enthusiastic anticipation, contrasting sharply with their actual performance later, match the Athenians' experience of the Spartan helots during the war? The lameness from which the satyrs claim to suffer at 637 may be another allusion to Sophocles' *Philoctetes*. The Chorus decide to let Odysseus/Alcibiades do all the work with an apparently dismissive "let the Carian do it" (654); Alcibiades had technically been a slave in Caria when he served at Tissaphernes' court.[18] The Homeric story is then played out, although with further likely allusions to Alcibiades. At 678, for example, wine is said to be a difficult thing to wrestle with;

---

17. Cf. K. J. Dover, *Greek Homosexuality* (London: Duckworth, 1978), 187.
18. Alcibiades' position as πρῶτος καί μέγιστος at Magnesia (Plut. *Alc.* 24.5) made him the δοῦλος of Tissaphernes; "δοῦλος is the regular word for the subjects of the Great King regardless of rank" (H. J. Rose, *A Commentary on the Surviving Plays of Aeschylus*, Verhandelingen der Koninklijke Nederlandse Akademie van Wetenschappen, Afd. Letterkunde 64, Amsterdam [1957], 1.242). Cf. Briant, *From Cyrus to Alexander*, 324, 347; Vickers, *Alcibiades on Stage*.

so too was Alcibiades if there is any truth in the story told about his having been so eager to win that he bit his opponent (Plut. *Alc.* 2.2). The blinded Cyclops' inability to find Odysseus presumably reflects the inability of the Spartans, bereft of Tissaphernes' help, to corner Alcibiades in the Hellespont and Bosphorus. At 694 and 695 there are final lambdacizing puns on Pylos and Sardian Tmolus: διεπυρώσαμεν/διεπυλώσαμεν and ἐτιμωρησάμεν/ἐτιμωλησάμεν (cf. 441). Alcibiades has already fulfilled the prophecy about Odysseus wandering the seas (700), and he is indeed within the year to return to his own country (703). When he does, it is largely with the support of his σύνναυταί (fellow sailors; 708), again recalling a significant element of *Philoctetes* performed the year before.

Alcibiades and Polyphemus

Would, however, that things were so simple, that matters were so straightforward. A well-known aspect of Alcibiades' chameleon-like progress through life was elsewhere lampooned by characterizing him as a domineering Spartan. Aristophanes does this in the figure of War in *Peace*,[19] and I shall be arguing elsewhere that he does the same with Wealth in *Plutus*.[20] It seems that Euripides' characterization of Polyphemus owes much to Alcibiades. For thanks to his Spartan name, his Spartan nannies and his Spartan sojourn, not to mention his current status as the presumptive father of a future king of Sparta, Alcibiades was well placed to be lampooned as an extreme Lacedaemonian. Polyphemus' name, the equivalent of "Greatly famed" or "Much talked about", is highly appropriate in the case of one who seems to have monopolized the stage for a decade or two. While the threat to give his servants a drubbing with his club (210–11) may well conjure up the periodic beating handed out to Spartan helots, it will also have recalled to an Athenian audience Alcibiades' propensity to violence, and in particular the way in which he had killed one of his servants with a club (Plut. *Alc.* 3.1). The Cyclops' stated desire for dairy-products (216–18) is in diametric opposition to Alcibiades' true tastes (but may have reflected those he chose to adopt in order to please his Spartan hosts). The Cyclops' having to be instructed in how to behave at a symposium later in the play is ironic if Alcibiades is in the picture, and recalls the education of Philocleon in *Wasps*.[21]

---

19. Vickers, *Pericles on Stage,* 147–9.
20. Vickers, *Alcibiades on Stage.*
21. Cf. R. G. Ussher (ed.), *Euripides* Cyclops: *Introduction and Commentary* (Rome: Edizioni dell' Ateneo e bizzarri, 1978), 203; Vickers, *Pericles on Stage,* 136.

The Cyclops' expression, when he first sees Odysseus and his mates, ἔα· τίν' ὄχλον τόνδ' ὁρῶ ... (Lo! What crowd is this I see ...?; 222) is, as we have already had occasion to note, a parody of one first used, so far as we know, in Euripides' *Andromeda*, ἔα· τίν' ὄχθον τόνδ' ὁρῶ (Lo! What crag is this I see ...?; *Fr.* 124), where it will have been spoken by Perseus. The same words are spoken by "Perseus" in Aristophanes' parody in *Thesmophoriazusae* (1105), and I shall be arguing elsewhere that it is probably a Perseus who also "comes forward" as Alcibiades.[22] If so, in each case, ὁρῶ will have been pronounced ὁλῶ, and if the Cyclops too was characterized as Alcibiades, he will have pronounced ὁρῶ in similar fashion. Polyphemus is stated to have been a god and descended from gods (231); within a year, Alcibiades was to receive divine honours (Just. *Epit.* 5.4; did Euripides already know of plans being made?), and he claimed descent from Zeus (Pl. *Alc.* 1.121a). The Cyclops' praise of ὁ πλοῦτος (wealth) is very much in keeping with Alcibiades' public image,[23] and his impious statements, listed above, for all that they are disguised as Spartan impiety, are appropriate in the context of Alcibiades. Alcibiades' vices are exaggerated: the Cyclops' "selfish hedonism"[24] matches that of Alcibiades (Plut. *Alc.* 6.1–2, where Alcibiades is said to have been very prone to pleasure [πρὸς ἡδονὰς ἀγώγιμος]) and is reduced to cannibalism. Alcibiades' sexual excesses (cf. Thuc. 6.28.1 on Alcibiades' exotic and perverse habits [τὰ ἐπιτηδεύματα οὐ δημοτικὴν παρανομίαν]) become "approbation of masturbation" (327–8)[25] and the sodomizing of Silenus (and thus, polymorphically and ironically, of himself).

Polyphemus' self-confessed *paranomia* does not simply include impiety, greed and vice, but his "incongruous urbanity" runs to a parody of current intellectual developments at Athens.[26] "He speaks and thinks like a sophisticated egoist, in the manner of those self-centred freethinkers whom Plato's Socrates liked to stump with his dialectic –Thrasymachus in the first book of Plato's *Republic*, for example, or the cynical Callicles in the *Gorgias*."[27] Seaford had already noted the similarity

---

22. Vickers, *Alcibiades on Stage*.

23. Alcibiades was, on occasion, very rich indeed. His inheritance (of 100 talents: Lys. 19.52) was one of the largest of which we hear. On entering politics he was said to be possessed of τοῦ τε γένους καὶ τοῦ πλούτου (noble birth and wealth; Plut. *Alc.* 10.3; cf. Diod. 13.37.2). Socrates brought down to earth an Alcibiades τετυφωμένον ἐπὶ τῷ πλούτῳ (full of over-weening pride on account of his wealth; Ael. *VH* 3.28), and for Constantine Porphyrogenitus Alcibiades was ἐν δὲ εὐγενείᾳ καὶ πλούτῳ πρῶτος Ἀθηναίων (in birth and wealth the first of the Athenians; *De virt. et vit.* 1.232).

24. Seaford, *Euripides Cyclops*, 53.

25. *Ibid.*, 55, cf. 166.

26. *Ibid.*, 52, 157.

27. Konstan, "Introduction", 13. It is also of interest to note that Alcibiades' speech in Plato's *Symposium* is closely modelled on a satyr play: F. C. C. Sheffield, "Alcibiades' Speech: A Satyric Drama", *Greece and Rome* **48** (2001), 193–209.

of Polyphemus to Callicles, "who argues that strong individuals have a duty, based on φύσις, to satisfy their desires at the expense of νόμοι, which are to be despised as the creation of the weak majority".[28] Callicles, it will be suggested in Chapter 12, is another who "comes forward" as Alcibiades (as does Thrasymachus; see p. 120, below, n.26). It very much looks as though Polyphemus is another character in the same vein, to stand alongside not simply Callicles and Thrasymachus, but "the Athenians" at Melos and the Weaker Argument in *Clouds* in that they are all the direct intellectual progeny of our unpleasant hero.

But it is Odysseus, the relatively civilized version of Alcibiades, who comes out on top. It is he who has got rid of those aspects of Alcibiades' recent history that showed him as a wannabe Spartan or Persian (or indeed, a decadent Athenian intellectual). The Lacedaemonian has been dispatched, or at least his power greatly weakened, the King's Eye has been put out, and the sophisticated arguments dealt with. The ξύμπασα γνώμη (bottom line) of Euripides' play is a subtle appeal for Alcibiades, his excesses behind him, to be allowed home from exile. The message is similar to that of Sophocles' play of the preceding year, but the tone is decidedly different.

---

28. Seaford, *Euripides Cyclops*, 52. Cf. H. North, *Sophrosyne* (Ithaca, NY: Cornell University Press, 1966), 97 n.44, who speaks of this scene as "a satire on the cult of *physis* and the right of the strong".

7

Oedipus at Colonus, Alcibiades and Critias

Sophocles' *Oedipus at Colonus* seems to fall into the same category as the other plays discussed in this book. In the spirit of Wilamowitz, Karl Reinhardt thought that it is "a play ... which is careful to avoid all political allusions",[1] but Lowell Edmunds' view that "the tragedy provides various models of acceptance and reconciliation pertinent to Athens in the aftermath of the revolution of the Four Hundred" in 411 BCE is probably closer to the truth.[2] Sophocles died in 406/5 having recently completed the text of *Oedipus at Colonus*. The play was only actually performed in 401. Oedipus again would appear to "come forward" as Alcibiades, an Alcibiades who had left Athens for the second time in the autumn of 407, never in fact to return. By the time of the likely composition of *Oedipus at Colonus* he had taken refuge in one of the fastnesses in the Thracian Chersonnese that he had thoughtfully prepared against such an eventuality. Deprived once again of his property in Attica, in the spring of 406 he was in as bad a position as he had been in the autumn of 415.[3]

Sophocles had been a *proboulos* in 412/11,[4] one of a board of ten appointed from men who were over the age of forty to stabilize the government of Athens in troublesome times. The high age qualification for this office and the lack of any time limit on tenure have been taken to be oligarchical features.[5] The *probouloi*

---

1. Reinhardt, *Sophocles*, 214.
2. L. Edmunds, *Theatrical Space and Historical Place in Sophocles' Oedipus at Colonus* (Lanham, MD: Rowman & Littlefield, 1996), 88. For a range of views of what the play might be about, see R. G. A. Buxton, *Sophocles* (Oxford: Clarendon Press, 1984), 29–31; A. Markantonatos, *Tragic Narrative: A Narratological Study of Sophocles' Oedipus at Colonus* (Berlin: de Gruyter, 2002) and *Oedipus at Colonus*.
3. Hatzfeld, *Alcibiade*, 317–24.
4. Foucart, "Le Poète Sophocle"; Wilamowitz, *Aristoteles und Athen*, 102 n.6; Calder, "Sophoclean Apologia: *Philoctetes*", 173–4, and *Theatrokratia*, 219–20 (with further literature).
5. C. Hignett, *A History of the Athenian Constitution to the End of the Fifth Century BC* (Oxford: Clarendon Press, 1952), 269.

were replaced in an oligarchic revolution by a group known as the Four Hundred. This was achieved by means of an irregular Assembly meeting held, not on the Pnyx, but in a shrine of Poseidon at Colonus, some ten stades outside the city (Thuc. 8.67.2). Colonus was sacred to the knights, the elite property class who might have been expected to favour the aims of an oligarchic conspiracy; attendance might well have been intimidating for any natural supporters of the democracy.[6] This meeting was probably a motivating factor in the choice of the setting for Sophocles' last play.[7] It has been well observed, by Edmunds, that the promise of *soteria*, "which was the ostensible agenda at the special meeting of the Assembly at Colonus in 411", is in *Oedipus at Colonus* "fulfilled by an exiled Theban king".[8] For us, aware of the reign of terror inflicted on Athens and the Athenians by the extreme oligarchs known as the Thirty between 405 and 403, Oedipus' claims do indeed seem, again in Edmunds' words, "inopportune"; but from the vantage point in 406 BCE of a Sophocles who had acquiesced – albeit with qualifications – in the oligarch Peisander's plans in 411,[9] matters might have looked different.

Alcibiades meanwhile was, without any doubt, still the most controversial figure of his age.[10] He had been persuaded to return to Athens from exile, and this he did, albeit briefly, in 407 BCE: in triumph as the city's potential saviour. In *Oedipus at Colonus*, Oedipus again "comes forward" as Alcibiades. Oedipus is once more an older man with a problematic past, and the interaction is principally with polymorphic evocations of another political figure, namely, Critias, with whom

---

6. Ostwald, *From Popular Sovereignty*, 373; P. Siewert, "Poseidon Hippios am Kolonos und die athenischen Hippeis", in *Arktouros: Hellenic Studies Presented to Bernard M. W. Knox on the Occasion of His Sixty-fifth Birthday*, G. W. Bowersock *et al.* (eds), 280–89 (Berlin: de Gruyter, 1979). Thousands of *thetes* were absent in Samos: M. Finley, *The Legacy of Greece: A New Appraisal* (Oxford: Clarendon Press, 1981), 29.

7. We might compare his choice of a play about Heracles at Trachis not long after the foundation in 427/6 BCE of the Spartan colony of Heraclea in Trachis: Vickers, "Heracles Lacedaemonius".

8. Edmunds, *Theatrical Space and Historical Place*, 145.

9. "Thus when Sophocles was asked by Peisander whether he had, like the other members of the Board of Safety, voted for setting up the Four Hundred, he said 'Yes.' – 'Why, did you not think it wicked?' – 'Yes,' – 'So *you* committed this wickedness?' 'Yes,' said Sophocles, 'for there was nothing better to do'" (Arist. *Rh.* 1419a). Cf. M. H. Jameson, "Sophocles and the Four Hundred", *Historia* 20 (1971), 541–68; W. M. Calder III, "The Political and Literary Sources of Sophocles' *Oedipus Coloneus*", in *HYPATIA: Essays in Classics, Comparative Literature, and Philosophy presented to Hazel E. Barnes on her Seventieth Birthday*, W. M. Calder III, U. K. Goldsmith & P. B. Kenevan (eds), 1–14 (Boulder, CO: Associated University Press, 1985) and *Theatrokratia*, 158–9.

10. For example, P. J. Rhodes, "What Alcibiades Did or What Happened to Him", inaugural lecture, University of Durham (1985); Ellis, *Alcibiades*; J. de Romilly, *Alcibiade, ou, Les dangers de l'ambition* (Paris: Editions de Fallois, 1993); Munn, *The School of History*.

Alcibiades had earlier had much in common. Both had fallen under the Sicilian sophist Gorgias of Leontini's spell when he visited Athens in 427 (Philostr. *VS* 1.492–3).[11] Then, it was Critias who proposed that Alcibiades should be allowed to return from exile (Plut. *Alc.* 33.1), and he even wrote verses in Alcibiades' honour (observing how difficult it was to fit his name into iambic verse: 88 B 4 DK). At some stage, however, there was a serious rift between them, to the extent that in 404 we hear of Critias appealing to Lysander to have Alcibiades put to death (Plut. *Alc.* 38.5–6. Cf. Nep. *Alc.* 10.1). Both Alcibiades and Critias were in exile in 406. If it is true that Lysias' assertion that the Thirty's initial policy "to purge the city of unjust men and to turn the rest of the citizens to goodness and justice" (Lys. 12.5) points to a puritanical streak in their ring-leader Critias,[12] then it is unlikely that he and an Alcibiades who was wedded to pleasure and self-gratification (cf. Plut. *Alc.* 6.1–2) were soulmates. And just as the real-life Critias was known to have presented two faces, one friendly and the other not, towards Alcibiades, so too Alcibiades' dramatic analogue appears to be confronted with the welcoming figure of Theseus and the manipulative and harsh Creon.

Theseus and Critias

It may at first sight seem odd to associate the bloodthirsty tyrant we know from 405–403 with the correct and traditional Theseus of *Oedipus at Colonus*, but we should remember that the play was written before all that happened. In any case, it is apparent from the language used on Theseus' re-entry at 887 ff. that he is characterized as Critias. But how? An aspect of Critias' personality that was well known before he went into exile in 408 was his philo-laconism. A "personal and sentimental" attachment to Sparta is clear from his having written two works, one in prose and the other in verse, on the customs of the Lacedaemonians (Crit. 88 B 6–9, 32–37 DK).[13] One of the characteristics of Critias' literary style was βραχυλογία (conciseness of expression; Philostr. *VS* 1.503; Crit. 88 A 1.37 DK), of a kind that was often associated with the Spartans.[14] This being the case, we can understand the otherwise unmotivated laconism of Theseus' lines τίς ποθ' ἡ βοή; τί τοὖργον (What on earth is this shouting? What is the matter?; 887) and τὰ ποῖα

---

11. On the date of Gorgias' visit, see Diod. 12.53.1–2.
12. Ostwald, *From Popular Sovereignty*, 465.
13. Ostwald, *From Popular Sovereignty*, 464.
14. See, for example, Francis, "Brachylogia Laconica"; Tompkins, "Archidamus and the Question of Characterization".

ταῦτα; τίς δ᾽ ὁ πημήνας; λέγε (What wrong? Who has committed it? Speak!; 893). We might tentatively see these expressions as deliberate, perhaps even exaggerated, evocations of Critias' own βραχυλογία. There is some, if slight, confirmation that laconism in the Spartan sense may have been intended in the use of βοή (shout) at the beginning, since "shouting" was a marker of Laconian practice. Spartans famously voted by means of shouts (Thuc. 1.87.1–2), and never knocked at doors, but shouted from outside (Plut. *Mor.* 239a). Five sentences in less than two lines of verse is brachylogy by any standards, and although we cannot be certain, it is possible that Theseus in the play "comes forward" as Critias. Otherwise, Critias atticized to a fault (Philostr. *VS* 1.503; Crit. 88 A 1 38 DK), again suitable for a Theseus.

Theseus is protective of Oedipus, as the latter declares, giving thanks for Theseus' generosity of spirit and "loyal care on [his] behalf" (1042–3). It has been said that lines 563–4, in which Theseus claims to have "suffered abroad as many dangers as a man could on my person" (χὣς τις πλεῖστ᾽ ἀνὴρ ἐπὶ ξένης / ἤθλησα κινδυνεύματ᾽ ἐν τὠμῷ κάρα·), must refer to Theseus' glory, rather than pollution and ignominy, as Oedipus' exploits did. "Thus", it has been argued by Sophie Mills, "Theseus' comparison is in fact entirely inexact".[15] It may be so in terms of what can be gleaned from within the play and the mythical tradition alone, but to charge Sophocles here with such a gross inexactitude is surely to wrong him grievously as a poet. The charge that he was ga-ga was dealt with long ago, by the poet himself, as Cicero and Plutarch report.[16] If instead we were to understand, along with the play's first audience, an equation between the political exiles of both Alcibiades and Critias, the problem would disappear. If Theseus represents the positive side of Critias' character as it appeared before he became the cruel local

---

15. S. Mills, *Theseus, Tragedy, and the Athenian Empire* (Oxford: Clarendon Press, 1997), 172.

16. "Sophocles composed tragedies to extreme old age; and since he was thought to neglect the care of his property owing to his devotion to his art, his sons brought him into court to get a judicial decision depriving him of the management of his property on the ground of weak intellect, just as in our law it is customary to deprive a paterfamilias of the management of his property if he is squandering it. Thereupon the old poet is said to have read to the judges the play he had on hand and had just composed, the Oedipus at Colonus, and to have asked them whether they thought that the work of a man of weak intellect. After the reading he was acquitted by the jury" (Cic. *Sen.* 7:). "Sophocles is said to have been brought to court by his sons on a charge of madness, and to have read the chorus in Oedipus at Colonus that begins ... When it became clear how wonderful the verses were, he was led from the court as though from the theatre to the clapping and shouts of the bystanders" (Plut. *Mor.* 785a–b). According to Satyrus (*FHG* 3.162), Sophocles is supposed to have said, "If I am Sophocles, I am not crazy; if I am crazy, I am not Sophocles".

representative of the Spartan coalition forces, this would be the Critias who had proposed Alcibiades' return and who was the author of verses in his honour. Once again, though, we have to remove Pericles from the scene, for he has been seen to lie behind Theseus in *Oedipus at Colonus*.[17] If he does, it is because the virtues Pericles once possessed are those that it was hoped that Critias might develop if only he could shed the characteristics embedded in the personality of Creon.

Creon and Critias

It was wisely written by Jebb that: "it is idle to look for the Creon of the *Tyrannus* in the Creon of the *Coloneus*: they are different men, and Sophocles has not cared to preserve even a semblance of identity ... the Creon of this play is a heartless and hypocritical villain".[18] Such is probably indeed the case, and instead of Cleon we have Critias. The spiritually blind Creon of *Oedipus at Colonus*, who "arrives in guile and departs in violence"[19] is arguably a Critias-the-tyrant-in-waiting. He even admits (851) to being a tyrant (καὶ τύραννος ὤν), but displays other characteristics too, for as Whitman has noted, he has much in common "with the clever, sophistically trained oligarchs of the war years".[20] Thus, for example, at 813 Creon characterizes what he takes as Oedipus' betrayal in terms of *philia*. "Oedipus ought to have replied differently to a *philos* like [C]reon" is the implicit meaning, as Edmunds has seen,[21] just as Critias must have assumed that in writing the verses addressed to Alcibiades reminding him who moved his recall, Alcibiades would be in his pocket. Then, at 947, Creon's appeal to the legislative traditions of the Areopagus reminds us that Critias was shortly to be one of the two legislators of the Thirty (Xen. *Mem.* 1.2.31), under whom the Areopagus was to be restored to its earlier predominance in the state.[22] These future developments were of course unknown to Sophocles, but Critias' existing position on such an issue will have been common knowledge in 406.

17. Reinhardt, *Sophocles*, 213.
18. R. C. Jebb (ed.), *Sophocles, the Plays and Fragments 2: Oedipus Coloneus* (Cambridge: Cambridge University Press, 1900), xxiii.
19. Whitman, *Sophocles*, 207.
20. *Ibid.*, 208.
21. Edmunds, *Theatrical Space and Historical Place*, 118.
22. Munn, *The School of History*, 266–7; R. W. Wallace, *The Areopagus Council to 307 BC* (Baltimore, MD: Johns Hopkins University Press, 1985).

Polyneices and Alcibiades Jr

There is then the Polyneices problem. Oedipus' speech in which he rejects his son Polyneices is written with such venom that some commentators have found it inexcusable.[23] But excusable or not the speech is there and its content *is* harsh. As Knox puts it: "In a final passage which clangs and rattles with massed, bristling consonants, an explosion of hate and fury, [Oedipus] curses his son: 'Get out. I spit on you. I am not your father. You vilest of all vile beings, take this curse with you, which I call down on you ...'".[24] But some have attempted to rationalize the speech, seeing it in the context of laws relating to Greek family life.[25] If Oedipus does once again "come forward" as Alcibiades, the laws concerning τροφή (upbringing) and θρεπτήρια (return made by children for their rearing) are very pertinent. Oedipus curses Polyneices because his son has been cruel and neglectful. We learn from Lysias how truly awful Alcibiades the younger had been to his father.

Alcibiades Jr was leading such a dissolute life in Athens ("keeping a mistress when under age, and imitating his ancestors"; Lys. 14.25) that he was sent for by his father in Thrace, presumably in 406. He did not go in a helpful spirit, but conspired to betray Orni, one of his father's strongholds, to an enemy. He was nevertheless imprisoned and held to ransom by his co-conspirator, and was only released after his father's death in 404. Alcibiades, we are told, "felt such a deep hatred of [his son] that he declared that even if he should die he would not recover his bones" (Lys. 14.26–7). The situation revealed by this story, not simply neglect of filial duties but actual betrayal, together with Alcibiades' rancour, probably informs the venomous tone of the speech that Sophocles makes Oedipus address to his son.

---

23. For example, Wilamowitz, *Die dramatische Technik des Sophokles*, 362. Cf. "[There is] no excuse for the savagery of his curses" (Reinhardt, *Sophocles*, 219); B. M. W. Knox refers to "this dreadful speech" (*The Heroic Temper: Studies in Sophoclean Tragedy* [Berkeley, CA: University of California Press, 1964], 160); P. E. Easterling quotes Pohlenz's observation that the curse is "unbegreiflich hart" ("Oedipus and Polyneices", *Proceedings of the Cambridge Philological Society* **13** [1967], 1–13, esp. 13).

24. Knox, *The Heroic Temper*, 159.

25. For example, Pohlenz, *Die griechische Tragödie*, 365; Bowra, *Sophoclean Tragedy*, 327–31. B. M. W. Knox, "Sophocles and the *Polis*", in *Sophocle*, J. de Romilly (ed.), 1–37 (Geneva: Fondation Hardt, 1983), 26, and M. W. Blundell, "The Ideal of Athens in Oedipus at Colonus", in *Tragedy, Comedy and the Polis,* Sommerstein *et al.* (eds), 287–306, esp. 304, it is interesting to note, see Alcibiades Senior lying behind Polyneices.

Oedipus, Alcibiades and the Mysteries

The mystical aspect of *Oedipus at Colonus* is by now almost a commonplace. The play is imbued with allusions to the cult of Demeter and Kore at Eleusis, either explicitly, as in the reference to the golden key with which the Eumolpid officials enjoined silence on initiates (χρυσέα κλὴς γλώσσα βέβακε προσπόλων Εὐμολπιδᾶν; 1049–53), or implicitly from the very beginning. Andreas Markantonatos has recently demonstrated this in detail:[26] how Oedipus' ξύνθημ' (watchword of his destiny; 46) corresponds to the σύνθημα (token) "by which the initiate proclaimed that he had performed the necessary preliminaries to initiation";[27] the repeated stress laid on the fact that Oedipus should sit, on a rock, recalls both Demeter's sitting on the Agelastos Petra and the sitting of the candidate during the mystical ceremony (we might compare Socrates' injunction to Strepsiades to "sit" in the mock initiation ceremony in *Clouds* [254–5]); the triple thunderclaps that precede Theseus' return are another reminder of the Eleusinian ritual, where three was a significant number and a thunderous noise from the ἠχεῖον was part of the initiation ceremony (we might again compare the imitation of thunder that occurs during Strepsiades' "initiation" in *Clouds* [290–92]); when Oedipus informs Theseus that he will keep him free from suffering so long as the place of his tomb is kept secret, his use of the word ἐξάγιστα (things that cannot be uttered with impunity) "intensifies the mystic tone of the scene";[28] the replacement of Oedipus' rags with a new garment recalls the fact that initiates wore special linen vestments;[29] when Oedipus asks his daughters to leave we are reminded that only initiates can witness the mystic rites, often called δρώμενα (e.g. Plut. *Alc.* 34.4), hence Oedipus' final word, δρώμενα, as quoted by the messenger; Theseus' shading of his eyes was perhaps to protect them from the great light that marked the climax of the initiation ceremony;[30] the Chorus's statement that Oedipus had found a blessed end is evocative of the traditional formula of μακαρισμός that proclaimed the happiness of those who had been initiated.[31]

If Oedipus does "come forward" here as Alcibiades, all these elements are highly appropriate. The reason why Alcibiades chose to go into exile in 415 was because he was accused of having profaned the Mysteries. He was condemned to death in his

---

26. Markantonatos, *Tragic Narrative*, 198–220 ("Colonus and Eleusis"), 208–20 ("Oedipus and Eleusis"), on which much of what follows depends. Cf. Seaford, "Sophokles and the Mysteries".

27. Richardson, *The Homeric Hymn to Demeter*, 22.

28. Markantonatos, *Tragic Narrative*, 210.

29. *Ibid.*, 213.

30. Richardson, *The Homeric Hymn to Demeter*, 209.

31. *Ibid.*, 310–11, 313–14, 316.

absence and cursed publicly by nearly all the Athenian priests and priestesses (Plut. *Alc.* 22.5).[32] By 407, however, he had returned to Athens and "the Eumolpidae and Kerykes were ordered to retract the curses which they had invoked upon him". All except one, Theodorus the hierophant, did so (Plut. *Alc.* 33.3). Alcibiades delayed his departure on campaign in order to celebrate the Mysteries in style; many of the regular rites (δρώμενα) had fallen into abeyance on account of the Spartan occupation of Decelea. Alcibiades must have undergone initiation on this occasion (he could hardly have done so before). If so, a remark of Markantonatos on 1641–2 is extremely pertinent: "Perhaps a more specific phase of the ritual is echoed here. The ἐποπτεῖα, the highest stage of the initiation ceremony, could only be attained by those who had already been initiated in the Mysteries in the previous year".[33] Assuming Sophocles to have been writing in 406, this would nicely fit Alcibiades' situation.

To elide Oedipus, who carries so much negative baggage, from the plot by fusing the quasi-death of the Mysteries with death itself was very skilful. It is not as though Sophocles was envisaging the physical death of Alcibiades, merely his having achieved, through the completion of his initiation at Eleusis, the promise of a blissful existence after death. Alcibiades was very much alive in 406, and even shortly before his actual death in 404, at the Athenians' lowest ebb, "a vague hope prevailed among them that Athens would not be utterly lost while [he] was still alive" (Plut. *Alc.* 38.3). Sophocles appears to envisage the city under the leadership and control of Critias in the person of Theseus, as representing Athens' best hope in troubled times, which tends to confirm the picture of Sophocles as a moderate oligarch that the sources suggest.[34]

In the event, everything went wrong. Alcibiades died in rather less happy circumstances than Oedipus' passing,[35] and a Creon, not a Theseus, came to power in Athens. Critias died in May 403, and one of the first decisions of the relevant officials of the "restored but now conservative democracy of 403/2"[36] must have

---

32. Cf. D. M. Lewis, "After the Profanation of the Mysteries", in *Ancient History and its Institutions: Studies Presented to Victor Ehrenberg on his 75th birthday*, 177–91 (Oxford: Blackwell, 1966), 177, 189, who adduces Lys. 6.51 as a closely parallel situation.

33. Markantonatos, *Tragic Narrative*, 213 n.96.

34. Calder, "The Political and Literary Sources" and *Theatrokratia*, 168–73, notes parallels between *Oedipus at Colonus* and *Philoctetes*; these might perhaps be explained on the grounds that Alcibiades probably underlies both plays.

35. B. Perrin, "The Death of Alcibiades", *Transactions of the American Philological Association* 37 (1906), 25–37; L. Robert, *À travers l'Asie Mineur: poètes et prosateurs, monnaies grecques, voyageurs et géographie* (Athens/Paris: École française d'Athènes/de Boccard, 1980), 257–307; Briant, *From Cyrus to Alexander*, 395, 618, 928 and 987.

36. Munn, *The School of History*, 272.

been that Sophocles' last play should be performed at the Dionysia of 401. What Sophocles had optimistically foreseen will, with hindsight, have been even more cathartic than a performance in 406 might have been.

8
Critias and Alcibiades: Euripides' *Bacchae*

There is rather more to be said about Critias, whom we met in Chapter 7 as an individual Sophocles thought might, under the right circumstances, be the saviour that Athens needed in troubled times. If the positive side of his character embodied in the Theseus of *Oedipus at Colonus* (as opposed to the negative aspects with which the manipulative and harsh Creon is imbued) were to come to the fore, and if Alcibiades were to accept his leadership, Athens might yet survive. There is a note of muted optimism in *Oedipus at Colonus* that was to prove to have been misplaced. For Critias gained notoriety as the lawmaker of the Thirty Tyrants, who ruled Athens with a bloody hand after the city's defeat by the Spartans in 405 BCE. The sources relating to Critias are few in number by comparison with those that tell us about Alcibiades. This is in large part owing to the fact that Critias' excesses towards the end of his life contributed to the deliberate excision of his actions from Athenian folk memory, formally enacted in the oaths "not to remember evils in the future" (μὴ μνησικακήσειν; Xen. *Hell.* 2.4.43) once democracy was restored after the fall of the tyrants in 402 BCE. This may have contributed to Plato's concealment of Critias' identity behind the figure of Polus in the *Gorgias*, discussed in Chapter 12.

We are here concerned with another manifestation of Critias, but one delineated in the years before he became a bloodthirsty tyrant. It was written at about the same time as *Oedipus at Colonus*, and like that work reflects a playwright's view of the relationship between Alcibiades and Critias, but from a rather different, pro-Alcibiadean, standpoint. If this analysis is correct, it can join the relatively few testimonia relating to Critias. Critias is slowly emerging from the shadows. Several works have recently been devoted to his influential, but ultimately deleterious role in Athenian life and politics during the later fifth century BCE.[1] Even the slight

---

1. M. Centanni, *Atene Assoluta: Crizia dalla Tragedia alla Storia* (Padua: Esedra, 1997); U. Bultrighini, *"Maledetta democrazia": studi su Crizia* (Alessandria: Edizioni dell'Orso, 1999); A.

existing testimonia can reveal fresh insights. It has been suggested, for example, that Critias' ostensibly light-hearted verses in praise of Alcibiades (88 B 4 DK) might be a parody of a sympotic praise poem of the kind Euripides composed for Alcibiades' Olympic victory in 416 BCE; they may, however, contain a violent threat at the end where Alcibiades' reclining position at this symposium will perhaps "be that of a dead man".[2] Critias and Alcibiades were ultimately to be mortal enemies; it is interesting to see the seeds of this apparently so early. Critias' claim (88 B 5 DK) to have sponsored the recall of Alcibiades in 411 makes best sense as an attempt by Critias to clean up his own image after his participation in the rule of the Four Hundred, and the occasion was probably when Critias himself had gone into exile in 407.[3] And although it has little to do with the topic under discussion, it is good to see the "inventions elegy" (88 B 2 DK), in which blessings including Athenian pottery are extolled, interpreted as an ironic critique of Athenian mercantilism, for this ties in nicely with the case for the essentially banausic and contemptible role (in the eyes of contemporaries) of Greek potters made by David Gill and myself over the past couple of decades.[4]

The hexameters devoted to Anacreon (88 B 1 DK) in which choruses of women perform nocturnal rites, have been interpreted as a negative caricature of the decadent Athenian symposium prevalent at the end of the fifth century, and which Critias wished to replace with a restrained Dorian symposium more in keeping with traditional values and his philo-Laconian principles.[5] These are well expressed in Critias' denunciation of current Athenian dining practices (88 B 6 DK). Vessels "which a Lydian hand, Asiatic-born [Ἀσιατογενής] invented" are spoken of disparagingly, as is the custom of multiple toasts, after which Athenians "loosen their tongues to tell disgraceful tales [αἰσχροὺς μύθους] and they enfeeble their bodies". Anacreon is described by Critias as the "enemy of the aulos [αὐλῶν ἀντίπαλον]" (88 B 1 DK) and Peter Wilson, following Alessandro Iannucci, suggests that we may be witnessing an attempt on the part of Critias to reclaim for the traditionalists an instrument that was no longer in favour among the trendy (cf. Plut.

Iannucci, *La parola e l'azione: i frammenti simposiali di Crizia* (Bologna: Edizioni Nautilus, 2002); P. Wilson, "The Sound of Cultural Conflict: Critias and the Culture of *Mousike* in Athens", in *The Cultures within Ancient Greek Culture: Contact, Conflict, Collaboration*, C. Dougherty & L. Kurke (eds), 181–206 (Cambridge: Cambridge University Press, 2003).

2. Ianucci, *La parola e l'azione*, 42–3; Wilson, "The Sound of Cultural Conflict".
3. Ianucci, *La parola e l'azione*, 55; Wilson, "The Sound of Cultural Conflict".
4. Vickers & Gill, *Artful Crafts*; Vickers, "Art or Kitsch?"; Ianucci, *La parola e l'azione*, 69–77.
5. Ianucci, *La parola e l'azione*, 130; Wilson, "The Sound of Cultural Conflict".

Alc. 2.5–7).[6] Critias' Anacreon is "a restrained pleasure seeker" by contrast with Athens' gilded youth.[7]

These works of Critias will have been composed before his appointment as one of the five ephors of Athens installed by the Spartans in 405, and before his bloody participation in the rule of the Thirty who controlled Athens until their fall, and Critias' death, in the winter of 404/3 BCE. But even before the truly violent phase of Critias' career there are indications of his zero-tolerant attitudes. His proposal after the overthrow of the Four Hundred at the end of 411 BCE that the body of the dead Phrynichus be put on trial for treason (Lycurg. *Leoc.* 113) bespeaks a tendency to go too far. Critias' role during the regime of the Four Hundred itself is far from certain,[8] but it would appear from a hitherto unconsidered document that his sanguinary proclivities were already in evidence. This document, if that is the word, is Euripides' *Pentheus*, often called *Bacchae*.

Euripides' politics

I shall argue elsewhere that in *Helen* and *Ion*, Euripides was peculiarly sympathetic towards Alcibiades' cause, exculpating him from some of his worst actions.[9] Euripides' motivation may even have been financial, for he composed an epinician ode in Simonidean style on the occasion of Alcibiades' flamboyant participation in the Olympic festival of 416 BCE. (Poets' fees might be considerable: Pindar was paid 43 kilos of silver for verses in honour of Athens [Isoc. 15.166]). In *Helen* (of 411 BCE), I believe that Euripides shows Alcibiades in the best possible light, given the misdeeds and misunderstandings of the previous few years. He seems to stress such topics as the embarrassment many thought Alcibiades had caused King Agis, Alcibiades' supposed influence with Tissaphernes, and the promise that Alcibiades might be another Themistocles. In *Ion* (of perhaps 408 or even 407 BCE), Euripides makes Alcibiades out to be the true heir of Pericles, and exculpates him from his transgressions. Aristophanes, meanwhile, consistently held an anti-Alcibiadean

---

6. P. Wilson, Review of Iannucci 2002, *Bryn Mawr Classical Review* (16 September 2004).

7. Wilson, "The Sound of Cultural Conflict", 192.

8. H. C. Avery, "Critias and the Four Hundred", *Classical Philology* **58** (1963), 166–7; G. Adeleye, "Critias: Member of the Four Hundred?", *Transactions of the American Philological Association* **104** (1974), 1–9; Bultrighini, *"Maledetta democrazia"*; Ianucci, *La parola e l'azione*, 13 n.54, 57.

9. Vickers, *Alcibiades on Stage*.

stance (*this* was Aristophanes' political position),[10] and he appears to have reacted against Euripides' propaganda in 410 BCE by using in *Thesmophoriazusae* Euripides' own plots to emphasize the more discreditable aspects of Alcibiades' recent history: his entanglement with the oligarchs, his imprisonment at the hands of Tissaphernes and his irresponsible lack of respect for hallowed custom.[11]

It is still widely held that it is "improper" to attribute political motives to Greek playwrights, at least to tragedians, and even more so to suggest that their plays might closely reflect current events. But in a world where Antigone, Oedipus, Ajax and Philoctetes were all based in one way or another on the complex and disturbed personality of Alcibiades, political allegory may have been the norm rather than the exception. Sophocles, like Aristophanes, usually took a dim view of Alcibiades. Tales of Alcibiades' teenage cross-dressing, his belligerent obstinacy, his desire always to win and come first and the rumour that he slept with his mother lie behind Sophocles' plotting and character-building, as we have seen.

Euripides, by contrast, might treat Alcibiades favourably, and this is certainly the case in his *Bacchae*. It has been said of the two main characters in this play that "Dionysus is the dispenser of natural joys, Pentheus the joy-hating Puritan".[12] We shall presently see how, in detail, Euripides envisages a worst-case scenario for the relationship between an Alcibiades who was very prone to pleasure (πρὸς ἡδονὰς ἀγώγιμος; Plut. *Alc.* 6.1–2), and a Critias who was possessed of "a strong puritanical streak";[13] between an Alcibiades who was "of all Athenians, the most notorious for various types of *hybris*",[14] and a Critias who saw "tyranny" and *nomos* as brakes on hubris.[15] In *Oedipus Coloneus*, Sophocles observes the same political scene but from a different standpoint. He sees both good and bad in Critias, showing the good side in Theseus and the bad in Creon. (That there was a quickly forgotten good side to Critias is apparent from Aristotle's choosing him as the exemplar of the famous man whose good actions had to be actively recalled "since not many people

---

10. A topic that has generated much discussion: for example, A. W. Gomme, "Aristophanes and Politics", *Classical Review* **52** (1938), 97–109; G. de Ste. Croix, *The Origins of the Peloponnesian War* (London: Duckworth, 1972); P. A. Cartledge, *Aristophanes and his Theatre of the Absurd* (Bristol: Bristol Classical Press, 1990); N. R. E. Fisher, "Multiple Personalities and Dionysiac Festivals: Dicaeopolis in Aristophanes' *Acharnians*", *Greece and Rome* **40** (1993), 31–47; J. Spielvogel, "Die politische Position des athenischen Komödiendichters Aristophanes", *Historia* **52** (2003), 1–22.

11. Vickers, *Alcibiades on Stage*.

12. E. R. Dodds (ed.), *Euripides Bacchae* (Oxford: Clarendon Press, 1960), 128. It is a pity that the moment has probably passed for a Blair–Brown revival of *Bacchae*.

13. Ostwald, *From Popular Sovereignty*, 465.

14. Fisher, *Hybris*, 461.

15. Centanni, *Atene Assoluta*, 151, citing Critias' *Sisyphus*.

know about them" [*Rh.* 1416b].) The aura of mystery cult that surrounds Oedipus reflects Alcibiades' recent revival of the Eleusinian celebrations. In *Oedipus Coloneus* Sophocles, whose sympathies lay with the oligarchs, expresses the hope that a moderate Critias (in the person of Theseus) might prove to be Athens' saviour, and that a reformed Alcibiades might cooperate with him. In the event, it was the butcher in Critias that came to the fore, and Alcibiades was murdered.[16] Euripides in *Bacchae* was also looking to the future, but gives an entirely different spin, and envisages a rather different outcome in having a pleasure-loving Alcibiades give a puritanical Critias the chop.

Euripides' final months, when he probably completed *Bacchae*, were spent at the court of Archelaus of Macedon. He left Athens in the summer of 408, and died in the winter of 407/6. Alcibiades returned from exile with great pomp in the summer of 407, and was active on several fronts. Notably, he caused the Eleusinian Mysteries to be celebrated in traditional fashion, with a procession to Eleusis held for the first time in several years (the Spartan occupation of Decelea having inhibited such activity). It was Alcibiades who appears to have proposed a grant of *euergesia* for Archelaus, Euripides' host, early in the archonship of Antigenes (407/6 BCE) for having supplied the Athenians with timber for ships (ML 91). Alcibiades was himself treated as a benefactor to Athens by many of its inhabitants, who granted him gold and bronze crowns (Nep. *Alc.* 6), and remarkably, "not only all human, but divine honours", having "looked upon him as if sent from heaven" (Just. *Epit.* 5.4). Alcibiades briefly had the populace eating out of his hand (Plut. *Alc.* 34.7), but was to leave the city for ever in October 407.

Dionysus and Alcibiades

It is possible to match most of the characteristics of Dionysus in *Bacchae* with those of Alcibiades, and these will have been readily picked up by the audience (and many will already be familiar to you, Dear Reader). They will have recognized in the god's vinosity an allusion to Alcibiades' having been given to heavy drinking (Pliny includes him in a list of the most famous drinkers of all time: *HN* 14.144; cf. Plut. *Mor.* 800d; Ath. 12.534b). Dionysus' beauty will have recalled that of Alcibiades, which was famous (he was ὡραιότατος καὶ ἐρασμιώτατος Ἑλλήνων [the

---

16. M. Vickers, *Oedipus and Alcibiades in Sophocles* (Toruń: Wydawnictwo Uniwersytetu Mikołaja Kopernika, 2005); Chapter 7.

handsomest and loveliest of the Greeks]).[17] Dionysus has long hair; Alcibiades "let his hair grow long during a great part of his life" (Ath. 12.534c). Dionysus has smooth cheeks; extant portraits of Alcibiades show him clean-shaven.[18] Dionysus' skin is white; so will that of Alcibiades have been after his Persian sojourn (Persians' bodies were white since they "never took their clothes off", at least in public; Xen. *Hell.* 3.4.19). Dionysus is effeminate (353), and his transvestism figures in modern criticism;[19] Alcibiades as a teenager boasted that "dressed in women's clothes ... he attended symposia undetected" (Lib. *Fr.* 50.2.13). Dionysus is no wrestler (455); Alcibiades disdained gymnastic contests (Isocr. 16.33). Dionysus is a womanizer; when Alcibiades "was a young boy he lured husbands away from their wives, but when he was a young man he lured wives away from their husbands" (Bion ap. D.L. 4.49). Dionysus is much given to luxury; when in Asia, Alcibiades "outdid even the Persian in splendour and pomp" (Plut. *Alc.* 23.5). Dionysus is forever laughing in ways that annoy Pentheus; Alcibiadean laughter was a by-word in later times for inappropriate behaviour.[20]

Dionysus was a god; Alcibiades was said, as we have already seen, to have been accorded divine honours during his brief stay in Athens in 407 (Just. *Epit.* 5.4). Whether this was in fact true, or the invention of the stage, is uncertain. What is the case is that there were divine claims made for mortals about the same time. The doctor Menecrates (*c.*390 BCE) believed himself to be Zeus after he was accredited with curing epileptics (Plut. *Ages.* 21), and Alcibiades' Spartan contemporary Lysander (d. 395 BCE) was worshipped as a god on Samos in his lifetime (Plut. *Lys.* 18.8),[21] the very place where the Samians had erected a bronze statue in honour of Alcibiades a few years earlier (Paus. 6.3.15). Alcibiades clearly attracted fervent support at times: Aelian reports Alcibiades' claim that "when he enjoyed favour among the people, he was considered equal to the gods" (*VH* 13.38), which was almost certainly rhetorical hyperbole;[22] perhaps the same was true of the supposed events of 407 BCE.

---

17. Ael. *VH* 12.14; cf. Plut. *Alc.* 1.4; cf. 4.1, 16.4; Pl. *Smp.* 216c–219e; *Prt.* 309a; Ath. 12.534c; Dio Chrys. 64.27; Gribble, *Alcibiades and Athens*, 39.

18. R. R. R. Smith, "Late Roman Philosopher Portraits from Aphrodisias", *Journal of Roman Studies* **80** (1990), 127–55.

19. J. N. Bremmer, "Transvestite Dionysus", in *Rites of Passage in Ancient Greece*, M. W. Padilla (ed.), 183–200 (Lewisburg, PA: Bucknell University Press, 1999).

20. For example, τὸ γὰρ γελᾶν τὸν Ἀλκιβιάδην ἢ δακρύειν τὸν πένητα ἑπόμενον τῷ πλουσίῳ, καὶ τὰ τοιαῦτα (Alcibiades' laughter, or weeping when poverty accompanies wealth, and the like; Sopat. Rh., Διαίρεσις ζητημάτων, 8.127).

21. P. A. Cartledge, *Agesilaos* (London: Duckworth, 1987), 83.

22. B. Currie, *Pindar and the Cult of Heroes* (Oxford: Oxford University Press, 2005), 185.

It is not difficult to see the analogies between Dionysus and Alcibiades in the opening lines of *Bacchae*. Alcibiades was the ward and *de facto* son of the "Olympian" Pericles, just as Dionysus was the son of Zeus, as we are reminded in the very first line of the play (cf. Διὸς παῖς; 1). Alcibiades was in any case supposedly descended from Zeus *via* Salaminian Ajax (cf. Plut. *Alc.* 1.1). He gained considerable notoriety by replacing the traditional emblem on his shield with an image of Eros brandishing thunderbolts (Plut. *Alc.* 16.1–2; cf. Ath. 12.534e), but again this may have been an invention of the stage.[23] Thunderbolt imagery figures large in Dionysus' speech. It was a thunderbolt that assisted Semele's *accouchement* (3), and there are successive references to Dionysus' "thundersmitten" mother (6) and the remains of the flame (8). If Alcibiades was in the frame, these allusions would have been both deft and appropriate.

Dionysus has left Asia behind him, described in terms that extend beyond Lydia and Phrygia to Bactria and Arabia Felix (13–16). This is an exaggerated image of the Asia from which Alcibiades had just come, similarly situated beside the salty sea and full of fine cities occupied by both Greeks and barbarians (17–19). The word Dionysus uses to describe these cities, καλλιπυργώτους (19), is a neologism, one of many in the play (there is said to be "an unusually high proportion of 'new' words" in *Bacchae*);[24] Alcibiades was famous for persuading his contemporaries to use newfangled words (Ar. *PCG* 205.6–7), and this may be an evocation of that phenomenon. Dionysus came to "this city of Greece" (Thebes, as often, is to be equated with Athens; cf. Beaumarchais' Seville as a calque of Paris) after he had "set Asia dancing [χορεύσας; 21], and established there [his] mysteries, that [he] might be manifest to mankind as a god" (20–21). Alcibiades had likewise made a triumphant journey to Athens after some years in Asia, at Magnesia-on-the-Meander, Sardis, Samos and elsewhere. He had been formally absolved of his sins by most of Athens' priesthood, and not only were the charges of impiety that had been laid against him dropped, but his magnificent celebration of the Eleusinian Mysteries will doubtless have involved his initiation. And if the tradition that he was granted divine honours only had its origins in an invention of the stage, perhaps here, it will be very pertinent in the present context.

Relevant here, in the context of the apparently innocuous word χορεύσας (dancing) is the information we receive in Plutarch about the way Alcibiades

---

23. D. A. Russell, "Plutarch, 'Alcibiades' 1–16", *Proceedings of the Cambridge Philological Society* **12** (1966), 37–47, esp. 45; R. J. Littmann, "The Loves of Alcibiades", *Transactions of the Americam Philological Association* **101** (1970), 263–76

24. Cf. Dodds, *Euripides Bacchae*, xxxvii, citing J. Smereka, *Studia Euripidea: De Sermone. De Vocabulorum copia. De Elocutionis consuetudinibus. De Genere dicendi sive "Stilo"* (Lwow: Sumptibus Societatis Litterarum, 1936), 241.

walked and spoke. His manner of walking was so distinctive that it was imitated by his son (Plut. *Alc.* 1.8). He probably owed his peculiar gait, however it might have looked, to a serious wound he had received at Potidaea in 432 (Plut. *Alc.* 7.4), and it contributed to Sophocles' characterizations of him as Oedipus (in 425) and Philoctetes (in 408); both characters were deficient in the leg department and walked with a limp. Alcibiades' son also imitated his father's distinctive manner of speaking. Alcibiades was unable to pronounce the letter *rho* and would lambdacise it, saying for example ὁλᾷς for ὁρᾷς (do you see?; Ar. *Vesp.* 44). This is to suggest that if Dionysus in *Bacchae* was indeed characterized as Alcibiades, he will have been heard describing his recent experience not so much as "having set Asia dancing" (χορεύσας; 21) but as "having set Asia limping" (χωλεύσας), extremely apposite in an Alcibiadean context (and not unparalleled). If ὡς ὁρᾷ at the end of Dionysus' opening speech (61) were to be pronounced ὡς ὁλᾷ, it would have been equally apposite. The parallels, echoes and resonances continue through the play.

Pentheus and Critias

Similarly, there are constant allusions to Critias' public image and career in the way Pentheus is represented. His very first words ἔκδημος ὤν (216) that J. E. Sandys translates as "Though at the moment absent from this land"[25] evoke an exiled existence (cf. Pl. *Lg.* 869e). Critias had been in exile since 408 BCE. He has heard of evil νεοχμά at Thebes, a word that smacks of political strife and upheaval (cf. Thuc. 1.12.2); this was Critias' special foible in the eyes of contemporaries, and was probably the reason why he had to go into exile in the first place. He objects to the women performing their nocturnal rites on the mountains, and suspects that they have base reasons for their activities; if the Anacreon hexameters (88 B 1 DK) were indeed intended to be "a caricature of the kind of decadent Athenian symposium against which he is raising the standard of the restrained Dorian alternative",[26] then "the women's nocturnal choruses" of which Critias complains will be pertinent to any interpretation of Euripides' *Bacchae*.

Pentheus has little time for Dionysus, and refuses to acknowledge his divine status; Critias by 407 will have had little time for Alcibiades, and if divine honours had been granted, we can be sure that Critias would not have been among the devotees. But there may be more at work than this, for Pentheus' unwillingness

---

25. J. E. Sandys (ed.), *The Bacchae of Euripides with Critical and Explanatory Notes* (Cambridge: Cambridge University Press, 1892), 131.
26. Iannucci, *La parola e l'azione*; Wilson, Review of Iannucci 2002.

to acknowledge Dionysus' status as a god may well reflect what has been called Critias' "functional atheism": his rejection of the gods of the democratic city[27] foremost among whom was Dionysus.[28] It should probably not be taken as a statement of Euripides' own religiosity. Pentheus disapproves of the Asiatic carryings-on of Dionysus and his followers; Critias by contrast was a proponent of the "Dorian muse".[29] "Bromios" as an epithet of Dionysus is a constant theme of *Bacchae* (84, 87, 115, 141, 329, 375, 446, 536, 546, 593, 629, 726, 412 (× 2), 584 (× 2), 790, 976, 1031, 1250); Critias describes in hyperbolic periphrastic fashion the game of kottabos: "the scale-pan, daughter of bronze, sits on the top of the high peaks of the kottabos, to receive the raindrops of Bromios" (88 B 1.10 DK). *Bacchae* begins with the story of a false accusation of rape (26–31); Critias had written a tragedy, *Tennes*, in which a false accusation of rape was made.[30] Pentheus' threats of imprisonment in chains and stoning to death (355–6) certainly foreshadow Critias' cruel role during the regime of the Thirty, and perhaps echo his behaviour as one of the Four Hundred. We might even preserve the disputed manuscript reading at *Bacchae* 466, where εὐσέβησ' (made me reverent) recalls Critias' claim that "Sobriety is the neighbour of Reverence [Εὐσεβίης]" (88 B 6.21 DK). Again, there are many more resonances between details of the play and the testimonia relating to Critias.

Dionysus tricks Pentheus into dressing up like a woman, in fine linen (821ff.), a far cry from the rough Spartan garb favoured by philo-Laconians like Critias. Likewise, the luxury (ἁβρότητα; 968, τρυφᾶν; 969) with which Pentheus is bedecked before his ill-fated rendezvous with his mother on the mountains is redolent of the East, and surely foreign to the Dorian ideology that Critias was zealous to inculcate even in the unwilling. Pentheus' pretty curls are the object of comment (928); we may well speculate that Critias kept his hair long in the Spartan manner (cf. Hdt 208.3; Xen. *Lac.* 9.3)). Topical elements will have added to the humour of the dressing-up scene,[31] and the total effect will have been to hold the historical Critias up to ridicule before an audience that had perhaps already suffered at his hands, and whose subsequent sufferings might well have been all the harsher thanks to Euripides' invidious imagery.

No enemy of the historical Critias could possibly devise a punishment that was more exquisitely cruel or shameful than the one that Euripides gives to his tragic

---

27. Bultrighini, *"Maledetta democrazia"*, 249–50.

28. Dodds, *Euripides Bacchae*, 127.

29. Wilson, "The Sound of Cultural Conflict", 190.

30. *Ibid.*, 188.

31. On which see B. Seidensticker, "Comic Elements in Euripides' *Bacchae*", *American Journal of Philology* **99** (1978), 303–20, and *Palintonos Harmonia: Studien zu komischen Elementen in der griechischen Tragödie* (Göttingen: Vandenhoeck & Ruprecht, 1982).

hero, Pentheus. To be torn down from his observation post by crazed Bacchants was bad enough, but to be torn limb from limb by his own mother and to have her brandish his head was just not cricket. Euripides arouses feelings of pity even for a Critias by dwelling on Agave's delusions, and on the grief shown by Cadmus for his dismembered grandson. Pity will, however, have been mitigated by those who recalled Critias' insistence that the corpse of Phrynichus should be put on trial in 411. Euripides' gruesome conceit was arguably informed by this event.

***

Bacchae won first prize, but one cannot help feeling that its subsequent survival was due to the fact that Euripides' analysis of the forthcoming political situation was in principle spot-on, but in fact a kind of mirror image of what actually happened. For it was Alcibiades who was the victim of an ambush in open country, and who was shot at with arrows. It was Alcibiades whose headless corpse was to be lovingly tended, not by his mother, but by camp-followers called Theodote and Timandra (Nep. *Alc.* 10.6; Plut. *Alc.* 39; cf. Ath. 13. 574e–f).

Aristophanes' *Frogs* was probably performed at the same festival, in 405. The precise relationship between it and *Bacchae* is uncertain, but it is likely that Aristophanes knew the broad outlines of the play at least,[32] for his Dionysus too "comes forward" as Alcibiades, as I have argued elsewhere.[33] Aristophanes' Dionysus is "supple, fickle, wayward, panicky, opportunistic, and unscrupulous" and "changes like a chameleon";[34] in other words, rather closer to the picture of Alcibiades that we receive in Plutarch. For him, "Alcibiades, among his other extraordinary qualities, had this especial art of captivating men by assimilating his own manners and habits to theirs, being able to change, more quickly than a chameleon, from one mode of life to another" (Plut. *Alc.* 23.4).

One wonders why the points made here are not commonplace (and there are plenty more in the play than are discussed here). It perhaps has much to do with what a recent editor of *Bacchae* wrote in another, but related, context: that "it is an essential critical principle that *what is not mentioned in the play does not exist*".[35] This critical principle underlies, and invalidates, much current scholarship. If the analysis presented here is correct, there is a huge job to be undertaken to restore the text of *Bacchae* – and other plays – and to further elucidate Euripides' delicate

---

32. R. Cantarella, "Dioniso, fra *Baccanti* e *Rane*", in *Serta Turyniana*, J. L. Heller (ed.), 291–310 (Urbana, IL: University of Illinois Press, 1974).
33. Vickers, "Aristophanes *Frogs*" and *Alcibiades on Stage*.
34. W. B. Stanford (ed.), *Aristophanes Frogs*, 2nd edn (London: Macmillan, 1973), xxix–xxx.
35. Dodds, "On Misunderstanding the *Oedipus Rex*", 40; *The Ancient Concept of Progress*, 68; *Oxford Readings in Greek Tragedy*, 180; original emphasis.

but incisive commentary on current affairs (Quintilian called him *sententiis densus* [*Inst.* 10.1.68] for good reason, since Euripides was indeed the master of oblique reference, of allusive resonance). That Euripides chose in this instance to fling a "disgraceful tale", an αἰσχρὸν μῦθον, at Critias – the mortal enemy of his patron Alcibiades who was also his current Macedonian patron's friend – was merely another example of the way political debate at Athens extended to the stage.

9
Alcibiades and Melos: Thucydides 5.84–116

The dramatists were not the only writers to face up to Athens' problematic citizen and the issues to which his erratic career gave rise. Thucydides and Plato did so in their respective ways, but often employing the language of subliminal suggestion, of innuendo. The form in which Thucydides reports the discussion between the Athenians and the Melians before the Athenians began besieging Melos in the summer of 416 has long been a problem. In place of set speeches usually delivered in public, we are given what purports to be a dialogue conducted in private. "An isolated Thucydidean experiment"[1] or the product of a crude insertion by a later editor,[2] are two recent explanations. Although, as seems possible, the headings that distinguish the speakers are indeed later interpolations (and early readers had to make the distinction themselves by "paying close attention to what was said"[3]), the passage is remarkable on several other counts. The conclusion here is that the Melian Dialogue was neither experimental nor a later addition, but was the result of Thucydides' careful, and clever, approach to his material, and that it has much to do with Alcibiades.

This aspect has already been noted. Ostwald rightly draws attention to the way in which the "design and execution" of the Melian Dialogue "breathes the spirit of the anti-Spartan war-mongering characteristic of Alcibiades",[4] but, it will be argued here, that far from suppressing Alcibiades' involvement as Ostwald suggests, Thucydides was employing the rhetorical device known as ἔμφασις: "the process of digging out some lurking meaning from something said" (Quint. *Inst.* 9.2.64).[5] A

---

1. Andrewes, in Gomme *et al.*, *A Historical Commentary on Thucydides*, 4.159.
2. L. Canfora, "Per una storia del dialogo dei Melii e degli Ateniesi", *Belfagor* **26** (1971), 409–26.
3. K. Maurer, *Interpolation in Thucydides* (Leiden: Brill, 1995), 79–80.
4. Ostwald, *From Popular Sovereignty*, 305.
5. Cf. Ahl, "The Art of Safe Criticism", and *Sophocles' Oedipus*, 22–5.

contemporary of Demetrius the rhetorician (writing in the fourth century) pointed out that "the effect of an argument is more formidable [δεινότερος] because it is achieved by letting the fact make itself manifest [ἐμφαίνοντος] rather than having the speaker make the point for himself" ([Demetr.] *Eloc.* 288). Regarding Thucydides' rhetorical skills there can be no doubt,[6] and his implicit inclusion of Alcibiades throughout the Melian Dialogue can be matched elsewhere in the "emphatic" character sketches in the "digressions-that-are-not-digressions" in Books 1 and 6.[7]

The account of the Melian campaign (5.84–116) follows the briefest of references to an attack on Argos, but one in which Alcibiades is specifically named. In the summer of 416, "Alcibiades", who was one of the generals for that year,[8] "sailed to Argos with twenty ships" and took three hundred captives, who "the Athenians" – by implication not including Alcibiades but presumably acting on his orders – deposited on nearby islands. "The Athenians", again not including Alcibiades, then "attacked the island of Melos with thirty ships of their own, six from Chios and two from Lesbos. There were also 1200 of their own hoplites, and three hundred archers and twenty mounted archers, as well as 1500 men, mostly hoplites supplied by their allies and islanders into the bargain" (5.84.1). Even if we did not know from another source that Alcibiades had already returned to Athens (Diod. 12.81.3), the fact that Thucydides names the generals who actually were present makes it clear that Alcibiades did not personally take part in the Melian campaign. The generals in question were Cleomedes son of Lycomedes and Teisias son of Teisimachus (Thuc. 5.85.3).

Much of our information regarding Alcibiades' direct concern with Melos comes from a diatribe attributed to Andocides: [Andoc.] 4. Scholars differ as to whether this speech was written in 417,[9] or whether it was composed as a literary exercise in the early fourth century.[10] Paradoxically, the later [Andoc.] 4 is, the more reliable a witness it becomes in the present context, for if it were indeed "late", it would serve as a useful index of the degree to which the memory of certain actions of Alcibiades

---

6. Cf. C. W. Macleod, "Form and Meaning in the Melian Dialogue", *Historia* **23** (1974), 385–400, and *Collected Essays* (Oxford: Clarendon Press, 1983), 52–67.

7. Vickers, "Thucydides 6.53.3–59"; Chapters 10–11.

8. Develin, *Athenian Officials 684–321 BC*, 148.

9. So Schroff, *Zur Echtheitsfrage*; Raubitschek, "The Case against Alcibiades"; reprinted in *The School of Hellas*, 116–31; Furley, "Andokides iv ('Against Alkibiades')" and *Andokides and the Herms*; Cobetto Ghiggia, *[Andocide] Contro Alcibiade*; F. Gazzano, *Contro Alcibiade* (Genova: Il melangolo, 1999).

10. For example, Maidment, *Minor Attic Orators*, 538–9; Andrewes, in Gomme *et al.*, *A Historical Commentary on Thucydides*, 4.287–8; Edwards, *Greek Orators 4*, 132–5; Gribble, "Rhetoric and History" and *Alcibiades and Athens*, 154–8; Heftner, "Ps.-Andokides' Rede gegen Alkibiades" and "Die pseudo-andokideische Rede".

remained alive in the public mind. Plutarch, too, is informative, describing how Alcibiades supported the motion that men of military age should be put to the sword (Plut. *Alc.* 16.5–6); Thucydides simply records the bloody consequence, without directly mentioning Alcibiades' involvement (Thuc. 5.116.4). Alcibiades is himself said to have presented a motion that the islanders be enslaved, but whether this was originally intended to be an alternative to slaughter, or was a proposal to deal with the surviving Melians is not clear ([Andoc.] 4.22). The same source informs us that Alcibiades bought one of the captive slavewomen, took her as a mistress and had a child by her. This was considered a scandalous business by his detractor: "a lawless outrage" of a kind more often "seen on the tragic stage" ([Andoc.] 4.23). Thucydides' apparent silence may well be an "emphatic" manifestation of the opposite: namely, a means of drawing attention to the enormity of Alcibiades' actions by innuendo, rather than the result of ignorance or suppression.

Alcibiades and Callicles

The Melian Dialogue is generally acknowledged to be couched in the form of a sophistic debate,[11] and its Athenian participants at least will have belonged to the social class that frequented the sophists. Where there is disagreement is the degree to which the views expressed by "the Athenians" correspond to those of other prominent exponents of power politics, Callicles in the *Gorgias* and Thrasymachus in the *Republic*. It is customary today to deny a progression from the views of "the Athenians" who state that the drive to rule is an inevitable fact of nature to those of Callicles' doctrine that might-makes-right,[12] and in terms of the principles actually enunciated this may well be correct. There are, however, other – Alcibiadean – reasons for associating them.

In Chapter 12, it will be argued that the *Gorgias* is Plato's equivalent of that part of Xenophon's *Memorabilia* where the attempt was made to exculpate Socrates from any blame for Alcibiades' political career (Xen. *Mem.* 2.1–48).[13] From Callicles' remark at the beginning that it were always best to be late for a battle (*Grg.* 447a) to the final myth where people are judged "naked and dead" (524a), Alcibiades is there (Alcibiades was notoriously late in arriving at the battle of Abydus [Xen.

---

11. For example, Macleod, "Form and Meaning in the Melian Dialogue", 387, and *Collected Essays*, 54; Ostwald, *From Popular Sovereignty*, 307.
12. For example, Gomme, in Gomme *et al.*, *A Historical Commentary on Thucydides*, 4.163; de Ste. Croix, *The Origins of the Peloponnesian War*, 14–15 n.30; Ostwald, *From Popular Sovereignty*, 309.
13. Vickers, "Alcibiades and Critias in the *Gorgias*"; Chapter 12, below.

Hell. 1.1.5–6; Diod. 13.46.2–3; Plut. *Alc.* 27.3–4],[14] and had in 404 been forced naked out of the house in which he was sleeping to his death [Plut. *Alc.* 39.3–7; Diod. 14.11; Nep. *Alc.* 10.2-6; Just. *Epit.* 5.8]). Plato puts the view that "might-makes-right" into the mouth of his Alcibiadean puppet,[15] Callicles, and makes his Socrates vehemently disagree with him. Xenophon had denied that Alcibiades' Socratic tuition was responsible for his later excesses, but Plato argues (by indirect means) that these excesses should indeed be laid at the door of a teacher, but of Gorgias rather than Socrates. The historical Gorgias claimed never to have spoken any of the lines attributed to him by Plato (Ath. 11.505e),[16] and it could well be that the views indirectly attributed to Alcibiades through the medium of Callicles were equally fictitious: that they represented an exaggeration of Alcibiades' position composed with a view to making the distinction that Plato wanted to draw between Socrates and Alcibiades as complete as possible. The *Gorgias* would in any case have been as carefully constructed a fiction as the *Symposium*,[17] and doubtless as carefully contrived as Thucydides' Melian Dialogue, where a less extreme version of the Calliclean position is put forward.

Xenophon records (or invents) a conversation between Pericles and Alcibiades, where Alcibiades speaks of force and lawlessness: "Is it not when the stronger [ὁ κρείττων] obliges the weaker [τὸν ἥττω], not by persuasion but by force [βιασάμενος] to do what he pleases?" (Xen. *Mem.* 1.2.40–46). Xenophon goes to great pains accurately to characterize Alcibiades, beginning his speech with a potential opta-tive (ἔχοις ἄν με διδάξαι; 41), and making frequent use of paratactic constructions and of initial καί, features that D. P. Tompkins has isolated as being characteristi-cally Alcibiadean.[18] Xenophon also employs βία as a play on Alc*ibia*des, using it five times in thirteen lines of text. Even – especially – if Xenophon's conversa-tion is an invention, he has clearly gone to some lengths to characterize not simply the form, but the content, of the kind of thing that Alcibiades was likely to say. Plato is even more ingenious than Xenophon. A pertinent instance is the way in which he makes Callicles misquote Pindar at *Grg.* 484b. One of the charges against Socrates was that he had "selected the worst passages of the most celebrated poets,

14. E. F. Bloedow, Alcibiades, A Review Article", *Ancient History Bulletin* 5 (1991), 17–29, esp. 25.
15. The phrase is that of E. A. Havelock, *The Liberal Temper in Greek Politics* (New Haven, CT: Yale University Press, 1957), 248.
16. See, however, A. Riginos, *Platonica: The Anecdotes Concerning the Life and Writings of Plato* (Leiden: Brill, 1976), no. 37 cf. 17 and 58 (who regards the tale as fictitious).
17. On which see P. von Blanckenhagen, "Stage and Actors in Plato's *Symposium*", *Greek, Roman and Byzantine Studies* 33 (1992), 51–68; Sheffield, 'Alcibiades' Speech".
18. Tompkins, "Stylistic Characterization in Thucydides".

and using them as argument, taught those who kept him company to be unprincipled and tyrannical" (Xen. *Mem.* 1.2.56). According to Libanius' fictional, but well-informed, *Apology of Socrates*, Socrates' intention was to indicate how silly were some of the things that poets said. He hoped thereby to prevent people from carrying out their injunctions. "And [Socrates] spoke thus about Pindar, fearing his teaching, and worried lest one of the young men on hearing that 'Justice yields to the force [βιάζεται τὸ δίκαιον] of a powerful hand', may think nothing of the laws and start getting his hands in practice" (Lib. *Decl.* 1.1.87).

This is a misrepresentation of lines of Pindar that read νόμος ... δικαίων τὸ βιαιότατον (Law ... justifies the extreme of violence),[19] and there has been much scholarly discussion over the issues involved.[20] Libanius' version is also close to what the manuscripts of the *Gorgias* unanimously record as βιαίων τὸ δικαιότατον (having Pindar say: "Law, which is king of all, whether mortal or immortal, makes violent even what is most just"), although editors today often print the Pindaric text unchanged.[21]

Alcibiades and the Weaker Argument

We happen to have the literary source (or a version of it) for both Plato's and Xenophon's conceits, and a case can be made for its having influenced Thucydides. We can be sure that Plato was familiar with Aristophanes' *Clouds*, for he is said to have presented a copy of the play to a tyrant of Syracuse (who "wanted to know about Athenian government"),[22] and when Plato's bed was being tidied up after his death, his attendants supposedly found a set of Aristophanes' plays (Olymp. *Vit. Pl.* 5).[23] I have argued elsewhere that *Clouds* was as political a play as the Syracusan anecdote suggests, that the principal participants (Socrates and the Clouds apart)

---

19. Pind. *Fr.* 169.1–7 Sn-M; correctly quoted by Plato at *Lg.* 715a.
20. Summarized by Dodds, *Plato: Gorgias*, 270–72; cf. C. Pavese, "The New Heracles Poem of Pindar", *Harvard Studies in Classical Philology* 72 (1987), 45–88.
21. For example, Dodds, *Plato: Gorgias*, 271, who (surely wrongly) remarks that "the misquotation would have no dramatic value (and would pass unnoticed by most readers) unless Socrates proceeded to correct it".
22. *Vit. Ar.* 28.46–48 (Koster); cf. 29a.33–5 (Koster); see further my *Pericles on Stage*, 1–2. On the date of the version we have, see J. Henderson, "Problems in Greek Literary History: The Case of Aristophanes *Clouds*", in *Nomodeiktes: Greek Studies in Honor of Martin Ostwald*, R. Rosen & J. Farrell (eds), 591–601 (Ann Arbor, MI: Michigan University Press, 1993).
23. Plato was said in antiquity to be the author of an epigram "saying that the Graces, when looking for a temple that would never fall ... found the soul of Aristophanes" (Murray, *Aristophanes, a Study*, 189; Pl. *Epigr.* 14).

are based on Pericles and his extended family, and that the twists in the plot correspond to what we hear about them in the anecdotal tradition. Strepsiades "comes
forward" as Pericles, and Pheidippides is an amalgam of individuals who bore
a filial relationship to him, and in particular Alcibiades. The scheme is a simple
device to personalize the generation gap.[24] Strepsiades' injunction at 887–8, that
Pheidippides should be able to argue against πάντα τὰ δίκαια (every kind of justice),
thus strongly recalls (and will doubtless have influenced) the way in which Callicles
argues that "might-makes-right" in the *Gorgias*, especially the observation that
"justice consists in the stronger [τὸν κρείττω] ruling over and having more than the
weaker [τοῦ ἥττονος]" (483d; cf. 484c).[25]

Then the encounter (*Nu.* 890–1114) between the Stronger (τὸν κρείττονα)
and Weaker (τὸν ἥττονα) Arguments, apart from being another debate across the
generation gap, also depends on characters who "come forward" as Pericles and
Alcibiades, according to the principle of "polymorphic characterization". The values
for which they stand correspond to (or are exaggerations of) those attested for the
historical individuals: the Stronger Argument's conservatism and respect for the
gods is an exaggeration of the public image of the man known as the "Olympian",
while the Weaker Argument's moral nihilism well matches Alcibiades' tendency
to παρανομία. Many examples could be cited of the way the lines spoken by the
two Arguments overlap with what is known about Pericles and Alcibiades in the
anecdotal tradition. "More than a thousand staters" at 1041, for example, recalls
Alcibiades' anonymous gift of a thousand gold coins to test his wife's virtue (Ath.
12.534c), and the Weaker Argument's expressed determination to win the contest
(1042), Alcibiades' predominant characteristic according to Plutarch – τὸ φιλόνικον
ἰσχυρότατον ... καὶ τὸ φιλόπρωτον (his extremely strong desire to win and to come
first), a trait that was apparent from his earliest youth (*Alc.* 2.1; cf. Thuc. 5.43.2).[26]
Characteristic mannerisms of speech also help make the point that the Weaker
Argument represents Alcibiades. His two long speeches (1036–45, 1068–82) both
begin with καί – that is, καί μήν and κᾆτ' – both have sentences beginning with καί

---

24. Vickers, Alcibiades in Cloudedoverland" and *Pericles on Stage*, 22–58; Strauss, *Fathers and
    Sons in Athens*, 166–75; Handley, "Aristophanes and the Generation Gap".
25. See Chapter 12.
26. Thrasymachus ("Bold in battle") in the *Republic* (1.328b), who adopts a similar stance to that of
    Callicles in the *Gorgias*, could well be another mask for Alcibiades (see Chapter 12, below). It
    was not simply that Alcibiades was extremely brave (in the fourth century, the Romans erected
    a statue of him in the Forum as "the bravest of the Greeks" [Plin. *HN* 34.12]; cf. Diodorus for
    whom Alcibiades was "by far the most outstanding citizen in daring" [13.37.2]), but he also had
    a tendency to insolent boldness. Plutarch called him θρασύτατος (extremely bold; *Alc.* 44.2; cf.
    18.1). Small wonder, therefore, that at 90 and 915, Aristophanes makes the Stronger Argument
    accuse his Alcibiadean opponent of being θρασύς (brazen).

halfway through (at 1041 and 1074), and both have last lines (and sentences) beginning καίτοι.[27] Line 1074, moreover, ends with a potential optative.[28] Alcibiades as reported verbatim by Thucydides uses very few abstract expressions; ἀνάγκη (necessity) and ἀναγκαῖον (necessary) account for four out of the six (Thuc. 6.16.1, 89.1 – both at the beginning of speeches).[29] The Weaker Argument refers to τῆς φύσεως ἀνάγκας (needs of nature) at 1075, here describing illicit lovemaking, but doubtless parodying views concerning *nomos* and *physis* of the kind put forward by Callicles (*Grg.* 482c–486d), who is also fond of the word ἀνάγκη and its cognates.[30]

Thucydides and Alcibiades

Xenophon and Plato were not the only writers to have relied on Aristophanes, for Thucydides seems to have used the work of the comic writer as an *aide-mémoire* in composing his history.[31] He did so at both the thematic and stylistic levels. In *Acharnians*, for example, the debate between Dicaeopolis and the Chorus of Acharnians closely resembles that between Pericles and his Acharnian critics,[32] and the Pythonesque parody of one suffering from the plague in the bedbug scene at *Clouds* 694–745 contributed to Thucydides' account of the Great Plague of Athens (2.48–9).[33] On the stylistic level, the fourteen initial καίs in forty-four sentences of Alcibiades' speech to the Spartan assembly (6.89–92) come at exactly the same rate as the seven initial καίs in twenty-two sentences in the first two-thirds of the Alcibiadean Sausage-seller's speech at *Knights* 624–82. Thucydides would appear to have employed Aristophanes' plays as a handy means of recalling significant historical events, and as a record of political gossip, rather as a modern historian might consult relevant copies of *Punch* or *Private Eye*.

Thucydides, moreover, may well have acquired information directly from Alcibiades,[34] and thus have had personal experience of his distinctive diction, and he indulges occasionally in *lambda*-engendered wordplay at Alcibiades' expense.

---

27. Cf. Tompkins, "Stylistic Characterization in Thucydides".
28. *Ibid.*, 214 n.58.
29. *Ibid.*, 189–90.
30. ἀναγκασθῆναι (Pl. *Gorg.* 482d), ἀναγκάζεται (483a), ἀνάγκη (484c). And cf. the stress on *physis* in the Sophocles' characterization of Neoptolemus in *Philoctetes* (Chapter 5, above).
31. Vickers, *Pericles on Stage, passim.*
32. *Ibid.*, 59–76.
33. M. Vickers, "A Contemporary Account of the Athenian Plague? Aristophanes *Clouds* 694–734", *Liverpool Classical Monthly* **16** (1991), 64, and *Pericles on Stage*, 39–41.
34. Cf. P. A. Brunt, "Thucydides and Alcibiades", *Revue des études grecques* **65** (1952), 59–96; E. Delebecque, *Thucydide et Alcibiade* (Aix-en-Provence: Éditions Ophrys, 1965); E. F. Bloedow,

The contemporary reader (who in any case read aloud) will have made the appropriate noises; W. B. Stanford once likened ancient texts to "a tape-recording waiting to be played on someone's vocal organs".[35] It was in any case Thucydides' practice to imitate the manner of speech of his speakers (Hermog. *Meth.* 31). A good example is the phrase Πελοποννησίων τε στορέσωμεν τὸ φρόνημα (let us lay low the pride of the Peloponnesians; Thuc. 6.18.4), said by a scholiast both to be one of the most unpleasant (σκληρότατον) metaphors used by Thucydides, and to be an expression κατ' Ἀλκιβιάδην. No one seems to have asked why the expression was considered to be so unpleasant,[36] but if the words in question were lambdacized, the "unpleasant" phrase would have sounded as Πελοποννησίων τε στολέσωμεν τὸ πλύνημα (and let us get the bath ready for the Peloponnesians).[37] If so, Thucydides may have been alluding both to Alcibiades' speech defect and his love of bathing (Plut. *Mor.* 235a), as well as to the fact that the Peloponnesians, or at least the Spartans, were unenthusiastic bathers (Xen. *Lac.* 2.4; Plut. *Lyc.* 10.1; *Mor.* 237b), and in consequence notoriously dirty (cf. Ar. *Av.* 1282). Thucydides even puts a similar pun into Alcibiades' mouth at the beginning of his speech to the Spartans (Thuc. 6.89.1), where there is a play on πρῶτον (first) and πλωτόν (afloat): Alcibiades had recently crossed from southern Italy to the Peloponnese "in a merchantman'" (Thuc. 6.88.9).

When Thucydides uses Aristophanic models, he tones them down. He preserves the essence, but serves it up in a considerably more restrained form. While the bedbug scene in *Clouds* provided a useful checklist of symptoms (for all that he will have experienced some of them at first hand himself), his own account of plague symptoms will also have been a discreet ("emphatic") way of describing the sufferings of a Pericles who had "exhibited many varieties of symptoms" (Plut. *Per.* 38), but whose memory he wished to honour.[38] Similarly, the content of the lines given to "the Athenians" in the Melian Dialogue is less extreme than either of the

---

Alcibiades Reexamined (Wiesbaden: Steiner, 1972); H. D. Westlake, *Studies in Thucydides and Greek History* (Bristol: Classical Press, 1989), 154-65.

35. W. B. Stanford, *The Sound of Greek: Studies in the Greek Theory and Practice of Euphony* (Berkeley, CA: University of California Press, 1967), 3.

36. Gomme *et al.*, *A Historical Commentary on Thucydides*, *ad loc.* do not even quote the relevant part of the scholion.

37. And note that the preceding three words: ποιώμεθα τὸν πλοῦν (let us make the voyage) may also play on the expression πλύνον ποεῖν τινα, literally "to make a wash" for someone, and metaphorically "to abuse", "give someone a dressing" (LSJ s.vv. πλύνος, πλύνω II).

38. For M. Marshall, "much pro-Periclean sentiment [in Thucydides] takes the form of implicit suggestion" ("Pericles and the Plague", in *"Owls to Athens": Essays on Classical Subjects Presented to Sir Kenneth Dover*, E. M. Craik [ed.], 163–70 [Oxford: Clarendon Press, 1990], 165). The same might be said about anti-Alcibiadean sentiment.

exaggerations for satirical purposes of Aristophanes in *Clouds*, or those of Plato in the *Gorgias* or the *Republic*.

Alcibiades at Olympia

Alcibiades would surely have gone to Melos himself, and delivered the lines Thucydides gives to "the Athenians" in person, were it not for one overriding factor. His main interest in life was horses.[39] He kept a stud farm (Thuc. 6.15.3), and had already won victories at the Pythian and Nemean games (Satyr. *FHG* 24 ap. Ath. 12.534d), as well as at Olympia.[40] He participated with a hitherto unparalled degree of flamboyance in the ninety-first Olympic games, which were held soon after mid-summer 416.[41] Alcibiades' preparations for this festival will have precluded his presence on Melos, but it will have been one of the best known facts in the Greek world that he was engaged in the Olympic games rather than taking a personal role in the negotiations with the Melians. Alcibiades entered seven teams, the only person ever to enter so many, and with them took the first, second and fourth places (Thuc. 6.16.2). He himself performed the sacrifice to Olympian Zeus, and gave a feast to the whole crowd (Ath. 1.3e; Plut. *Alc.* 11.1–3; Thuc. 6.16.2). Earlier victors had commissioned epinician odes from Pindar, Simonides or Bacchylides. Alcibiades commissioned such an ode from Euripides, who obsequiously (and inaccurately) stated that his patron's horses came in first, second and third (Ath. 1.3e; Plut. *Alc.* 11.1–3; cf. Isocr. 16.34). Ephesus provided a magnificent Persian tent for the occasion, Chios fodder for Alcibiades' horses and victims for sacrifice, and Lesbos wine and everything necessary for the banquet ([Andoc.] 4.30; Plut. *Alc.* 12).[42] According to Satyrus, four allied cities, Ephesus, Chios, Lesbos and Cyzicus (the last of which he has supplying Alcibiades with animals for sacrifice at Olympia [Ath. 12.534d]), were regularly used "as so many handmaidens" whenever Alcibiades travelled abroad (*ibid.*). It is interesting to note

---

39. For a brilliant evocation of the role of horses in the aristocratic world of late-fifth-century Greece, see A. Schaeffer, "Alkibiades und Lysander in Ionien", *Würzburger Jahrbücher für die Altertumswissenschaft* 4 (1949/50), 287–308.
40. For Alcibiades' earlier victory, see p. 37, above.
41. The Olympic games took place in the eighth month of the Elian calendar (= July and August), and at the first full moon after the summer solstice: E. Spathari, *The Olympic Spirit* (Athens: Adam Publications, 1992), 68.
42. Briant observes that Alcibiades at Olympia was trying "to profit from the symbolism proclaimed by the rules of Achaemenid court nomadism" (*From Cyrus to Alexander*, 202); cf. his "Dons de terres et de villes: l'Asie Mineure dans le contexte achéménide", *Revue des études anciennes* 87 (1985), 53–71, esp. 59.

that Chian and Lesbian ships were on hand assisting the Athenians at Melos, and their presence is further evidence of a strong Alcibiadean element in the planning of the Melian operation.

During his flamboyant visit to Olympia in 416 BCE, Alcibiades had gained further notoriety, and had provided further ammunition for his enemies, by seizing the processional vessels belonging to the Athenian state in order to add magnificence to what he possessed himself. Not only did he borrow the official vessels, but the result was that people thought, when they saw them in the official procession, that the Athenians were using Alcibiades' plate and not the other way round ([Andoc.] 4.29; Plut. *Alc.* 13.3). This, however, was not the only act of dishonesty that Alcibiades performed at Olympia, for one of the teams of horses that he entered in the chariot race consisted of Argive horses said to have belonged to "Diomedes, a man of moderate means ... who was a citizen of Athens". But, "thanks to his influence with the judges of the games at [Olympia], Alcibiades stole [Diomedes'] team and raced it himself" ([Andoc.] 4.26). Elsewhere, we learn that "Diomedes was a respectable person and a friend of Alcibiades desirous of winning an Olympic victory" (Plut. *Alc.* 12.3). The "horses of Diomedes" appear to have been the winning team, since "Alcibiades took for himself the glory of the victory" (Diod. 13.74.3). Ownership was disputed in 408 (*ibid.*), and again in *c.*397 when Alcibiades' son was sued by Teisias (Isocr. 16), who may well have been the real owner (and the Argive horses direct descendants of the mares believed to be those that Heracles stole from Diomedes).[43]

That there may indeed have been a genuine confusion between the historical Teisias and the mythical Diomedes receives support from the recent discovery of a papyrus version of the complete ode that Plato made Callicles misquote (Pind. *Fr.* 169.8ff. Sn-M; *POxy* 26.2450). It shows how Pindar used the story of Heracles and the horses of Diomedes "to prove the proposition that *nomos*, king of all gods and men (that is, custom or conventional belief) justifies the greatest violence. The theft of the horses, although apparently unjust, was approved by Zeus".[44] The lines immediately following those exploited by Plato refer to the ἀπριάτας ... Διομήδεος ἵππους (the horses of Diomedes that were not paid for). Plato's misquotation brings this ode into the world of Alcibiades, as do "the horses that were not paid for";

---

43. Ostwald, *From Popular Sovereignty*, 311, and J. K. Davies, *Athenian Propertied Families 600–300 BC* (Oxford: Clarendon Press, 1971), 501–2, following R. Münsterberg, "Zum Renstallprozess des Alkibiades (Isokrates περὶ τοῦ ζεύγους)", in *Festschrift Theodor Gomperz dargebracht zum siebzigsten Geburtstage am 29 März 1902 von Schülern, Freunden, Collegen*, 298–9 (Vienna: Alfred Hölder, 1902).

44. A. Lintott, *Violence, Civil Strife and Revolution in the Classical City, 750–330 BC* (London: Croom Helm, 1982), 169.

they perhaps also help to explain how the name of Teisias came to be confused with the mythical Diomedes. If so, the inevitable conclusion is that [Andoc.] 4 was composed years, rather than months, after Alcibiades' Olympic embezzlement. Of even greater interest in the present context, Teisias is the name of Alcibiades' co-general for 416 in command on Melos, and he was almost certainly the plaintiff in *c.*396. Alcibiades' theft must have rankled from the start, but Teisias only began to react officially when Alcibiades' star was on the wane in 408. If he was afraid to protest until then, it is possible that he was under Alcibiades' thumb, and the executor of Alcibiadean policy in the matter of Melos in 416.

Teisias' absence from Olympia, and his inability to prevent Alcibiades' chicanery, has been noted in the past,[45] but the converse – Alcibiades' absence from Melos and his inability to participate in the Melian Dialogue – has not received nearly as much attention. And yet it is a fact of central importance for the elucidation of Thucydides' account. Although Alcibiades was away at Olympia, there is more than enough evidence to suggest that the Melian business was largely his affair. The forces ranged against Melos included Chios and Lesbos, cities that were in his pocket, and they were led in part by Teisias, who was foolhardy enough to trust him in a deal over horses, and fearful enough not to involve the law until it seemed safe to do so. It is likely, therefore, that the attack on Melos only took place with Alcibiades' active encouragement.

The attack on Melos may even have taken place on account of a personal grudge on the part of Alcibiades. Far from it being impossible now to "expect to discover what ... [were] the specific grounds for an attack in 416",[46] it is more than likely that Alcibiades' pique at having been thwarted by the islanders in 425 lay behind the siege and merciless punishment of Melos. For Alcibiades had probably been a τάκτης: a member of the commission sent by the Athenians to reassess the tribute throughout the empire in 425 ([Andoc.] 4.11).[47] Melos was not a tributary state, but had nevertheless been had been treated harshly in 426 by Nicias, and in 425 had had its tribute assessed at the very large figure of 15 talents.[48] This sum was never

45. For example, by Davies, *Athenian Propertied Families 600–300 BC*, 503, and Ostwald, *From Popular Sovereignty*, 311.
46. Gomme, in Gomme *et al.*, *A Historical Commentary on Thucydides*, 4.157.
47. Alcibiades' participation has been doubted, by, for example, Maidment, *Minor Attic Orators*, 551; Andrewes, in Gomme *et al.*, *A Historical Commentary on Thucydides*, 4, 49, and believed in, by, for example, Ostwald, *From Popular Sovereignty*, 293; Develin, "Age Qualifications for Athenian Magistrates", 149–59, cf. Develin, *Athenian Officials 684–321 BC*, 131; Ellis, *Alcibiades*, 31; Vickers, *Pericles on Stage*, 20, 24, 32, 99.
48. Meiggs, *The Athenian Empire*, 327–8; *IG* I3 71.65.

paid, not in 425 nor in subsequent years.[49] The lack of compliance will hardly have been forgotten, still less by those, perhaps including Alcibiades, who had imposed such a crippling burden in the first place.

Alcibiades and Melos

It is time to bring these disparate threads together. To the knowing reader, Thucydides' account of the Melian campaign would resonate with *Alcibiadiana*. Although Alcibiades soon leaves the scene physically (at the beginning of 5.84.1), it is left to the reader to deduce the fact. His moral presence continues in the description of the make-up of the forces that attacked Melos. The Chians and Lesbians were Alcibiades' regular "handmaidens", and their mention at 5.84.1 will not only have reminded the contemporary reader of this, but will also have recalled the services that Chios and Lesbos were simultaneously supplying to Alcibiades at Olympia. The reluctance of the Melians to belong to the Athenian confederacy, in contrast to the attitude of "the other islanders" (5.84.2), may have brought to mind the earlier harsh treatment of the island and the punitive tribute assessment that Alcibiades and others had tried to impose in 425. The method the Athenians chose to adopt towards Melos was coercion; if Thucydides (and Plato) had aptly characterized Alcibiades by having him (and Callicles) make frequent use of ἀνάγκη and its cognates, then ἠνάγκαζον οἱ Ἀθηναῖοι (5.84.2) will have possessed a certain Alcibiadean resonance. It also makes the point, "emphatically", that the Athenians in general had been taken in by Alcibiades. "The whole weight of imperial ἀνάγκη" is indeed articulated in the Melian Dialogue,[50] but Thucydides personalizes the affair, and does so in such a way that the ground is prepared for the full enormity of the Sicilian campaign in the next book of the *Histories* and Alcibiades' role therein. Munn perceptively notes the congruence of the case made by "the Athenians" at 5.29, that in effect "those who can objectively be deemed more powerful than others are beyond the bounds of equality with them", with Alcibiades' claim in his speech in the Athenian assembly in 415 to "have a better right to command than others" (6.16.1).[51]

At least one of the generals, Teisias, was close to Alcibiades. The word Thucydides uses to describe the action that Teisias and Cleomedes were going to carry out on the territory of the Melians was to ἀδικεῖν it (treat it with injustice). Thucydides

---

49. Gomme, in Gomme *et al.*, *A Historical Commentary on Thucydides*, 4.156.
50. M. Ostwald, *ANAΓΚΗ in Thucydides* (Atlanta, GA: Scholars Press, 1988), 40.
51. Munn, *The School of History*, 120.

prejudges the whole episode in terms that recall (but that are even harsher than) the way more responsible Athenians viewed Alcibiades' private conduct around this time (Plut. *Alc.* 16.2). In Aristophanes' early plays (or those we have), Alcibiadean characters are frequently foils for figures based on Pericles.[52] Pericles' public life was characterized by the virtue of δικαιοσύνη (righteousness or justice) (Plut. *Per.* 2.5), and δίκαιον (just) is a word that occurs in the mouth of Thucydides' version of the statesman.[53] Δίκη (justice), moreover, was a concept closely linked with Zeus (e.g. *Nu.* 902),[54] and this will have greatly contributed to Pericles' Olympian nickname (Plut. *Per.* 8.3). Ἀδικία well epitomized the unjust, and lawless, tendencies in Alcibiades, as was evident to Aristophanes, who exploited the fact in creating the Alcibiadean Weaker Argument in *Clouds*,[55] a version of which was known to Thucydides, as we have seen.

Another way in which Thucydides indicates that many Athenians were won over by Alcibiades was to make "the Athenians" in the Melian Dialogue speak in a suitably Alcibiadean manner. The knowing contemporary reader will thus have spoken the words of "the Athenians" τραυλίζων, or pronouncing *rho* as *lambda*. If the opening words of the first speech of "the Athenians" were thus lambdacized, they would quickly produce a disagreeable jingle: πλὸς τὸ πλῆθος is the kind of expression for which Alcibiades' teacher Gorgias was famous but which good Attic stylists tried to avoid (cf. Plato's satirical ὦ λῷστε Πῶλε at *Grg.* 467b,[56] or the χάλιν καλόν he puts into Callicles' mouth at 485a).[57]

The way in which "the Athenians" say that they fully understand why the Melians have chosen to conduct negotiations in private, and not "before the people", lest the latter be deceived having heard their ἐπαγωγὰ καὶ ἀνέλεγκτα (persuasive and unchallenged) words in a continuous discourse, is remarkably (and no doubt deliberately) similar to the way in which Thucydides had described Alcibiades' deception of the Spartan ambassadors to Athens in 420. On that occasion, Alcibiades had been afraid lest the ambassadors ἐπαγάγωνται τὸ πλῆθος (should persuade the people) if they spoke in public (Thuc. 5.45.2).

ξυνεχεῖ ῥήσει (continuous discourse), when lambdacized, would produce ξυνεχεὶ λήσει (continuous seizure). λῆσις, according to Hesychius, meant the same as

---

52. Vickers, *Pericles on Stage, passim*.
53. Cf. Tompkins, "Stylistic Characterization in Thucydides", 189.
54. Also, H. Lloyd-Jones, *The Justice of Zeus*, 2nd edn (Los Angeles, CA: University of California Press, 1971); Ostwald, *From Popular Sovereignty*, 143–4.
55. Vickers, *Pericles on Stage*, 42–58. The Stronger Argument promises to win by τὸ δίκαια λέγων (speaking what is just; *Nu.* 900).
56. Cf. Dodds, *Plato: Gorgias*, 235.
57. Chapter 12, below.

αἴρεσις. αἴρεσις δυνάμεως (seizure of power) is actually included in Socrates' address to Callicles in the *Gorgias* (513a). The last sentence of the same short speech (Thuc. 5.85), καὶ πρῶτον εἰ ἀρέσκει ὡς λέγομεν εἴπατε (And first tell us if you like what we say), includes initial καί followed by a πρῶτον, which, if lambdacized, would be heard as πλῶτον. Thucydides is here playing on the notion of πλωτόν (afloat), and had sown the seeds of the idea at the beginning of Chapter 84 with Ἀλκιβιάδης τε πλεύσας (Alcibiades having sailed). ἀλέσκει does not produce a pun, but is simply there for the sake of cacophony (as, to a large extent, is πλῶτον). The sentence as it stands can also mean "And first tell us if you like the way we speak"; for it to be read as καὶ πλῶτον εἰ ἀλέσκει ὡς λέγομεν εἴπατε would have done Alcibiades no credit at all.

The *locus classicus* for Alcibiades-speak is at *Wasps* 44–5, where a slave is made to imitate his characteristic mode of speech. Alcibiades is supposed to have said to him τραυλίσας (lambdacizing): ὁλᾷς; Θέολος τὴν κεφάλην κόλακος ἔχει (Do you see Theolus? He has the head of a flatterer). Aristophanes elsewhere makes great play with jokes on ὁρᾶν at Alcibiades' expense; it becomes a *topos*. Thucydides too executes one in the second speech of "the Athenians", in a sentence that would have been full of awkward jingles in any case: καὶ ὧν ὁλᾶτε πελὶ σωτηλίας – if the speech were indeed lambdacized.

The unrestrained aggression of "the Athenians" reaches a peak in Chapter 105. There we learn that both gods and men exercise power by the sanction of superior natural strength, ὑπὸ φύσεως ἀναγκαίας (105.2).[58] This is a restrained, toned down version of Aristophanes' Weaker Argument's reference to τῆς φύσεως ἀνάγκας (needs of nature; *Nu.* 1075), itself doubtless a lampoon of a theme that was evidently popular in the circle of Gorgias (he wrote a study Περὶ φύσεως [On Nature]; Grg. 82 B 1 DK).[59] J. H. Finley's judgement is very much to the point: "In attributing to the gods their own belief that superior power sanctions any conduct, [the Athenians] reveal the total disappearance of higher standards".[60] This is the same criticism as Plato's, when he makes Callicles misquote Pindar (*Grg.* 484b). Thucydides' passage in which the statement of mocking scepticism appears (5.10) is also rich in sentences beginning καί. There are eight sentences in all, the fourth and the fifth begin καί, and the eighth and final sentence begins καίτοι: the same pattern as in the Alcibiadean Weaker Argument's long speeches (*Nu.* 1036–45, 1068–82). Moreover, the frequency rate (employing Tompkins' criteria) of initial

---

58. Cf. ἀνάγκης (5.89), ἀναγκαίῳ (5.99), not to mention the Melians' ἀνάγκη γὰρ ... (5.90).
59. Cf. Guthrie, *A History of Greek Philosophy*, 3.55–134.
60. J. H. Finley, *Thucydides* (Cambridge, MA: Harvard University Press, 1942), 211; cf. Furley, *Andokides and the Herms*, 77–8.

καῖ's in 5.105 is, at 0.375, even higher than that of Alcibiades' two speeches at 6.16–18 and 6.89–92, where it is 0.368 and 0.318 respectively.[61]

Pericles and the Melians

But are "the Melians" really Melians, or do they provide a dramatic front for other interests? "The Athenians" have so much in common with the Weaker Argument in *Clouds* that it is possible that Thucydides used Aristophanes' play to remind himself what the philosophical issues were. He toned the content down, but the viewpoint is essentially the same. The Weaker Argument "came forward" as Alcibiades, the Stronger Argument as Pericles. In this way, the generation gap, and the contrast between the old ways and the new, were effectively personalized. Xenophon's conversation between Alcibiades and Pericles (characterized by the latter as σοφίζεσθαι [philosophiz(ing)]; Xen. *Mem.* 1.2.46) is relevant here, and since the Weaker Argument reflects views that Alcibiades must have received from Gorgias, and Gorgias did not visit Athens until after Pericles' death, Xenophon's conversation must be a contrivance based on *Clouds* or something similar. Just as Xenophon apparently follows the idolopoieïc tradition of bringing Pericles back from the dead as the spokesman for old-fashioned values, so too did Eupolis in *Demi* in perhaps 417 (Eup. *PCG* 110); so too does Thucydides, who puts such views in the mouth of "the Melians".

In his representation of the Stronger Argument, Aristophanes seems to have attributed to him extremely exaggerated, and frequently Spartan, versions of known positions of Pericles.[62] Pericles' anti-Laconism was well known (Plut. *Per.* 21.1, 31.10); for Aristophanes to make the Stronger Argument put forward his views in a Spartan guise would not only have been funny, but in keeping with Gilbert Murray's spendthrift Aberdonian principle, whereby writers of comedy made their audiences laugh by means of images diametrically opposed to what was being represented. Thucydides' Melians express far less exaggerated views, and we might even assume them to be intended to be an accurate statement of what Pericles would have said in response to the arguments put by "the Athenians". To put Periclean arguments in the mouths of Spartan colonists (as the Melians were;

---

61. Tompkins, "Stylistic Characterization in Thucydides", 206.
62. This hypothesis can be tested against K. J. Dover's useful checklist of the values for which the Stronger Argument stands (*Aristophanes Clouds* [Oxford: Clarendon Press, 1968], lix); see my *Pericles on Stage*, 43–52, for a full discussion.

Thuc. 5.84.2), would have been a knowing – and witty – nod in the direction of *Clouds*.

While Thucydides stands back from the encounter between "the Athenians" and "the Melians",[63] his sympathies tend towards the latter. Not only are "the Athenians" revealed from the outset as bent on reducing Melos to servitude at best and utter destruction at worst, but Thucydides allows "the Melians" to conduct the debate, and quickly gives them the upper hand morally speaking so that their adversaries are forced to justify their policies at every step.[64] The motives and weaknesses of "the Athenians" are unmasked by these means. "The very hate of their subjects which is the source of their fear [and which] they take to be the guarantee of their security (5.95)"[65] is in marked contrast to Pericles' admission (2.64.5) that "to be hateful and offensive has ever been the fate of those who have aspired to empire".[66] The reluctance of "the Melians" to be cowardly (5.100) and their constant (and understandable) concern for σωτηρία (safety) play allusively on the charges of cowardice laid against Pericles during his declining years (Plut. *Per.* 33.7); their faith in the gods, and their belief that they are righteously contending against those who are οὐ δικαίους (unjust; 5.104) relates to Pericles' δικαιοσύνη (justice); their phrase "ὁ πόνος ὑμῖν ἔσται [your task will be to fight; 5.110]" over land closer to home than Melos includes a word, πόνος, that Thucydides' Pericles employs five times in his last formal speech (2.62.1, 62.3, 63.1, 63.3, 64.6).[67]

***

The knowing contemporary reader presumably changed voices according to whether "the Athenians" or "the Melians" were speaking (and would indeed have had to "pay close attention to what was said": the tenor of the argument would have been a sure guide).[68] The contemporary reader will have been aided by the fact that Alcibiades-speak was well-known from the theatre, but so too must Pericles' mode of speech have been: we know that it was "sweet", and that it was distinctive enough

63. H.-P. Stahl, *Thukydides: Die Stellung des Menschen im geschichtlichen Prozess* (Munich: Beck, 1966), 164.
64. Cf. M. Amit, "The Melian Dialogue and History", *Athenaeum* **46** (1968), 216–35.
65. Macleod, "Form and Meaning in the Melian Dialogue", 392, and *Collected Essays*, 59.
66. Cf. Gomme, in Gomme *et al.*, *A Historical Commentary on Thucydides*, 4.167; Macleod, "Form and Meaning in the Melian Dialogue", 392; *Collected Essays*, 59.
67. Boegehold, "A Dissent at Athens *ca.* 424–421 BC", 154–5.
68. See J. Svenbro, *Phrasikleia: An Anthropology of Reading in Ancient Greece* (Ithaca, NY: Cornell University Press, 1993), introduction and Chapter 3 on writing in ancient Greece having depended on the reader's voice to complete the text.

to have been held to resemble that of Peisistratus (Plut. *Per.* 7.1; Val. Max. 8.9. ext. 2); it will also have been widely lampooned by actors.[69]

But how do these personalizations help our understanding of the Melian episode? Having "the Athenians" personalized as Alcibiades certainly explains why Thucydides did not explicitly mention how the Athenians starved the Melians to death, for the reference to the Melians breaking out from the siege to steal food (5.115.4) makes the point implicitly.[70] Implicit too is Alcibiades' involvement in the slaughter and enslavement of the Melians. Thucydides' account of the Melian campaign may moreover be an "emphatic" commentary on Pericles' Samian campaign many years earlier. Both involved revolts by islanders, Athenian reversals, siege operations and (if adverse Samian sources are to be believed; Plut. *Per.* 28.2–7) the cruel treatment of survivors. If we today can recreate the broad outlines of the situation, how much more would the ancients, Thucydides and his audience included, have known of the details? Athenians will have been used to seeing Pericles on stage serving as a foil to Alcibiadean characters; it is understandable why Thucydides followed suit. It is not as though the events of 416 were a passing wonder; their consequences were still a live issue when Thucydides was writing his account of the Melian Dialogue, as (the presumably later) [Andoc.] 4 and Isoc. 16 indicate. Whether this was before or after the end of the Peloponnesian War (and the death of Alcibiades) in 404,[71] is a moot point. It could be that Thucydides had to tread with caution, so that he could, if challenged by Alcibiades or one of his supporters after his death, absolve himself from the charge of explicitly implicating Alcibiades in what had occurred. What he does implicitly is, however, all the more powerful.

It is surely wrong to believe that "Thucydides simply did not realise that most of his readers would be unable to forget the massacre that was to come and would therefore feel strongly prejudiced against the Athenian speakers".[72] And yet, G. de Ste. Croix is essentially correct in his view that the Melian Dialogue "has nothing whatever to do with the massacre of the Melians".[73] It was composed with a view

---

69. See my *Pericles on Stage, passim*, and Chapters 5 and 7 above.
70. Cf. the heartless λιμῷ Μηλίῳ on the lips of the Alcibiadeanizing Peisthetaerus at *Av.* 186 (performed in 414); cf. Vickers, "Heracles Lacedaemonius" and *Pericles on Stage*, 154–70. The reference is far from "casual" (Andrewes in Gomme *et al.*, *A Historical Commentary on Thucydides*, 4.187), nor does it indicate that the Athenians did not feel "any remorse for their treatment of Melos" (Gomme in *ibid.*, 4.189); rather, the opposite.
71. For discussions of the date of composition see: J. de Romilly, *Thucydides and Athenian Imperialism* (Oxford: Blackwell, 1963), 313–15; Macleod, "Form and Meaning in the Melian Dialogue", 397–8, and *Collected Essays*, 64–5; Munn, *The School of History*, 292–329.
72. de Ste. Croix, *The Origins of the Peloponnesian War*, 16.
73. *Ibid.*, 14.

to demonstrate the principles according to which the Athenians operated in the mid-teens of the fifth century.[74] War had indeed taught men to be violent (cf. βίαιος διδάσκαλος, Thuc. 3.82.2).[75] In closely identifying Alcibiades with "the Athenians", Thucydides is making the point that philosophical ideas of the early 420s (when Gorgias first came to Athens), which were well enough known to be lampooned on the comic stage in 424, had by now gained acceptance among the *demos*. Thucydides succeeds in universalizing the particular: "'the universal' consist[ing] in describing the kind of things that a person of a certain character would say or do probably or necessarily ... [and] an example of the particular [being] what Alcibiades did, or what was done to him" (Arist. *Poet.* 9.1–4). Discussion of Thucydides' practice of giving the ξύμπασα γνώμη (entire intention; Thuc. 1.22.1)[76] of what a speech contained has hitherto been confined to the intention of the speaker. The ξύμπασα γνώμη of the Melian episode, including the Dialogue, is to make the reader reflect on the nature of Athenian imperialism once it had turned really nasty.

---

74. Cf. Finley, *Thucydides*, 212.
75. An expression that itself might play on Ἀλκιβιάδης, as an anonymous referee kindly notes.
76. E. Badian, "Thucydides on Rendering Speeches", *Athenaeum* **80** (1992), 187–90.

10
Thucydides on tyrannicides: not a "digression"

Certain passages in Thucydides have caused a good deal of scholarly embarrassment. To the literal-minded they are distracting excrescences that should not be there. The passages in question are the account of Harmodius and Aristogeiton (6.53.3–59), the discussion of the origins of the Cylonian revolt and the subsequent Alcmaeonid curse (1.126.2–12), the end of Pausanias (1.128–135.1) and the fate of Themistocles (1.135.2–138). There is no shortage of critics who have used the terms "digression" or "excursus" to describe these passages. It will be argued here and in Chapter 11 that they are, instead, central to Thucydides' narrative.

In the case of the Harmodius and Aristogeiton passage that comes in the middle of Thucydides' account of Alcibiades' summons from Catana, his escape from his escort, and his exile in the Peloponnese (6.53.1–2, 60–61), "scholars have been puzzled by Thucydides' inclusion of a lengthy and somewhat loosely connected digression in an otherwise tightly-knit narrative that shuns extraneous material",[1] and the chapters in question have either been held to "provide an historical model for a crucial issue" on which the Peloponnesian War would turn,[2] or else to have nothing whatever to do with the events of 415.[3] On the latter view, Thucydides simply succumbed "to the temptation before which all historians and commentators

---

1. H. R. Rawlings, *The Structure of Thucydides's History* (Princeton, NJ: Princeton University Press, 1981), 90–91.
2. *Ibid.* For S. Hornblower, "[Alcibiades'] 'tyrannical' life-style awoke memories and fears of the Pisistratids" (*Thucydides* [London: Duckworth, 1987], 6); cf. the *logos* of the tyrants in Herodotus, which K. Raaflaub, "Herodotus, Political Thought, and the Meaning of History", *Arethusa* 20 (1987), 221–48, esp. 225, has argued had a bearing on the meeting of the Peloponnesian League at Sparta in 432, when bitter complaints were made about Athenian aggression. Raaflaub has well shown how Herodotus here "connects the events of the past with the experiences of the present".
3. Dover, in Gomme *et al.*, *A Historical Commentary on Thucydides*, 4.328–9; Stahl, *Thukydides*, 7.

are by their very nature weak, the temptation to correct historical error wherever they find it, regardless of its relevance to their immediate purpose".[4] But no matter how sensitive[5] (or insensitive) their treatment of the issue, commentators on both sides of the argument err in calling Thucydides' tyrannicide story a digression.[6] It is a necessary part of the narrative, and by his careful choice of language, by means of "emphasis",[7] Thucydides succeeds in saying rather more about Alcibiades than might otherwise be possible. The passage was carefully composed in order to enrich the surrounding narrative.[8]

Similarly, in the context of the Cylon episode (2) it has been asserted that "this whole digression is irrelevant to [Thucydides'] main narrative", while the "excursus" on Pausanias and Themistocles is "for his purpose quite unnecessary".[9] The "excursus" on Pausanias is said to be "unsatisfactory ... [and since it stands out from most of the rest of Thucydides' *oeuvre* it] can hardly stand as it is .... One may seek to excuse it as early work that he never got round to revising, but excuses are certainly due".[10] Rather, Thucydides knew full well what he was doing when he wrote of Cylon, Pausanias and Themistocles, and the accounts were of fundamental importance for contemporary readers' understanding of the *History*.

It was possible, as we have seen in Chapter 9, for Thucydides to devote pages to Alcibiadean policy without even mentioning him by name: in 416, Alcibiades was unable to be present at the sacking and cruel punishment of Melos because he was engaged elsewhere, in flamboyant and controversial attendance at the Olympic games. Since he was unable to take a personal role in the negotiations with the Melians, his words are put anonymously into the mouths of "the Athenians" (Thuc. 5.84–116). Likewise, the way in which Thucydides describes the negotiations with Segesta before the outbreak of hostilities in Sicily is done in such a way

---

4. Dover, in Gomme *et al.*, *A Historical Commentary on Thucydides*, 4.329.
5. Rawlings, *The Structure of Thucydides's History*, 100–117, makes some excellent points demonstrating formal links between the tyrannicide passage and its Alcibiadean setting. See too W. Schadewaldt, *Die Geschichtschreibung des Thukydides: Ein Versuch* (Berlin: Weidmann, 1929), 91–5.
6. For example, Dover, in Gomme *et al.*, *A Historical Commentary on Thucydides*, 4.317; Rawlings, *The Structure of Thucydides's History*, 59, 64, 90–117; S. Forde, *The Ambition to Rule: Alcibiades and the Politics of Imperialism in Thucydides* (Ithaca, NY: Cornell University Press, 1989), 95.
7. See p. 8, above.
8. Cf. the analysis of ring composition in Book 6: W. R. Connor, *Thucydides* (Princeton, NJ: Princeton University Press, 1984), 257.
9. Gomme *et al.*, *A Historical Commentary on Thucydides*, 1, 425.
10. G. Cawkwell, *Thucydides and the Peloponnesian War* (London: Routledge, 1997), 11, 125 n.37.

that Alcibiades' influence is felt, and his involvement criticized, without his name being mentioned.[11] It has recently been said that "Thucydides' most trenchant statements about the nature of Athenian politics and the fate of Athens were made with Alcibiades clearly in mind";[12] the "digressions" are – strange to say – where he is most outspoken in this respect.

Thucydides 6.53.3–59

The passage in Thucydides Book 6 (53.3–59) dealing with Harmodius and Aristogeiton ostensibly describes the circumstances in which Hipparchus, the son of the sixth-century Athenian tyrant Pesistratus, had been assassinated, but it comes in the middle of Thucydides' account of Alcibiades' arrest and escape into exile. Far from being a "digression" unconnected with the rest of the narrative, it was carefully composed in order to enrich it. Thucydides was a more subtle writer than many commentators allow.[13]

In his *Life*, in which he "brings out the political fears and nervy religious atmosphere" that prevailed in Athens in 415,[14] Plutarch indicates how Alcibiades' extravagant and intemperate behaviour alienated substantial portions of the population: both the "leading men" of Athens, who "viewed his conduct with disgust and apprehension, fear[ed] his scornful and unlawful behaviour, as tyrannical and portentous" (Plut. *Alc.* 16.2), and the "older men", who expressed similar sentiments (Plut. *Alc.* 16.5). Thucydides' narrative makes it clear that it was owing to the fear of tyrannical ambitions on Alcibiades' part, as well as to personal objections concerning his private life, that the Athenians "entrusted the administration of the war to others" (6.15.4). This in turn explains why there was a general readiness a few weeks later

---

11. G. Mader, "Rogues' Comedy at Segesta (Thukydides 6.46): Alcibiades Exposed?", *Hermes* **121** (1993), 181–95.

12. Munn, *The School of History*, 7.

13. Cf. E. Badian, *From Plataea to Potidaea: Studies in the History and Historiography of the Pentecontaetia* (Baltimore, MD: Johns Hopkins University Press, 1993), 125–62, 223–36 (who shows how much artifice went into the composition of the *History*); Francis, "Brachylogia Laconica", presents cogent arguments against the view that "All [Thucydides'] speakers talk the same language, irrespective of nationality and cultural milieu" [Dover, in Gomme *et al.*, *A Historical Commentary on Thucydides*, 5.395], and in support of the case for individualization made by Tompkins, "Stylistic Characterization in Thucydides" and "Archidamus and the Question of Characterization".

14. C. B. R. Pelling, *Plutarch and History: Eighteen Studies* (London/Swansea: Duckworth/Classical Press of Wales, 2002), 128.

to believe that Alcibiades might have been involved both in the mutilation of the Herms and the profanation of the Mysteries.[15] Private morality was of the essence here, as has often been noted.[16]

Without saying so explicitly, and leaving the alert reader to "dig out some lurking meaning" (Quint. *Inst.* 9.2.64), Thucydides equates Hipparchus and Hippias, the sons of Peisistratus, with Alcibiades, the *de facto* son of a Pericles[17] who was supposedly similar to Peisistratus in voice and physical appearance (Plut. *Per.* 7.1), whose followers were known as the New Peisistratidae (Plut. *Per.* 16.1), and whose own regime was regarded by its enemies as a tyranny (e.g. Crat 258 *PCG* ap. Plut. *Per.* 7.1; Plut. *Per.* 12.2, 16.1). The whole business of the death of Hipparchus is said by Thucydides to have arisen δι' ἐρωτικὴν ξυντυχίαν (from an erotic entanglement; 6.54.1), and the view is repeated throughout the account (ἐρωτικῶς περιαλγήσας [greatly hurt in love; 6.54.3], δι' ὀργῆς ... ἐρωτικῆς [as the result of erotically induced anger; 6.57.3], δι' ἐρωτικὴν λύπην [through erotic grief; 6.59.1]). The stress on ἔρως may be Thucydides' way of alluding to a feature of Alcibiades' private life that was well-known both to his peers (*vide* the play Plato makes of Eros in a specifically Alcibiadean context in the *Symposium*), and to the world at large: Alcibiades' shield, was "not emblazoned with the ancestral bearings of his family, but with an Eros wielding a thunderbolt" (Plut. *Alc.* 16.1; Satyr. ap. Ath. 12.534e), and if the image was one that owed its origins to an invention of the comic stage, so much the better. This was one of the specific reasons listed by Plutarch to explain why the "leading men" of Athens regarded Alcibiades' behaviour as "tyrannical" (Plut. *Alc.* 16.2). Moreover, as we have frequently had occasion to note, Alcibiades' youthful erotic career was later aptly to be epitomized in these words: "When he was a young boy he lured husbands away from their wives, but when he was a young man he lured wives away from their husbands" (Bion ap. Diog. 4.49).[18]

A reference to the innocent Harmodius' "good looks" (6.54.2) may have been included to recall the physical beauty for which the dissolute Alcibiades was

---

15. Alcibiades was probably not involved in the mutilation of the Herms, but Plutarch states (*Alc.* 20.5) that his enemies put about the story that he was (cf. Dem. 21.147). R. Osborne notes "how limited is the overlap between those named in connection with the mutilation and those named in connection with the profanation" ("The Erection and Mutilation of the Hermai", *Proceedings of the Cambridge Philological Society* 211 [1985], 47–73, esp. 73 n.97).

16. For example, R. Seager, "Alcibiades and the Charge of Aiming at Tyranny", *Historia* 16 (1967), 6–18; Forde, *The Ambition to Rule*, 95; Gribble, *Alcibiades and Athens*, 69–79, 131–6; Munn, *The School of History*, 95–126.

17. Cf. N. Loraux, *L'Invention d'Athènes: histoire de l'oraison funèbre dans la "cité classique"* (Paris: Mouton, 1981), 467; Strauss, *Fathers and Sons in Athens*, 133–4.

18. Cf. Gribble, *Alcibiades and Athens*; V. Wohl, "The Eros of Alcibiades", *Classical Antiquity* 18 (1999), 349–85; Munn, *The School of History*; Sheffield, "Alcibiades' Speech".

famous (Pl. *Prt* 309a; *Alc.* 1.113b, 123a; *Smp.* 216c–219e; Plut. *Alc.* 4.1, 16.4; Ath. 12.534c, etc.). The young Harmodius was not seduced (οὐ πεισθείς; 6.54.3) by Hipparchus, whereas the boy Alcibiades was notoriously seduced by his admirers (Plut. *Alc.* 3.1; 6.1). βίᾳ (violently) and βίαιον (violent) in the first passage of the narrative (6.54.3 and 4) may allude to the "violent" element in Alci*biades*' name, and the relative lack of violence that characterized the Peisistratean regime before the assassination (which Thucydides stresses; 6.54.4) may have been an intentional contrast to the behaviour of an ostensibly tyrannically disposed individual whose thuggery was well known;[19] just as the demands made by taxation were light under the Peisistratids (6.54.5), in contrast with Alcibiades' doubling of the tribute in 425 ([Andoc.] 4.11).

Thucydides' *logos* on the tyrannicides is not simply embedded within his account of the recall of Alcibiades, but it occurs in the very centre of Book 6. At the mid-point of the story itself is a brief description of the act of hubris (cf. ὑβρισμένος at 6.57.3)[20] that led to the formal breach between Hipparchus on the one hand and Harmodius and Aristogeiton on the other. Harmodius' younger sister had been invited to carry a sacred basket in a procession, but Hipparchus ἀπήλεσαν (dismissed) her, on the grounds that she was not ἀξίαν (worthy) (6.56.1). Again there may be specific Alcibiadean resonances, in that the word for "dismiss" was regularly used to describe those who had been forced into exile from their city,[21] while ἀξίαν, apart from being a "social slur against the rank of Harmodius' family" (only girls of a certain status could act as κανηφόροι [bearers of the sacred baskets]),[22] is full of additional meaning, as we have often had occasion to note.

When Thucydides introduces Alcibiades into his *History*, he states that although he was young by the standards of any other city, he was nevertheless influential on account of the reputation (ἀξιώματι; 5.43.2) of his forbears. Then, when Alcibiades is introduced again to take part in the debate over the Sicilian expedition, Thucydides reminds his readers that he was held in high esteem (ἀξιώματι; 6.15.3) by the citizenry. And again, when Thucydides makes Alcibiades recall his triumphs

---

19. In addition to his future father-in-law (Plut. *Alc.* 8.1), Alcibiades had once beaten up a rival *choregus* ([Andoc.] 4.20–21; Plut. *Alc.* 16.5; Dem. 21.147), a schoolmaster (Plut. *Alc.* 7.1), and one of his servants (Plut. *Alc.* 3.2); the latter died from his injuries. Alcibiades and his circle are said to have prevented Aristophanes from winning first prize for *Clouds* in 423 by intimidating the judges (Ar. *Nu.* Hyp. 5 Coulon; cf. Vickers, "Alcibiades in Cloudedoverland" and *Pericles on Stage*, 57).

20. Cf. Fisher, *Hybris*, 29 n.62, 109, 386.

21. LSJ s.v. ἀπελαύνω I.

22. Rawlings, *The Structure of Thucydides's History*, 106; Dover in Gomme *et al.*, *A Historical Commentary on Thucydides*, 4.334.

at Olympia when he entered seven teams in the chariot event, and was placed first, second and fourth, he "ordered everything in a style worthy [ἀξιῶς; 6.16.2] of the victory".[23] These may in turn have been "emphatic" allusions on Thucydides' part to Alcibiades' usurping Socrates' prize for valour at Potidaea in 431 on account of his ἀξίωμα (worth, reputation, social clout) "in the eyes of the generals" (Pl. *Smp.* 219*e*; Diog. 2.23; Plut. *Alc.* 7). If this is what is "lurking for the reader to dig out" in the tyrannicide section, Thucydides' language is exquisitely chosen in order to draw attention to Alcibiades' utter worthlessness in the eyes of his fellow citizens after he had been condemned to death and had curses called down upon his head in a public ceremony (Plut. *Alc.* 22.5).[24]

Harmodius' sister was to carry a basket in a procession (πομπῇ; 6.56.1). Alcibiades' behaviour in the context of a particular procession was described by one of his critics as an act of hubris directed against the city of Athens as a whole ([Andoc.] 4.29). In 416, when celebrating his Olympic victory ἀξιῶς (in a worthy style), he had seized the πομπεῖα (processional vessels) belonging to the Athenian state in order to add magnificence to what he had already. Not only did he borrow the official vessels, but the result was that people thought, when they saw them in the πομπήν (official procession), that the Athenians were using Alcibiades' plate and not the other way round ([Andoc.] 4.29; Plut. *Alc.* 13.3).

The references to the attempts of Hippias, the surviving tyrant, to create a safe haven abroad should he need it (6.59.2), perhaps hint at Alcibiades' impending need (in terms of Thucydides' narrative) to find a bolt-hole from his fellow citizens.[25] Hippias' medizing – marrying his daughter to a member of the family of Hippocles of Lampsacus, who had influence with the Persian king, and his subsequent exile at the latter's court (6.59.3-4) – may be a glance forward to Alcibiades' imminent fraternization with Athens' current enemy, not to mention his eventual ἀσφάλεια (refuge; Plut. *Alc.* 24.4)[26] at the court of a Persian satrap (Thuc. 8.45–7; Plut. *Alc.* 24.4–7; cf. 23.5). The meekness of Hippias' daughter, who was not given to ἀτασθαλίην (recklessness; 6.59.3) may be an implicit nod in the direction of Alcibiades' insolent boldness (e.g. Plut. *Alc.* 44.2). Herodotus' main objective in telling the story of the tyrannicides was to give credit to the Alcmaeonid clan for having eventually overthrown Hippias with the aid of the Spartans (Hdt. 5.62–5).

---

23. Rawlings, *The Structure of Thucydides's History*, 115, notes that the use of the word ἀξιώματος at Thuc. 8.73.3 is a reminder of Alcibiades.

24. Cf. Lewis, "After the Profanation of the Mysteries", 177, 189. Plato uses the same conceit in his satirical account of the relations between Socrates and Alcibiades (at *Grg.* 485c, 497c, 492c, 520a, 527e), on which see Chapter 12, below.

25. Alcibiades is actually stated to be an exile at 6.61.7.

26. Cf. ἀσφαλείαν at Thuc. 6.59.2.

Thucydides barely mentions the role of the Alcmaeonids and Spartans at all in his much longer narrative, but when he eventually does so, towards the end (6.59.4), it will have been as an "emphatic" reminder of Alcibiades' Alcmaeonid ancestry (Plut. *Alc.* 1.1), and of his supposed collusion with the Spartans even before he went into exile (6.61.2). Finally, Hippias' journey to the Persians was made ὑπόσπονδος (under safe-conduct; 6.59.4), which may be a deliberate anticipation of Alcibiades' refuge (also ὑπόσπονδος; 6.88.9) at Sparta in 415.

If these parallels are not contrived, Thucydides was being singularly – and uncharacteristically – insensitive; and it is perhaps preferable to see the tyrannicide story as a sophisticated means of suggesting that Alcibiades was considerably more tyrannical in his behaviour than even the Peisistratids had been. Physical safety may have been another reason why Thucydides might have wanted to conceal this view beneath what amounts to an allegorical judgement on an individual who could, if aroused, do a lot of damage. If Thucydides wrote Book 6 between 413 and 411/10,[27] Alcibiades was still very much alive and liable to kick; if, however, he wrote the whole of the *History* in 396–395 as has recently been argued,[28] then the unpredictable Alcibiades Jr who traded on his father's reputation (Archipp. *PCG* 48 ap. Plut. *Alc.* 1.8), not to mention those who subscribed to the "cult" of Alcibiades,[29] were perhaps to be feared. Like Aristophanes, and indeed Sophocles and Euripides, Thucydides knew how to write "figuratively and not openly" (Ttetz. XIAi 97–8 Koster). This is especially important in view of the most serious conclusion that could be drawn from the story, namely that it might have been a good thing if Alcibiades had been assassinated as well. That this may well have been in Thucydides' mind is suggested by his statement at the end of the following chapter that the fact that so many (including Alcibiades) had been condemned to death "had a clearly beneficial effect on the city" (6.60.5).[30] It has been well said that "tyrants and terrorists pun sparingly"[31] but their opponents often find ambiguity to be an effective means of safe criticism.

Thucydides seems to distance himself by employing allegory. Or rather, he does not distance himself, but engages in an analysis of what happened that is richer and more evocative (and safer) than any explicit account of Alcibiades' tyrannical tendencies might have been. Nor can it reasonably be claimed that "the passage

---

27. Hornblower, *Thucydides*, 150.
28. Munn, *The School of History*, 292–329.
29. Gribble, *Alcibiades and Athens*, 3, 137–43.
30. And it may also account for the polemical tone of the tyrannicide section noted by Rawlings, *The Structure of Thucydides's History*, 101.
31. H. Gaston Hall, *Comedy in Context: Essays on Molière* (Jackson, MI: University Press of Mississippi, 1984), 100.

do[es] not inevitably call Alcibiades to mind, and need not do so to be dramatically effective".[32] Thucydides' allegorizing *logos* is firmly embedded in what is an account of Alcibiades and no one else, the dramatic effectiveness of which is greatly enriched by its presence.

---

32. R. F. Moorton, "Aristophanes on Alcibiades", *Greek, Roman and Byzantine Studies* **29** (1988), 345–59, esp. 348, epitomizing H. D. Westlake ("The *Lysistrata* and the War", *Phoenix* **34** (1980), 38–54, esp. 42, 47, 49 n.32) on a different, but related, topic.

11
Alcibiades and Persia
(and more Thucydidean "digressions")

There is no end to the roll call of scholars who have dismissed the cluster of stories in Thucydides dealing with Cylon, Pausanias and Themistocles (1.126.2–138) – as well as the account of Harmodius and Aristogeiton discussed in Chapter 10 – as "digressions" or "excursuses". A case can, however, be made for their being necessary parts of the narrative; by his careful choice of language, by means of "emphasis" ("the process of digging out some lurking meaning from something said"; Quint. *Inst.* 9.2.64[1]), Thucydides succeeds in saying rather more about Alcibiades than might otherwise be possible. The passages were carefully composed in order to enrich the surrounding narrative.

As we have already seen, Thucydides could in any case devote pages to Alcibiadean policy without even mentioning him by name, whether it was his involvement in the campaign against Melos[2] and the cruel treatment of the inhabitants, or the negotiations between the Athenians and the inhabitants of Segesta[3] a year later; or, indeed, in the passage on Harmodius and Aristogeiton, which is redolent of an Alcibiades who lies hidden beneath the text.[4] It has recently been said that "Thucydides' most trenchant statements about the nature of Athenian politics and the fate of Athens were made with Alcibiades clearly in mind";[5] the "digressions" are where – paradoxically – he is most outspoken in this respect.

H. W. Westlake once noted that the passage in which Thucydides mentions Alcibiades for the first time (at 5.43.2–3) "is remarkable for its exceptionally personal tone", and went on to remark that in the first half of the *History* Thucydides

---

1. Translated by Ahl, "The Art of Safe Criticism", 176.
2. Vickers, "Alcibiades and Melos"; Chapter 9, above.
3. Mader, "Rogues' Comedy at Segesta".
4. Vickers, "Thucydides 6.53.3–59; Chapter 10.
5. Munn, *The School of History*, 7.

"includes hardly any personal detail and seems to have deliberately excluded it, even when it might have been relevant, except in excursuses when writing about persons long dead such as Pausanias and Themistocles".[6] But it is not simply a similarity in the register that Thucydides chooses to employ that alerts us to something special in the Cylon–Pausanias–Themistocles cluster, but by employing "emphasis" the historian creates resonances that would have been even more informative to his readers (and safer for himself) than a bald narrative would have been. Isocrates explains the contexts in which "emphasis" might legitimately be used, when speaking of λόγους ἀμφιβόλους (ambiguous words): "arguments the employment of which, when one contends in court over contracts for his own advantage, is shameful and no slight token of depravity but, when one discourses on the nature of man and of things, is fine and philosophical" (Isocr. 21.240).

One might put Thucydides in "Thucydidean" mode in the former category. When, however, he chooses to be "emphatic", he adopts a clearly different style, since it would have been "shameful" not to have done so. He thus alerts his readers to what is going on.

The Cylon passage

The Cylon episode begins with the Spartans' demand that the Athenians should expiate the pollution that had fallen on the Alcmaeonid clan as a result of the way in which suppliants had been treated after the Cylonian conspiracy. The Athenians must drive out τὸ ἄγος ... τῆς θεοῦ (the curse of the goddess; 126.2). The ostensible target here was of course Pericles, whom the Spartans wished to embarrass, but the phraseology will have reminded Thucydides' later readers of Pericles' impious Alcmaeonid ward, Alcibiades. When he was indicted *in absentia* on a charge of sacrilege in 415 BCE, not only was Alcibiades was condemned to death, but his property was confiscated, and it was voted that all the priests and priestesses should curse him publicly (Plut. *Alc.* 22). That it is unlikely that Thucydides was unaware of his readers making this connection is indicated by the way in which he shores up the idea in the next sentence. Cylon was an Ὀλυμπιονίκης, "an Olympic victor" (and so important was this concept that Thucydides placed it first among Cylon's attributes – Ὀλυμπιονίκης ἀνὴρ Ἀθηναῖος; modern critics, however, miss the point and emend the text in cavalier fashion to Ἀθηναῖος ἀνὴρ Ὀλυμπιονίκης); Alcibiades too fitted these criteria, having taken first, second and fourth places in the chariot

---

6. H. D. Westlake, *Individuals in Thucydides* (Cambridge: Cambridge University Press, 1968), 212.

event at Olympia in 416 BCE (when, as we saw in Chapter 9, he spectacularly entered seven teams; Thuc. 6.16.2). Cylon was of noble birth, and was powerful, εὐγενής καὶ δυνατός; Alcibiades' aristocratic lineage gave him great advantages in politics (Thuc. 5.43.2), and the way in which he wielded "his tremendous personal power" was a cause of deep anxiety during the last couple of decades of the fifth century.[7]

Furthermore, Cylon "seized the Acropolis, intending to make himself tyrant"; fears were expressed on the departure of the Athenian fleet for Sicily that Alcibiades was aiming at tyranny (Thuc. 6.15.4). There is talk of a local Attic festival of Zeus and attendant sacrifices in the Cylon passage (1.124.6); Alcibiades sacrificed at Olympia in 416 (Ath. 1.3e), and his interest in the sacrificial arrangements at another Attic cult centre is indicated by his having proposed a decree for providing monthly sacrifices at the Temple of Heracles at Cynosarges (Ath. 6.234d–e). He had apparently been given to φιλοθυσία (a love of sacrificing) since boyhood: witness the tale (Schol. Luc. 20.16) of the young Alcibiades strolling into "the fields of his admirers, and having selected the most beautiful bulls, sacrific[ing] them".

The conspirators were besieged on the acropolis by the citizenry, but these eventually tired of their task and entrusted it to the nine archons, giving them autocratic or plenipotentiary powers to do whatever they thought was appropriate. The word Thucydides uses, αὐτοκράτορσι, is also redolent with likely Alcibiadean allusion. In 420 BCE, Alcibiades had caused great embarrassment by persuading Spartan ambassadors plenipotentiary (αὐτοκράτορες), come to discuss outstanding differences after the Peace of Nicias, publicly to deny their true position; as a result the Peace broke down, and a treaty was made with Argos instead (Thuc. 5.45–6). Then it was as a στρατηγὸς αὐτοκράτωρ that Alcibiades had gone to Sicily in 415 BCE (Thuc. 6.8.2). Finally, Alcibiades' triumphant return to Athens in 407 BCE saw his status variously characterized as ἡγεμών αὐτοκράτωρ (Xen. 1.4.21) or στρατηγὸς αὐτοκράτωρ (Diod. 13.69.3). Either way (and his precise status is disputed),[8] Alcibiades' plenipotentiary role was paramount, and Thucydides again is striking an Alcibiadean note.

The expulsion of the ἀλιτήριοι τῆς θεοῦ (offenders against the goddess) is thorough (126.11–12). It will have recalled the solemn ritual purifications carried out when Alcibiades was cursed *in absentia* in 415 BCE. We get a glimpse of what happened from Lysias' description of Andocides' punishment: "And for such a deed priestesses and priests stood up and cursed him, facing the west, and shook

---

7. Gribble, *Alcibiades and Athens*, 139.
8. B. Bleckmann, *Athens Weg in die Niederlage: Die letzten Jahre des Peloponnesischen Krieges*, Beiträge zur Altertumskunde 99 (Stuttgart: B. G. Teubner, 1998), 480ff.

out their purple vestments according to the ancient and time-honoured custom"
(Lys. 6.51).[9] These events will not have been forgotten by Thucydides' readers. I
have argued elsewhere that Thucydides probably used the texts of Aristophanes'
plays as an *aide-mémoire*, in order to refresh his memory as to what were current
concerns a few years back.[10] Thus, if in Aristophanes' *Knights* the Sausage-seller
"comes forward" as Alcibiades (as Paphlagon "is" Cleon), then it is possible to
make sense of the allusion to the Alcmaeonid curse in lines 445–6.[11] These lines,
Ἐκ τῶν ἀλιτηρίων σέ φημί γεγονέναι τῶν τῆς θεοῦ (I declare you to be descended
from the offenders against the goddess), have in the past caused great puzzlement
to commentators.[12] If, however, Aristophanes' lines refer to Alcibiades' ancestral
curse, not only do they make sense but they also explain why Thucydides uses them
in order to create a similar resonance in another likely Alcibiadean context.

Nowhere in the Cylon passage are the Alcmaeonids mentioned by name; nor
is Herodotus, whose pro-Alcmaeonid account (5.70–72) of the same incident it
is often maintained Thucydides is correcting, echoing or parodying.[13] Readers are
intended to "dig out the lurking meaning" themselves. In similar fashion, they were
probably meant to discover for themselves the deft, but unmistakable, allusions to
Alcibiades, whom Thucydides wanted to bring into his narrative at an early stage.
These are not mutually incompatible aims; rather, such allusions perform the role
of chords in music and employ the economy of wit.

The Pausanias passage

There are strong Alcibiadean resonances in the Pausanias passage too, in that the
accounts of Pausanias' activities and of his excesses are highly reminiscent of those
of Alcibiades. Pausanias' freebooting in the Hellespont (when he commanded his
own trireme [ἰδίᾳ; Thuc. 128.3], independent of Sparta) recalls Alcibiades' activities in the area, from his naval victory in 411 (Plut. *Alc.* 27.3–6), and the occupation of forts near Bisanthe in 406 (Plut. *Alc.* 36.3; Nep. *Alc.* 7.4), as well as his
private warfare (ἰδίᾳ; Plut. *Alc.* 36.5) against Thracian tribes. Pausanias' capture of

---

9. Cf. Lewis, "After the Profanation of the Mysteries".
10. Vickers, *Pericles on Stage, passim*.
11. *Ibid.*, 97–120.
12. For example, Knox, "The Date of the *Oedipus Tyrannus*", 145; *Word and Action*, 121; Sommerstein,
    The Comedies of Aristophanes, 167.
13. For example, C. Patterson, "'Here the Lion Smiled': A Note on Thuc. 1.127–38", in
    Nomodeiktes, Rosen & Farrell (eds), 145–52.

Byzantium in 478/7 (Thuc. 1. 128.5), moreover, parallels Alcibiades' seizure of the city in 408 (Plut. *Alc.* 31.3–6).

The allusion to Gongylus of Eretria (Thuc. 128.6) is perhaps not so much to explain Pausanias' means of communication with Artaxerxes as to remind the reader of Gongylus of Corinth, who, on arriving in Sicily in 414, brought news of the imminent arrival of Gylippus the Spartan (Thuc. 7.2.1), sent as the direct result of Alcibiades' advice to provide the Syracusans with strong leadership (Thuc. 6.91.2–5). Then, the exchange of letters with the satrap Artaxerxes is unrealistic as reported ("it is most improbable either that Thucydides obtained a copy of the letter sent to Xerxes or that Pausanias did not promptly destroy such incriminating material")[14] but if the reader was really intended to reflect on Alcibiades' correspondence with the Great King, it makes a certain sense. We cannot know what such correspondence contained, but Thucydides perhaps gives us the essence of it. Pausanias gets his own direct link (cf. ἄνδρα πιστὸν; 128.7) with the Great King in the person of Artabazus, son of Pharnaces, satrap of Phrygia; Alcibiades had his royal representatives in Tissaphernes and later on Pharnabazus.

When Thucydides formally introduces Alcibiades at 5.43.2, he slyly states that he was respected ἀξιώματι ... προγόνων (through the reputation of his ancestors): a deft allusion to his having, as we saw in Chapter 4, been awarded the prize of honour at Potidaea διὰ τὸ ἀξίωμα (on account of his fame), even though Socrates had really won it (Plut. *Alc.* 7.5.3). Later, at 6.16.2, Thucydides speaks of the high esteem (ἀξιώματι) in which Alcibiades was held by the Athenian citizenry (just after he had claimed to be ἄξιος of being given the command in Sicily; 6.16.1), and of the way in which at Olympia in 416 he ordered everything in a style worthy (ἀξίως) of his victory. It has even been suggested that Thucydides' use of the word ἀξίωμα in the context of Hyperbolus, ostracized not διὰ δυνάμεως καὶ ἀξιώματος φόβον (for any fear of his power and influence) but for villainy (8.73.3), was a deliberate reminder of Alcibiades.[15] Moreover, Alcibiades' μεγαλοπραγμοσύνη (tendency to vast projects) was legendary (Plut. *Alc.* 6.4; cf. *POxy.* 411, 20–22). By contrast, by pointed contrast, Pausanias is said in the passage under discussion to have been held ἐν μεγάλῳ ἀξιώματι (in great respect) by the Greeks on account of his valour in the field (Thuc. 1.130.1). The implicit comparison with Alcibiades is no less potent for its being "emphatic".

On leaving Byzantium, Pausanias wore Persian costume, and was attended by Median and Egyptian bodyguards; in addition, he kept a Persian table (Thuc. 1.130.1). Alcibiades too adopted a Persian way of life when he lived for a time at

---

14. Cawkwell, *Thucydides and the Peloponnesian War*, 125.
15. Rawlings, *The Structure of Thucydides's History*, 115.

the court of Tissaphernes. Similarly, Pausanias' παρανομία (disregard of propriety) (in addition to his affecting Persian fashions), which gave rise to suspicion that he was not altogether loyal to the Spartan state (Thuc. 1.132.2), was nowhere nearly as serious as Alcibiades' utter disregard for convention, again παρανομία, the precise nature of which Thucydides draws explicit attention to at 6.15.4. It was his physical depravity as much as anything else that made people fear that he was aiming at tyranny.[16] The precise example of Pausanias' going beyond the norm that Thucydides produces is his hubristic inscription on the golden tripod at Delphi, in which he drew attention to his personal role at Plataea (Thuc. 1.132.2), an inscription that the Spartans replaced with something that spread the glory more widely. An Alcibiadean equivalent was the commissioning (albeit by others) of a bronze statue on Samos (Paus. 6.3.15), which probably represented another Persian practice on Alcibiades' part; satraps in Asia Minor had no compunction about allowing statues of themselves to be set up in sanctuaries.[17]

In his treatment of the tyrannicide story, Thucydides implicitly suggests that Alcibiades was considerably more tyrannical in his behaviour than even the Peisistratids had been; he perhaps goes even further in implying that it might have been a good thing if Alcibiades had been assassinated as well (Chapter 10). If so, it might explain why Thucydides dwells on the effective way in which the authorities at Sparta disposed of their awkward citizen. The ignominious death suffered by Pausanias – starvation as opposed to a glorious death on the battlefield – in many ways parallels Alcibiades' less than heroic end in north-west Asia Minor while on the run from his enemies. Smoked out naked from his cabin in a nocturnal raid, he was shot down with arrows while trying to escape. Pausanias' body was about to be cast into a chasm, but was then given a respectable burial where he died, the place being adorned with statues (Thuc. 1.134.5); Alcibiades' headless body was reverently cremated in the embers of his cabin by an attendant (Nep. *Alc.* 10.2–6) and the spot became a place of pilgrimage thereafter (Ath. 13.574f). These are generic parallels that will have resonated with the contemporary reader attuned to such a form of discourse.

David Gribble has also seen a connection between the Pausanias passage and Alcibiades, but he views it from the vantage point of Book 6: "Alcibiades' speech and the attitude it reveals recall Thucydides' description of the behaviour of Pausanias

---

16. See further: Wohl, "The Eros of Alcibiades"; Munn, *The School of History*; J. Davidson, "Dover, Foucault and Greek Homosexuality: Penetration and the Truth of Sex", *Past and Present* **170** (2001), 3–51.

17. Cf. P. Briant, "Droaphernès et la statue de Sardes", in *Studies in Persian History: Essays in Memory of David M. Lewis*, M. Brosius & A. Kuhrt (eds), 205–26 (Leiden: Nederlands Instituut voor het Nabjie Oosten, 1998).

the regent".[18] The parallels he draws are extremely pertinent: Alcibiades' attitude, whereby he regarded himself as superior to his fellow citizens, did indeed resemble that of Pausanias; Alcibiades' medizing did imitate that of Pausanias; Alcibiades' παρανομία does recall that of Pausanias.[19] But these resemblances are already lurking in the Pausanias passage, ready to be dug out by the reader. Matters are, however, not nearly as simple as this; there are further levels of complexity in the Pausanias passage which will be discussed presently.

The Themistocles passage

The suggestion has already been made that Thucydides' other "digression" on the career of Themistocles is a paradigm of Alcibiades.[20] The route of Themistocles' flight as described by Thucydides (from Argos to Corcyra, Epirus, Macedonia, the Greek islands and Ephesus; 1.135–137.2), carries certain Alcibiadean resonances. Argos figures large in the exile of both. Themistocles was resident there when accusations of treason were laid against him (Thuc. 1.135.3); not only did Alcibiades take refuge at Argos during his flight (Isoc. 16.9; Plut. *Alc.* 23.1), but he had famously tried to foster an Argive alliance at the expense of peace with Sparta in 421 (Thuc. 5.43–8). Thucydides is said not to have alluded to Alcibiades' stay at Argos;[21] perhaps he did so here, but "emphatically". Corcyra, the lynchpin of the Athenians' Sicilian campaign and Alcibiades' brainchild, was Themistocles' next port of call (Thuc. 1.136.1).

Themistocles' visit to the Molossians, where he begs for protection from king Admetus – "with whom he was not actually friends" (Thuc. 1.136.2) – is a lightly disguised commentary on Alcibiades' relations with the royal house of Sparta. There was no love lost between King Agis of Sparta and Alcibiades (cf. Thuc. 8.45.1), and the reason given by gossips was that Alcibiades had seduced and got with child Agis' wife Timaea (Xen. *Hell.* 3.3.2; Plut. *Ages.* 3.1–2; Plut. *Alc.* 23.7; Ath. 12.535b). Themistocles arrives to find Admetus away from home and presents himself as a suppliant to his wife. She bids him take their child and await her husband's return; in Sparta, Alcibiades had supposedly profited by the king's absence to take his wife

---

18. Gribble, *Alcibiades and Athens*, 60–61.
19. *Ibid.*
20. J. B. Bury, *The Ancient Greek Historians* (London: Macmillan, 1909), 127–8; A. G. Woodhead, *Thucydides on the Nature of Power* (Cambridge, MA: Harvard University Press, 1970), 81; Rawlings, *The Structure of Thucydides's History*, 97–8; cf. Gribble, *Alcibiades and Athens*, 193 n.92.
21. Hatzfeld, *Alcibiade*, 207 n.2.

and to give her a child. Themistocles' eloquent speech to Admetus, in which he intimates that if the king gave him up he would be signing his death warrant, plays on the fact that according to some reports Agis was instrumental in arranging for Alcibiades eventually to be put to death (Plut. *Alc.* 38.6).

Most commentators, however, believe that the Pausanias and Themistocles passages are "early",[22] but this view derives from their supposed simplicity, their unschooled nature; they are said to be juvenile pieces, written at a time when Thucydides had not yet learned to write in a Thucydidean manner.[23] Better H. R. Rawlings (on the Themistocles passage): "It is rather a historical paradigm, a *Tendenzschrift*, written to prove a point".[24] Both passages are indeed extremely subtle and complex, and if they refer "emphatically" to the death of Alcibiades, as they perhaps seem to, then they must have been written at least soon after that event in 404. As we shall presently see, it now seems likely that they were written later still.

In crossing the Aegean by boat, Themistocles calls at the island of Naxos (Thuc. 1.137.2); "Naxos" may well have reminded the contemporary reader that Sicilian Naxos was the one city on the island that was easily won over to the Athenian side in the opening stages of the expedition of 415 (thanks, it would seem, to Alcibiades' persuasive powers; Thuc. 6.50.2–3). Themistocles then makes his way to Ephesus (Thuc. 1.137.3); it was the Ephesians who had provided a magnificent Persian tent for Alcibiades' victory celebrations at Olympia in 416 ([Andoc.] 4.30; Satyr. ap. Ath. 12.534d; Alc. 12), and the Ephesians who (together with the Chians, Lesbians, and Cyzicenes) were regularly used "as so many handmaidens" whenever Alcibiades travelled abroad (Satyr. ap. Ath. 12.534d). Alcibiades was also instrumental in bringing about the revolt of Ephesus from Athens in 412 (Thuc. 8.19.3; cf. 109.1).

Having arrived in Ionia, Themistocles rewards the sea-captain who had brought him there with money that he received from friends, "property that he had deposited at Athens and Argos": Argos again. He then enters into correspondence with the Great King; whether or not Alcibiades did the same, the impression that he tried to put across to the Athenians in 411 was that he had great influence with the Persian court (albeit via the satrap Tissaphernes; Thuc. 8.81–2). It was on a journey to meet the Great King in 404 that Alcibiades met his death (Nep. *Alc.*

---

22. For example, F. E. Adcock, *Thucydides and His History* (Cambridge: Cambridge University Press, 1963), 23–4; Westlake, *Studies in Thucydides and Greek History*, 1; Cawkwell, *Thucydides and the Peloponnesian War*, 125.

23. K. von Fritz, *Die griechische Geschichtsschreibung* (Berlin: de Gruyter, 1967), Ia, 616–17.

24. Rawlings, *The Structure of Thucydides's History*, 98 n.45.

8–9). Themistocles learned Persian (Thuc. 1.138.1); so, eventually, did Alcibiades (Ath. 12.535e).[25] Themistocles owed his subsequent success at the Persian court to his former ἀξίωσις, the expression frequently used in Alcibiadean contexts.

Thucydides then describes Themistocles' σύνεσις (intelligence; 1.138.2), and continues with a passage extolling his natural authority, his powers of prognostication and his gifts of extemporization (1.138.3). If this is also a character sketch of Alcibiades, it is an interesting one, for there is a growing consensus that while Alcibiades was held to be brilliant by his contemporaries, he was not as intelligent as the likes of Themistocles, or Phrynichus.[26] Even Pericles was said to be only μὴ ἀξύνετος (not unintelligent; Thuc. 2.34.6). If this passage alludes to Alcibiades, it is, in part at least, perhaps an ironic comment. With regard to the rest, we might note Plutarch's quotation from Theophrastus, "who has enquired more diligently into these various tales [stories told about Alcibiades] than anyone else", saying that "Alcibiades excelled all men of his time in readiness of invention and resource" (Plut. *Alc.* 10.4), which is close to Thucydides' stated view of Themistocles.

Themistocles' death is quickly passed over (1.138.4), having little bearing on that of Alcibiades. It serves to introduce the monument in the agora at Magnesia-on-the-Maeander set up in order to commemorate Themistocles' importance there (1.138.5). The Great King had given him Magnesia for his bread, with an annual income of fifty talents, Lampsacus for his wine (a place that was πολυοινότατον [extremely rich in wine]), and Myous for meat. In 411 also, Alcibiades was resident at Magnesia-on-the-Maeander (Thuc. 8.50.3; cf. 48.1),[27] and was the recipient of a luxuriously appointed garden there, as we have seen. Themistocles' descendants still had certain privileges at Magnesia in Plutarch's day (Plut. *Them.* 32), and we might well suppose that Alcibiades enjoyed the society of Athenians who had "gone Persian". Themistocles' income of fifty talents recalls that of five hundred (or fifty) that Alcibiades received from his Persian patron Pharnabazus.[28] Lampsacus had been the place of exile of the tyrant Hippias (and much is made of the fact in Thucydides' other Alcibiades "digression" in Book 6 [59.1–4]; Chapter 10); it was also Alcibiades' winter quarters in 409/8 (Xen. *Hell.* 1.2.15). Furthermore, that carefully placed πολυοινότατον will have brought to mind Alcibiades' reputation as a phenomenal drinker (cf. Plin. *HN* 14.144).

---

25. For more information on Alcibiades' "Themistokles-Nachahmung", see Schneider, "Eine Polemik Polemons in den Propyläen", 23 n.40.
26. E. F. Bloedow, "Alcibiades 'Brilliant' or 'Intelligent'?", *Historia* **41** (1992), 139–57.
27. See further: Briant, "Dons de terres et de villes", 58–62.
28. A story that Hatzfeld believed was a calque of that of Thucydides on Themistocles: (*Alcibiade*, 342 n.3).

Lysander

The complexities continue. E. Schwartz recognized that Thucydides' account of Themistocles played on the career of Alcibiades, but also saw allusions to Alcibiades' nemesis in the Pausanias passage, namely to the Spartan general Lysander.[29] His brief arguments were either ignored[30] or dismissed,[31] but they were revived by Rawlings in 1981 with rather more in the way of supporting evidence. In brief, the case is as follows: not only do the Pausanias and Themistocles episodes reflect the different ways in which the Spartans and Athenians dealt with recalcitrant generals (the Spartans by a strict regard for legal procedures, the Athenians "shabbily, even disastrously"), but the experiences of Lysander and Alcibiades "repeat, to a remarkable degree, the careers of Pausanias and Themistocles", and "their treatment at the hands of their respective states mirrors the treatment that their two predecessors received". The Themistocles passage provides many points of comparison with the career of Alcibiades. They:

> were both leading men of their time, were both implicated in supposed crimes, were both recalled to Athens to face trial, escaped their would-be guards, found refuge first in Greece and then in Persia, used merchantmen for one of their escapades, promised a Persian king that they would help him conquer Greece, found great favor in the Persian court, died in Asia as exiles.

Furthermore, "both were brilliant men who could adapt to any circumstance".[32]

At the end of the Themistocles passage, Thucydides declares that Pausanias and Themistocles were "the most illustrious [λαμπροτάτους] of the Greeks of their time" (1.138.6). Rawlings observes that in Book 6 Alcibiades defends himself against Nicias' charge that he was privately glorifying (ἐλλαμπρύνεσθαι; 6.12.2) himself at the city's expense, by justifying "whatever splendour I have exhibited [ὅσα ... λαμπρύνομαι; 6.16.3]", and pointing out that those who in the past had achieved distinction (ὅσοι ἔν τινος λαμπρότητι; 6.16.5) won the approval of posterity (16.3).

---

29. E. Schwartz, *Das Geschichtswerk des Thukydides* (Bonn: F. Cohen, 1919), 158–62.
30. Gomme *et al.*, *A Historical Commentary on Thucydides*, 1.
31. A. Lippold, "Pausanias von Sparta und die Perser", *Rheinisches Museum* (new series) **108** (1965), 320–41, esp. 337.
32. Rawlings, *The Structure of Thucydides's History*, 95–6.

It is likely that Alcibiades here was referring to Themistocles,[33] who was indeed one of his personal heroes.[34]

The two most illustrious Greeks in the closing years of the fifth century BCE were undoubtedly Alcibiades and Lysander. And:

> like Pausanias, Lysander won the final victory of a great war, received extravagant honours throughout Greece as a result, dedicated offerings at Delphi in his own name, began soon to act arrogantly and ambitiously, angered Greek opinion by his private and public insolence, and was said to be planning to establish himself as tyrant of Greece. He was recalled to Sparta by the ephors, who sent a herald bearing a skytale to get him back, was tried by ephors, and schemed to overthrow the Spartan government.[35]

Rawlings' analysis is fundamentally sound, but there was, until recently, an overriding problem, namely, that Thucydides was widely believed to have been dead by c.400,[36] and Lysander did not die until 396. Now, though, Munn has made a plausible case for Thucydides having written the *History* in one go in 396–395 BCE in the months preceding the Corinthian War, the events of that period providing the occasion for him to write up the notes he had accumulated ever since the outbreak of the war between Athens and Sparta, and the historian having at his disposal the written media that were becoming increasingly available.

> In the events and circumstances of 396 and the following year, when war broke out, we find the clearest indications that both major and minor themes occurring in Thucydides' account of the previous war were at the center of public attention ... The salient characteristics of Thucydides' work as a whole are entirely comprehensible from the perspective of Athens on the brink of renewed war ...

and even features which have encouraged some scholars to believe that the *History* was composed over decades "are accountable when we recognize that Thucydides began writing in 396 and stopped, probably, in 395".[37] It is significant too that this

33. Rawlings, *The Structure of Thucydides's History*, 97.
34. Cf. Podlecki, *The Life of Themistocles*, 139 n.9; Schneider, "Eine Polemik Polemons in den Propyläen, 23 n.40.
35. Rawlings, *The Structure of Thucydides's History*, 99.
36. For example, O. Luschnat, *Thukydides der Historiker*, (Stuttgart: J. B. Metzler, 1970), 1094; H. T. Wade-Gery, "Thucydides", in *OCD*³, 1516–19, esp. 1517.
37. Munn, *The School of History*, 317, 320.

period witnessed two trials of Alcibiades Jr ([Lys.] 15; Isocr. 16) which will have placed the spotlight once again on "the career and reputation of his father, the senior Alcibiades".[38] Alcibiades will thus have been "at the center of public debate" at the very time that Thucydides was writing.

There is room, moreover, for both Alcibiades and Lysander to "come forward" in the Pausanias passage. Thucydides seems to have created a portmanteau figure of Pausanias, incorporating in his characterization aspects of both Alcibiades and Lysander, rather along the lines of such characters in comedy as Socrates in *Clouds* (who is made in the image of several philosophers prominent in Pericles' day), or Pheidippides (who is based on two individuals who bore a filial relationship to Pericles, namely Alcibiades and Xanthippus); we might well call the dramatic device "Arcimboldesque".[39] There are features of "Pausanias" that fit ill with Alcibiades, but that correspond closely with what we know of Lysander (for example, Pausanias is said to have been "difficult of access" and to have "displayed such a violent temper towards everybody that no one could come near him"; Thuc. 1.130.2). Lysander was of "a harsh, merciless disposition" (Plut. *Alc.* 19.6), while Alcibiades by contrast "tried to make himself acceptable to all with whom he had to do" (Plut. *Alc.* 44.2). A different spin is being given to the Pausanias image here, and the knowing reader would naturally have thought of Lysander as well as Alcibiades.

If these parallels are not merely coincidental, Thucydides was being unusually insensitive. Both Alcibiades and Lysander are alluded to "emphatically" in the Pausanias passage, while Alcibiades is paramount in the Cylonian and Themistoclean equivalents. Thucydides thus did not wait until Book 5 before introducing Alcibiades to his audience, but made clear from the start the disturbing role he played in the history of Athens in the last quarter of the fifth century, a role that at times involved behaving as the slave of the Great King. Although not the only Greek who "became" Persian, he was the one who did so most flamboyantly and controversially.

---

38. Munn, *The School of History*, 322; cf. Davies, *Athenian Propertied Families 600–300 BC*, 21.
39. After Giuseppe Arcimboldo (*c.*1530–93), who diverted the emperor Rudolph II with composite images made up of such things as fruit, flowers and vegetables; cf. Vickers, *Pericles on Stage*, 31.

12

Alcibiades and Critias in the *Gorgias*: Plato's "fine satire"

The dominant personality in Plato's *Gorgias* is Callicles, the man who argues forcefully that "might is right". It is also widely believed that the issues involved have been exhaustively analysed by Dodds in his edition and commentary on the *Gorgias*, and that little more need be said. There remains, however, much disagreement as to quite who Callicles is, or whom he represents. Callicles is so carefully delineated that it is difficult to believe that he is wholly fictitious (and if he were, he would be the only such example in the whole of Plato).[1] He is said to come from the deme of Acharnae (495d), and to be the *erastes* of the known individual Demus (481d). The names of his acquaintances (487c) suggest that he belongs to the Athenian aristocracy, the younger members of which came under the influence of the sophists in the 420s.[2] And yet there are problems. Unusually, his patronymic is not given,[3] and perhaps surprisingly for such a forthright individual, Callicles is not heard of in Athenian politics outside the *Gorgias*.

It has been suggested that Callicles died young, "before he had time to make his mark on history".[4] Many have been tempted to see Callicles as a mask for some historical individual, but some suggestions are less likely than others.[5] Alcibiades would appear at first sight to have a strong case, but there is an apparently insuperable obstacle in that Plato draws a careful distinction between him and Callicles (481c–d). Alcibiades, however, occupies the high ground of the fallback position:

1. O. Apelt, *Platonische Aufsätze* (Leipzig: B. G. Teubner, 1912), 106.
2. Dodds, *Plato: Gorgias*, 282–3. For excellent discussions of the *milieu*, see Ostwald, *From Popular Sovereignty*, 199–333; Munn, *The School of History*, 15–94.
3. As noted by Wilamowitz, cited by Dodds, *Plato: Gorgias*, 3.
4. Guthrie, *A History of Greek Philosophy*, 102, citing Dodds, *Plato: Gorgias*, 13, with evident approval.
5. They include Aristippus, Critias, Isocrates, Theramenes, Charicles, Polycrates and Alcibiades (M. Untersteiner, *The Sophists* [Oxford: Blackwell, 1957], 344–5 n.40).

for example, "There is no doubt that [Callicles] represented real conceptions of the period such as are found in Alcibiades";[6] and "If Callicles was not a historical person but was created in Plato's powerful imagination to embody the corruption with which sophistic education had tainted Athenian politics, Plato's model in provenance, training, political purpose, and political method may well have been Alcibiades".[7] Alcibiades, it will be recalled, was the most controversial individual of his age, having been elected one of the three generals for the Sicilian expedition (a campaign he had done much to promote); having been suspected of involvement in various acts of impiety on the eve of the fleet's departure; having been recalled from Sicily to stand trial; having jumped ship and gone into exile at Sparta; having advised the Spartans on the most effective ways to defeat Athens; having eventually, albeit briefly, returned to Athens in triumph as the city's potential saviour; and having finally died an ignominious death in north-west Asia Minor while on the run from his enemies.[8] Even more to the point in the present context, one of the charges made against Socrates was that he had been responsible for the education of Alcibiades and his erstwhile ally, the tyrant Critias.

Callicles and Alcibiades

Another thorny problem in *Gorgias* scholarship is the presence in the text of apparently confusing chronological pointers to the dramatic date of the dialogue, which could be anywhere between 427 and 405.[9] The evidence is internally inconsistent, as was noted even in antiquity.[10] (i) Pericles, who died in the late summer or autumn of 429,[11] is said to have died recently (νεωστί; 503c). (ii) The presence of Gorgias in Athens, where the dialogue takes place (in Callicles' house; 447b),

---

6. Untersteiner, *The Sophists*, 344 n.40, citing S. Kriegbaum, *Der Ursprung der von Kallikles in Platons Gorgias vertretenen Anschauungen* (Paderborn: F. Schöningh, 1913).

7. Ostwald, *From Popular Sovereignty*, 291. Cf. "So close is this passage to some of the words of Plato's Callicles in the *Gorgias* (484a, 492c) that someone, Plutarch or a source, seems to have identified Callicles, who is rather a mystery, with the historical Alcibiades" (Russell, *Plutarch*, 127, commenting on Plut. *Alc.* 34.7). Gribble, *Alcibiades and Athens*, 231–40, argues that Callicles cannot be identical to Alcibiades but is certainly meant to remind us of him.

8. For Alcibiades in general, see: Thuc. 5-8; Plut., *Alc.*; Hatzfeld, *Alcibiade*; Ellis, *Alcibiades*; Forde, *The Ambition to Rule*; Vickers, *Pericles on Stage*; Munn, *The School of History*; Duff, "Plutarch on the Childhood of Alkibiades"; and this book, *passim*.

9. G. Stallbaum, *Platonis Gorgias*, 3rd edn (Göttingen: Hennings, 1861), 51–72; Dodds, *Plato: Gorgias*, 17–18.

10. Herodicus of Babylon ap. Ath. 5.217c–218a.

11. Stadter, *A Commentary on Plutarch's* Pericles, 341–2.

is attested for 427/6 (Diod. 12.53, cf. Thuc. 3.86). (iii) Alcibiades is described as the *eromenos* of Socrates (481d). According to Xenophon, this relationship ceased when Alcibiades went into politics (Xen. *Mem.* 1.1.24). This will have been in the mid- to late-420s.[12] (iv) Demus, son of Pyrilampes, is said to be the *eromenos* of Callicles (481d). This individual is not attested as *kalos* (and thus "available") until 422 (Ar. *Vesp.* 97). (v) Socrates' forecast of the Athenian public's change of heart with regard to Alcibiades (519a) must relate to the events of 415. (vi) Archelaus of Macedon is said to have come to power "only the other day" (470d); the earliest this could occur is in 414/13.[13] (vii) There are several quotations from Euripides' *Antiope* (484e, 485e-486a, 486b, 486c), a play performed between 412 and 408.[14] (viii) At 473e, Socrates appears to say that the condemnation of the generals from Arginusae had taken place in the preceding year (πέρυσι), in 406 (Xen. *Hell.* 1.7.2, 33). It is clearly impossible to rationalize these data, although attempts have been made.[15] It could be, however, that what has been called "timelessness"[16] was a deliberate spread of allusions across the last three decades of the fifth century. Rather than being a morass of chronological discrepancies, the *Gorgias* may prove to have been carefully contrived, to have been composed with considerable *deinotes*.[17]

If so, this may be the clue to the understanding of Callicles, for it will be argued presently that the portrait painted of him reflects not simply the Alcibiades of the 420s, but Alcibiades' whole career from childhood to maturity and death. This will

---

12. Stallbaum, *Platonis Gorgias*, 59–60, places Alcibiades' entry on the political stage in 420 (cf. Bloedow, "On Nurturing Lions in the State"), but this is when he was first elected general, an office that presumably had to be worked for. Plutarch states that "when still immature Alcibiades plunged into political life, and at once surpassed most of the statesmen of his age" (*Alc.* 13.1), and seems to place his emergence shortly after Sphacteria (425): "About this time Alcibiades began to gain credit in Athens as a public speaker" (*Nic.* 9.1). Cf. "Alcibiades began his active political career ... around 425 ... but there can be little doubt that he had aspirations, from an early age, to rise to a position of leadership" (Ellis, *Alcibiades*, 24, citing Pl. *Alc.*, the dramatic date of which is 432). Hatzfeld places "[la] première manifestation de l'activité politique d'Alcibiade" in 425 (*Alcibiade*, 69). Thucydides mentions his activities on behalf of the Spartan captives in Athens (5.43) and Alcibiades was probably also, in 425/4, one of the *taktai* entrusted with the reassessment of the tribute of Athens' subject allies ([Andoc.] 4.11; cf. Hatzfeld, *Alcibiade*, 68–9; Ostwald, *From Popular Sovereignty*, 293; Munn, *The School of History*, 75–6, 322, 374).

13. Archelaus' predecessor Perdiccas is recorded in the field at the end of the summer of 414 (Thuc. 7.9.1). Cf. Hornblower, *A Commentary on Thucydides*, 376.

14. Schol. Ar. *Ran.* 53; L. B. Carter, *The Quiet Athenian* (Oxford: Clarendon Press, 1986), 163.

15. For example, A. E. Taylor, *Plato, the Man and his Work* (London: Methuen, 1926), 104–5; and note "There are no anachronisms in Plato" (U. von Wilamowitz-Moellendorff, "Die Xenophontische Apologie", *Hermes* **36** [1897], 99–106, 102n.).

16. Dodds, *Plato: Gorgias*, 18.

17. Cf. the "startling", but contrived, anachronisms in Polycrates' *Accusation of Socrates* (brought to my attention by David Gribble).

be argued in detail presently: but first credit must be paid where credit is due, for Otto Apelt once put forward powerful arguments to support an equation between Callicles and Alcibiades[18] that have not received the attention they deserve.[19] He noted that the historical Alcibiades is discussed in two places in the *Gorgias*, once in the passage 481c–482c, and again at 519a–b. In both places Alcibiades is closely associated with Callicles, but does not take part in the action. Apelt's view was that "it looks very much as though Plato had deliberately arranged for him to appear only in the shadow of Callicles".[20] He observes that the point where the love of Socrates for Alcibiades is equated with Callicles' love for the Athenian *demos*, is highly reminiscent of the fear expressed by Socrates in Plato's *Alcibiades* that Alcibiades might become a δημεραστής (a lover of the *demos*; Pl. *Alc.* 1.132a).

Apelt makes a nice point concerning Callicles' name, which he thinks was intended to recall the κάλλος (beauty) for which Alcibiades was famous (Pl. *Prt.* 309a; *Alc.* 1. 113b, 123a; *Smp.* 216c–219e; Plut. *Alc.* 4.1, 16.4; Ath. 12.534c, etc.). "If Callicles were a mask for Alcibiades, 'Famous for his Beauty' would certainly not have been a bad name for him". Apelt answers the obvious question – "Why did not Plato introduce Alcibiades himself?" – by suggesting that in what is in a special sense a dialogue dedicated to Socrates' memory, Plato might have felt it inappropriate to place the person who had been Socrates' "Liebling" in sharp opposition to his teacher.[21] Ten years later Apelt added the suggestion that if the *Gorgias* was written as a response to an anti-Socratic pamphlet written by one Polycrates (Xen. *Mem.* 1.2.12),[22] then the introduction of Alcibiades in the guise of Callicles would be perfectly logical. One of the charges laid against Socrates by Polycrates was that he had taught the young Alcibiades. To refer directly to Alcibiades in *Gorgias* would have descended to the level of pamphleteering; Plato, like Thucydides, wanted to write something more than that.[23]

If this were indeed the case, the *Gorgias* would have been Plato's equivalent of that part of Xenophon's *Memorabilia* in which he attempted to exculpate Socrates from

---

18. Apelt, *Platonische Aufsätze*, 106–8, and *Platon Gorgias* (Leipzig: Felix Meiner, 1922), 168.
19. Neither of Apelt's works is referred to in Untersteiner's ostensibly comprehensive bibliography (*The Sophists*, 344 n.40, cited by Guthrie, *A History of Greek Philosophy*, 102); Dodds only refers – dismissively – to the brief notes in Apelt, *Platon Gorgias*; see Dodds, *Plato: Gorgias*, 12, 392.
20. Apelt, *Platonische Aufsätze*, 108.
21. *Ibid.*, 105–8.
22. On Polycrates in general, see A. H. Chroust, *Socrates, Man and Myth: The Two Socratic Apologies of Xenophon* (London: Routledge, 1957); M. Montuori, *Socrate: fisiologia di un mito* (Florence: G.C. Sansoni, 1974); Gribble, *Alcibiades and Athens*, 226–30.
23. Apelt, *Platon Gorgias*, 168.

any blame for Critias' and Alcibiades' political careers (Xen. *Mem.* 2.1–48).[24] To show Alcibiades as Callicles, as a separate individual from the young man Socrates taught and loved, and as a person with whom Socrates is made strongly to disagree, would make the same point as Xenophon's, but even more effectively. "The failure of Socrates really to convince Callicles, despite using every sort of means of persuasion at his disposal",[25] is therefore deliberate. And just as the "dramatic date" of the *Gorgias* could be any time between 427 and 405, the implicit allusions to Alcibiades cover the period from his childhood, through the mid-twenties when he began his political career, to his death in 404. The whole man is encapsulated in the picture Plato gives us in *Gorgias*.

Plato does all this with a deft touch. At the beginning, he makes Callicles express the view that it were always best to be late for "a battle or for war" (447a): Alcibiades was notoriously late in arriving at the battle of Abydus (Xen. *Hell.* 1.1.5–6; Diod. 13.46.2–3; Plut. *Alc.* 27.3–4),[26] and the reason he had been deprived of his last generalship was his apparently careless absence from his fleet during a crucial action (Xen. *Hell.* 1.5.11–15; Diod. 13.71; Plut. *Alc.* 35.5–8). Similar considerations may underlie Alcibiades' late arrival in Plato's "historical fiction",[27] the *Symposium*. In the middle of the *Gorgias*, immediately after Callicles completes his speech (482c–486d), Socrates speaks of his need for a touchstone with which to test the purity of his own soul. "I think that in meeting you," he tells Callicles, "I have met such a ἑρμαῖον [gift of Hermes]". Although Alcibiades was probably not involved in the mutilation of the Herms on the eve of the Athenians' departure for Sicily, his enemies put about the story that he was (Plut. *Alc.* 20.5; cf. Thuc. 6.28.1–2). Demosthenes, writing later in the fourth century, certainly believed that Alcibiades was thus involved (Dem. 21.147). An ironic reminder of Alcibiades' apparent disrespect for traditional values, for *nomos*, may thus have been placed at the very centre of the *Gorgias*, to serve as a kind of *sphragis* for the whole work.[28] There is great skilfulness employed at the end of the dialogue too, as we shall see.

Plato's subtlety is also apparent from the way he causes Callicles to misquote Pindar at 484b. One of the charges against Socrates was that he had "selected the worst passages of the most celebrated poets, and using them as argument, taught

---

24. Cf. R. Hunter, *Plato's Symposium* (Oxford: Oxford University Press, 2004), esp. 102, on Pl. *Smp.* 218b–219e, where, with a "master stroke", Plato makes Alcibiades' own words exonerate Socrates of the charge of corruption of the young.
25. Gribble, *Alcibiades and Athens*, 231.
26. Cf. Bloedow, "Alcibiades, A Review Article", 25.
27. von Blanckenhagen, "Stage and Actors in Plato's *Symposium*", 62.
28. Alternatively (or in addition), the tradition that sculptors of his day used Alcibiades' features for those of Hermes (Clem. Al. *Protr.* 4.53.6) may lie behind Plato's conceit.

those who kept him company to be unprincipled and tyrannical" (Xen. *Mem.* 1.2.56). According to Libanius, Socrates' purpose was to show that some of the things poets said were laughable, so that people would not be encouraged to carry out their injunctions. "And [Socrates] spoke thus about Pindar," says Libanius, "fearing his teaching, and worried lest one of the young men on hearing that 'Justice yields to the force [βιάζεται τὸ δίκαιον] of a powerful hand', may think nothing of the laws and start getting his hands in practice" (Lib. *Apol. Socr.* 87). This is, it is agreed on all sides, a misrepresentation of lines of Pindar that read νόμος ... δικαιῶν τὸ βιαιότατον (Law ... justifies the extreme of violence; Pind. *Fr.* 169.1–7 Sn-M; correctly quoted by Plato at *Lg.* 715a), and there has been a long debate over the issues involved.[29] Libanius' version is also close to what the manuscripts of the *Gorgias* unanimously record as βιαίων τὸ δικαιότατον. Dodds, however, printed the true Pindaric text, arguing that "the misquotation would have no dramatic value (and would pass unnoticed by most readers) unless Socrates proceeded to correct it [which he did not]".[30]

If, however, Callicles was cast in the role of an Alcibiades who had turned against Socrates' teachings, then there would have been immense dramatic value in making him thus to misquote Pindar, and to do so with a skilful play on words. For βιαίων would have drawn "emphatic" attention to the element in Alcibiades' name that actually means "force" or "violence", namely -*bia*-; and far from passing unnoticed by ancient readers of the *Gorgias*, would have been recognized as a clever means of passing whatever blame had attached itself to Socrates on to his wayward pupil. Libanius too probably had Alcibiades in mind, and was expressing Socrates' fears about what he might do once he turned to politics.

That such was probably the intention of Plato's quotation of Pindar is confirmed by the recent discovery of a papyrus version of the complete ode. "This showed how Pindar had used the story of Herakles and the horses of Diomedes to prove the proposition that *nomos*, king of all gods and men (that is, custom or conventional belief) justifies the greatest violence. The theft of the horses, although apparently unjust, was approved by Zeus".[31] The lines immediately following those exploited by Plato refer to the ἀπριάτας ... Διομήδεος ἵππους (the horses of Diomedes that were not paid for). At the Olympic games of 416, Alcibiades entered seven teams of horses in the chariot event. As we saw in Chapter 9, one of these was a team of

---

29. Summarized by Dodds, *Plato: Gorgias* 9, 270–72; cf. Pavese, "The New Heracles Poem of Pindar".
30. Dodds, *Plato: Gorgias*, 271.
31. Lintott, *Violence, Civil Strife and Revolution*, 169, citing *POxy* 26.2450 (= Pind *Fr.* 169 Sn-M).

Argive horses that belonged to an Athenian of modest means named Diomedes. Alcibiades played on his ἀξίωμα with the judges and raced the team in his own name, taking credit for their victory. The subject was still topical in the fourth century for an action was brought against Alcibiades' son by Teisias in *c*.397.[32] The subject would thus have still been topical in the fourth century, and any confusion between Teisias and Diomedes may have been due to the quotation of Pindar's lines by amused, or concerned, contemporaries.[33]

Βία (force) is not the only word that Plato seems to use to play on Alcibiades' name. Βίος (life) is another. From βίον βιῶναι (live one's life) within Callicles' speech (485d), and βίος in the last line (486d), to the numerous allusions to "life" elsewhere (e.g. 492d, 492e, 493c [× 2], 494a [× 2], 494b, 494c, 494d, 494e, 500c, 500d, 507e), the dialogue is full of the kind of wordplay used of Alcibiades by other writers, by Xenophon and Sophocles.[34]

The passage in which the seemliness of a devotion to philosophy on the part of older men is discussed (485a–486e) may also contain deliberate Alcibiadean resonances. A perennial problem here has been the presence of the expressions καὶ παίζοντας, καὶ παῖζον (485b), and ἢ παίζοντα (485c), meaning "and/or fooling around" or "playing jokes". Some editors have been so mystified by these expressions that they either deleted them from the text or changed it to read πταίοντας (stumble in speech) or the like.[35] If, however, the passage concerns the man who hit his future father-in-law "as a joke" (Plut. *Alc.* 8.1), and who was much given to horseplay (Plut. *Alc.* 40.3), and if Plato was in turn ridiculing him, then the expressions should perhaps stand.

Plato's purpose is wholly serious, but his portrait of Callicles seems to include examples of Alcibiadean buffoonery in which the object of Plato's attack is made to ridicule himself from his own mouth. In other contexts, Plato has been described as "a good caricaturist [who] reduces his victims to a few readily recognizable features".[36] This is what Plato does here. Callicles describes the lot of the philosopher as "living the rest of his life ψιθυρίζοντα [whispering] in a corner ..."; ψιθυρίζω, however, was also used for the twittering of swallows (Poll. 5.90; cf. *Anth. Pal.*

---

32. Ostwald, *From Popular Sovereignty*, 311, has a good exposition of the issues involved.

33. On fourth-century interest in Alcibiades, see Bruns, *Das literarische Porträt der Griechen*, 509–21; Gribble, *Alcibiades and Athens, passim*. On Teisias and Diomedes, see pp. 124–5, above.

34. For example, the account of a conversation between Pericles and Alcibiades at Xen. *Mem.* 1.2.40–46, where βία occurs five times in thirteen lines of text. On Soph. *Ph.*, see Henry, "Bios in Sophocles' *Philoctetes*"; Vickers, "Alcibiades on Stage", 171–97, and Chapter 5, above.

35. See Dodds, *Plato: Gorgias*, 274.

36. R. Brock, "Plato and Comedy", in *"Owls to Athens": Essays on Classical Subjects Presented to Sir Kenneth Dover*, E. M. Craik (ed.), 39–49 (Oxford: Clarendon Press, 1990), 47.

12.136, and Plut. *Alc.* 24.8),[37] as was τραυλίζω, the term that was also applied to the speech defect for which Alcibiades was lampooned by Aristophanes.[38] The words Plato puts into Callicles' mouth are suspectable of double meanings resulting from a confusion of *lambda* and *rho*. For example, if we assume that the sentence beginning φιλοσοφίας μέν (485a) were spoken in an Alcibiadean manner, there would be a disagreeable jingle at χάλιν καλόν, the kind of expression for which Gorgias was famous but that good Attic stylists tried to avoid, and that Plato had already put into Gorgias' own mouth at 467b (ὦ λῷστε Πῶλε [my good friend Polus]).[39]

The sticking point for some, however, will come when it is realized that the particular speech defect Callicles refers to, ψελλότης (cf. ψελλιζομένους, ψελλιζομένον [485b], ψελλιζομένον [485c]), was different from τραυλότης, which was Alcibiades' particular affliction (or affectation). ψελλότης was "the omission of some particular letter or syllable", while τραυλότης was "the inability to master ... a particular letter".[40] All is not lost, however, for if Alcibiades' idiolect was in question here, ψελλιζομένος pronounced as it should be would nevertheless allow the listener to understand ψηριζομένος, meaning "twittering like a starling [ψήρ]", a rather less exalted bird than the swallow. Starlings were, moreover, taught to speak in antiquity (Plut. *Mor.* 927f), and there may thus be an additional jibe at the nature of Gorgias' rhetorical tuition.

What Plato gives us at 485b–c would seem to be an insight into the development of the child Alcibiades: (i) the playful child with a speech defect, (ii) the older child attempting to enunciate his words clearly, and (iii) the grown man with a speech defect again, but this time playing practical jokes. Callicles' comments are ironic: while the first is perfectly normal, indeed charming and proper for the age (but if the hypothesis presented here is correct, there is a cruel piling up of a cacophony of *lambdas* [χαίλω τε καὶ χαλίεν ... καὶ ἐλευθέλιον καὶ πλέπον, for χαίρω τε καὶ χαρίεν ... καὶ ἐλευθέριον καὶ πρέπον] at 485b), the second smacks of slavery,[41] and the third is ridiculous (καταγέλαστον), unmanly (ἄνανδρον) and ought to be punished with "blows" (πληγῶν). The historical Alcibiades had once been a *de facto* slave (at the court of Tissaphernes) and was the object of ridicule on the Athenian

---

37. It was also, perhaps significantly, the word used to describe the Spartan Timaea's confiding to her intimates that her son's name was really Alcibiades, not Leotychidas (Plut. *Alc.* 23.7).

38. Ar. *Vesp.* 44 where Alcibiades is quoted as τραυλίσας (pronouncing *rho* as *lambda*). Cf. ἐτραύλισεν at 46, and LSJ s.vv. τραυλίζω, τραυλός.

39. Cf. Dodds, *Plato: Gorgias*, 235n.

40. O'Neill, *Speech and Speech Disorders*, 40, citing Arist. *Pr.* 902b23–5.

41. Cf. Callicles' statement at 491e: "How can a man be happy who is the servant of anything?"

stage.[42] His posthumous reputation for ἀνδρεία (courage) meant that by the end of the fourth century his statue had been erected in the Forum at Rome as "the bravest of the Greeks" (Plut. *Num.* 8.20; Plin. *HN* 34.12). Alcibiades, moreover, was not averse to handing out blows, and is recorded as having done so on several occasions. There was his attack "as a joke", as he put it, on his future father-in-law Hipponicus (Plut. *Alc.* 8.1), as well as assaults on a rival *choregus* ([Andoc.] 4.20–21), a schoolmaster (Plut. *Alc.* 7.1), and a servant (Plut. *Alc.* 3.2). Plato emphasizes this particular aspect of Alcibiades' personality by repeating talk of "blows" at 485d, and driving the point home with what is clearly a very crude expression[43] for a "crack on the jaw [ἐπὶ κόρρης]" at 486c. But even here, Plato is being playful, at Alcibiades' expense, for ἐπὶ κόλλης would have conjured up an image of the game κολλαβίζειν, "in which one holds his eyes, while the other strikes him, and bids him guess which hand he has been struck with" (Poll. 9.129; LSJ s.v. κολλαβίζω). It is in any case a fact that when Alcibiades attacked the *choregus*, he is said to have hit him precisely ἐπὶ κόρρης (Dem. 21.147).

There are some other choice puns in Callicles' speech: ληρήματα (follies) spoken Alcibiades-wise would generate a play on λαλήματα (prattlings), an appropriate image for one who had been implicitly described as a λάλος (prattler) in his lifetime (Ar. *Ach.* 716). Callicles' philosopher is said at 485d to "flee from the city centre and the agora, which as the poet says makes men ἀριπρεπεῖς (distinguished)". *ἁλιπρεπεῖς, however, would mean "fit for the briny", and if a poetic and Alcibiadean context is called for, one need look no further than the events surrounding the performance of Eupolis' *Baptae*, when Alcibiades is said to have been so put out by the way he had been lampooned that he caused Eupolis to be dipped in the sea, "Alcibiades saying the while 'Baptise me on stage, and I will soak you in salt water'" (Tzetz., ap. Kaibel 20).[44] Then there is the pun generated from προπηλακιζόμενος (disparage, literally "trampled in the mud") at 483b, where if *προπηρακιζόμενος were understood by the hearer, it would produce the meaning "trampled in the shit".[45] προπηλακισθείς was, moreover, Alcibiades' own word to describe how the

---

42. Vickers, *Pericles on Stage, passim.*

43. For which Callicles actually apologizes.

44. The story was later exaggerated so that Eupolis was said to have drowned. Cf. H.-G. Nesselrath, "Eupolis and the Periodization of Athenian Comedy", in *The Rival of Aristophanes: Studies in Athenian Old Comedy*, D. Harvey & J. Wilkins (eds), 233–46 (London: Duckworth and the Classical Press of Wales, 2000) (who, however, seems to think that the story of the dipping was a "toned-down" version of a late tradition that Eupolis was drowned by Alcibiades; less likely, in my view).

45. Cf. πῆραξον = ἀφόδευσον (excrement), Hsch.

Athenian generals at Aegospotami had told him to go away and not come near them again (Plut. *Alc.* 37.2; cf. Diod. 13.105.4).[46]

The reference to young lions (483e) not only recalls the Chorus in the *Agamemnon* (717–36) but the scene in *Frogs* where Dionysus asks Aeschylus and Euripides what they would do about Alcibiades, and Aeschylus replies that "It were best not to raise a lion cub in the city, but having done so, to indulge his ways" (Ar. *Ra.* 1431–2; Plut. *Alc.* 16.3).[47] Callicles' image of the lion that society tries to civilize is probably the source of Nietzsche's "magnificent blond beast that prowls in search of booty and victory";[48] interesting, if *that* was part of Alcibiades' intellectual progeny. Later on, the description of someone deprived of their goods and their citizenship (486c) recalls what happened to Alcibiades when his property was confiscated, and he was condemned to death *in absentia*.

Plato cleverly makes Callicles impute to Socrates elements of the historical Alcibiades' character, and he does so in such a way that, each time, Socrates emerges with an enhanced reputation. Thus, at the very beginning of his long speech (482c), Callicles accuses Socrates of "behaving like a hot-headed youth in the argument" (νεανιεύσθαι ἐν τοῖς λόγοις), and of being a real δημηγόρος (popular orator; cf. 482e, 494d). Neither accusation could possibly apply to Socrates, while both expressions well encapsulate a popular view of Alcibiades.[49] At 489b, Callicles asks whether Socrates will stop φλυαρῶν (fooling around). Again, this is an Alcibiadean, not a Socratic, failing. At 494e, Callicles asks whether Socrates is "ashamed" (αἰσχύνη) of running a particular argument. This recalls the way in which Socrates induced feelings of shame regarding his virtue (αἰσχυνόμενος τὴν ἀρετήν) in the young Alcibiades (Plut. *Alc.* 4.4). "How βίαιος [forceful] you are", says Callicles of Socrates at 505d, unjustly imputing to him the characteristic embodied in Alcibiades' name, already shown up by Plato in Callicles' main speech.[50] At 515, Callicles accuses Socrates of being φιλόνικος. According to Plutarch, Alcibiades' predominant characteristic from his earliest youth was τὸ φιλόνικον ἰσχυρότατον ... καὶ τὸ φιλόπρωτον

---

46. The study of the *aulos* was also "trampled in the mud" (προεπηλακίσθη) when the youthful Alcibiades took against it (Plut. *Alc.* 2.7).

47. The line is attributed by Valerius Maximus (7.2.7), perhaps correctly, to Pericles (Vickers, "Aristophanes *Frogs*"). If so, there should be a further link with the dream of Agariste (Hdt. 6.131.2). On Alcibiades' leonine characteristics, see Bloedow, "On Nurturing Lions in the State"; Munn, *The School of History*, 193–4; Duff, "Plutarch on the Childhood of Alkibiades", 98–9.

48. Cf. Dodds, *Plato: Gorgias*, 269, 389.

49. Thus Plutarch refers to τὰ ... Ἀλκιβιάδου νεανιεύματα (the youthful excesses of Alcibiades; *Mor.* 345a).

50. See pp. 158–9, above.

(an extremely strong desire to win and to come first; Plut. *Alc.* 2.1; cf. Thuc. 5.43.2), while Socrates prided himself on his humility.

What Socrates says to Callicles is also full of Alcibiadean meaning. For example, the frequent references made to κολακεία (fawning; e.g. 501c, 502d, 502c, 503a, 513d, 517a, 521b, 522d, 527c) recall the attention the young Alcibiades received from τοῖς κόλαξι (flatterers) who "would bribe him with the offer of many pleasures [πολλὰς ἡδονάς] to which he would yield and slip away from Socrates ... and indeed Alcibiades was very prone to pleasure [πρὸς ἡδονὰς ἀγώγιμος]" (Plut. *Alc.* 6.1–2). "Pleasure" is, of course, another major concern of the *Gorgias*, but it may be relevant that in the part of the dialogue concerned with Callicles, "pleasures" – in the plural – are the norm.

When Socrates congratulates his interlocutor on having been initiated into the Greater Mysteries before the Lesser, he adds: "I did not think it was θεμιτόν [allowed]" (497c). This is a crucial point for any association of Callicles with Alcibiades, for it can only apply to Alcibiades' highly peculiar status with regard to the Eleusinian Mysteries. Condemned *in absentia* for profanation in 415, and cursed by practically all the Athenian clerisy in a dramatic ceremony,[51] he lived in exile until 407. After his triumphant return, not only was he pardoned, but he stage-managed a magnificent celebration of the Mysteries: "all those who did not envy him said that he had performed the office of high priest as well as that of a general" (Plut. *Alc.* 34). We can hardly imagine that Alcibiades had been initiated before 415 BCE, but he presumably was in 407 BCE. Since he made his triumphal return to Athens in the late spring, he would have been five or six months late for the Lesser Mysteries (assuming they were still being celebrated),[52] and would thus have missed them, hence perhaps the ironic reference to Callicles' irregular initiation.

Granted gold and bronze crowns by the Athenians on his return (Nep., *Alc.* 6), and "not only all human, but divine honours" (Just. *Epit.* 5.4), we might well expect Alcibiades to have been called μέγιστος εὐεργέτης (great benefactor; cf. 506c) by a populace that he had, for the moment at least, eating out of his hand (Plut. *Alc.* 34.7). Alcibiades was probably behind the grant of *euergesia* voted in 407 to Archelaus of Macedon,[53] a figure who plays a prominent role in the *Gorgias*. So popular was Alcibiades at the time that "many even besought him to overcome the

---

51. Lewis, "After the Profanation of the Mysteries", 177, 189; cf. pp. 102, 138, above.
52. For the timetable, see Richardson, *The Homeric Hymn to Demeter*, 20; for the concepts underlying θεμιτόν, see *ibid.* 224; cf. the discussion of θεμίς at Soph. *Ph.* 660–61, p. 74, above.
53. M. Walbank, *Athenian Proxenies of the Fifth Century BC* (Toronto: Samuel Stevens, 1978), 460–9; R. Meiggs & D. Lewis, *A Selection of Greek Historical Inscriptions to the End of the Fifth Century BC*, rev. edn (Oxford: Clarendon Press, 1988), 91.

malice of his personal enemies, and sweep away ψηφίσματα [statutes] and νόμους [customary laws]", and assume sole power (Plut. *Alc*. 34.7). Although he was given plenipotentiary powers (στρατηγὸν ... αὐτοκράτορα; Diod. 12.69), enough influential people were alarmed at the prospect of an Alcibiades in Athens that he was sent off to sea as quickly as possible (Plut. *Alc*. 35.1), never in fact to return. It is the danger presented by an autocratic Alcibiades that Plato emphasizes in the *Gorgias*.

There are many more points that could be made to support the view that into the person of Callicles Plato built all the characteristics of Alcibiades that were at variance with Socrates' teaching. While Callicles expresses himself well disposed towards Socrates (485e), reflecting perhaps the sense of loyalty that motivated the by-then alienated Alcibiades to save Socrates' life at the battle of Delium in 424 (Plut. *Alc*. 7; Pl. *Smp*. 221a), Socrates is clearly shown to differ, and to differ insistently, with the turn that his erstwhile pupil has taken in the direction of tyranny. This is made absolutely clear in Socrates' closing words (527e): "the way you encourage me to follow you ... is οὐδενὸς ἄξιος [worth nothing]". This does indeed "formally reverse the judgement of Callicles that the principles of morality are οὐδενὸς ἄξια (492c)",[54] but does so in terms that both recur throughout the dialogue (485c, 497c, 492c, 520a, 527e), and recall an expression used in an important event in the relationship between Socrates and Alcibiades, namely, when Alcibiades received the prize of honour rightly due to Socrates, thanks to the ἀξίωμα (reputation) of his forbears in the eyes of the generals (Pl. *Smp*. 219e; DL 2.23; Plut. *Alc*. 7). Plato's phraseology is carefully chosen to demonstrate that the gulf between the values for which Socrates stood and those of the older Alcibiades was unbridgeable.

There remains the problem of Callicles' name. Apart from the possible reference to Alcibiades' beauty, it may be that Plato was also using a real person's name, using its literal meaning, coupled with elements of its owner's character or reputation, rather as Aristophanes did in characterizing his principal κωμῳδούμενοι.[55] The contemporary sculptor Callicles is known to have made statues of Olympic victors (Paus. 6.7.1, 9; Schol. Pind. *Ol*. 7.158), and could also have worked on the golden statue of Gorgias that was set up in the sanctuary at Delphi (Philostr. *VS* 1.9.4). If the name of a real individual is indeed in question here – in addition to the name being employed as a mask for Alcibiades – it may help to explain the use of the name of Polus for Socrates' other principal interlocutor. Polus was the name of a

---

54. Dodds, *Plato: Gorgias*, 386.
55. Cf. Vickers, *Pericles on Stage* and *Alcibiades on Stage*.

Sicilian teacher of rhetoric (cf. Pl. *Phdr.* 267b–c),[56] but a case can also be made for its use in the *Gorgias* as a mask for Socrates' other wayward pupil, Critias.

Polus and Critias

The image of Critias in the fourth century – and later[57] – was primarily that of an extraordinarily bloodthirsty tyrant, made somehow worse because his blood-thirstiness was the result of policy as much as bloodlust. He had been appointed one of the five ephors of the puppet government when Athens was in the hands of the Spartans after their victory in 405, and was subsequently one of the Thirty who inflicted the cruellest punishments even on members of their own faction. Hundreds were put to death, including three hundred Eleusinians at Critias' direct instigation, before the Thirty were ousted in the autumn of 403. Critias himself was killed in the Thirty's last stand at Munychia.[58]

Critias was coupled with Alcibiades in the accusations that were levelled against Socrates in 399 (Xen. *Mem.* 1.2.12); Polycrates apparently made the same association;[59] and Aeschines even gives Critias' education at the feet of Socrates as the sole grounds for the latter's execution (Aesch. in 1.173). The young Critias plays a prominent role in Plato's *Charmides*, set in the aftermath of Potidaea in 431 BCE. Critias brings to Socrates his cousin Charmides (who was Plato's uncle, and was later to die during the overthrow of the Thirty). The discussion is wholly concerned with σωφροσύνη, and it is hinted that for Critias the virtue in question is to be equated with the life of leisure, of non-engagement in day-to-day politics (Pl. *Chrm.* 161b).[60] Quite how long the association of Critias with Socrates lasted is uncertain. According to Xenophon there was a formal break when Socrates rebuked him for his incontinent behaviour over a boy (Xen. *Mem.* 1.2.29–30), and relations were certainly bad when the tyrant Critias legislated that "none should teach the art of disputation" out of spite towards Socrates (Xen. *Mem.* 1.2.29–31). Gorgias too figures in the testimonia relating to Critias: he is said to have enthralled

---

56. Cf. L. Radermacher, *Artium Scriptores (Reste der voraristotelische Rhetorik)*, Sitzungsberichte der Akademie der Wissenschaften in Wien, Philosophisch-Historische Klasse 227/3 (1951), 112–14.

57. Plut. *Mor.* 171c, in an elaborate metaphor, accuses Critias of human sacrifice.

58. On Critias in general, see Centanni, *Atene Assoluta*; Bultrighini, *"Maledetta democrazia"*; Ianucci, *La parola e l'azione*; Wilson, "The Sound of Cultural Conflict"; and Chapters 7 and 8, above.

59. Gribble, *Alcibiades and Athens*, 228.

60. Carter, *The Quiet Athenian*, 73.

both Critias and Alcibiades during his visit to Athens in 427 BCE (Philostr. *VS* 1.9). Gorgias was later established in Thessaly (although exactly when cannot be determined; he died there in the 370s aged 109),[61] and he may have been there when Critias went into exile in 407.[62]

Critias' relations with Alcibiades were, it would seem, never close. Even Critias' apparently lighthearted verses in praise of Alcibiades (88 B 4 DK) may contain a hint of menace.[63] Both were implicated in the desecration of the Herms in 415, and in Critias' case he was probably guilty (Andoc. 1.47 [Critias]; Plut. *Alc.* 20.5 [Alcibiades]). Critias moved that Alcibiades should be allowed to return from exile in 408/7,[64] and he even wrote elegiac verses drawing attention to the fact (88 B 4 DK),[65] but this was probably, as we saw in Chapter 8, an attempt by Critias to improve his own image after his participation in the rule of the Four Hundred.[66] For whatever reason, Critias was banished ὑπὸ τοῦ δήμου (by the people; Xen. *Hell.* 2.3.15) after Alcibiades' fall from favour in 407. Their relationship was certainly sour by 405. By this time, Critias was so committed to his role of *de facto* Spartan governor that he must have been among those members of the Thirty who were most wary about what Alcibiades might be prepared to do; for there were "vague hopes" that Alcibiades might yet save his city (Plut. *Alc.* 38.3–4). Critias' colleague Theramenes, who had in the past been well disposed towards Alcibiades,[67] was executed in the most irregular circumstances (Xen. *Hell.* 2.4.50–56), and we next hear of Critias appealing to the Spartan admiral Lysander to have Alcibiades put to death as a danger to the Athenian state (Plut. *Alc.* 38.5–6; cf. Nep., *Alc.* 10.1).

But how does this relate to Polus in *Gorgias*? It probably does so both in general terms and in detail. In the first place, there is so much talk about tyranny. From 466b to 480d there are more than a dozen places where tyranny is discussed at some length.[68] The first occasion is brief but typical. Polus tries to refute Socrates'

---

61. See Untersteiner, *The Sophists*, 94.
62. This may provide the answer to Ostwald's question, "Why did Critias not join Alcibiades in Thrace but rather go to Thessaly?" (*From Popular Sovereignty*, 464).
63. Ianucci, *La parola e l'azione*, 42–3; Wilson, "The Sound of Cultural Conflict".
64. Having already done so in 411: see Ostwald, *From Popular Sovereignty*, 400 n.215.
65. The verse begins – significantly perhaps, in view of Alcibiades' habit of beginning sentences with καί (Tompkins, "Stylistic Characterization in Thucydides", 181–214) – καὶ νῦν (88 B 4 DK).
66. Ianucci, *La parola e l'azione*, 55; Wilson, "The Sound of Cultural Conflict".
67. Theramenes is the only person actually mentioned in the sources as advocating the recall of Alcibiades in 411: Diod. 13.38; P. J. Rhodes, *A Commentary on the Aristotelian* Athenaion Politeia (Oxford: Clarendon Press, 1981), 413.
68. There are no words beginning τυρανν- in Gorgias' part of the *Gorgias*, fourteen in Polus' part, and seven in Callicles'.

criticisms of rhetoricians by maintaining that rather than being the least powerful of citizens, they are surely "like tyrants who kill whomsoever they want, and despoil and send into exile anyone they wish to" (466b–c). For Polus, tyranny means "the power of doing whatever seems good to you in a state, killing, banishing, doing all the things you like" (469c). Although Polus' point is of more general application, this is precisely what Critias and his fellow members of the Thirty had done in 405–403 BCE. Polycrates had accused Socrates of being τυραννικός (inclined to tyranny; Plut. *Alc.* 38.5–6; cf. Nep. *Alc.* 10.1); Socrates' absolute rejection of tyranny in the *Gorgias* is part of Plato's rejoinder to the charge.

Plato goes even further in alluding to the events of this time and Socrates' part in them, and does so not without wit. Critias' law that "none should teach the art of disputation" was passed with Socrates specifically in mind (Xen. *Mem.* 1.2.31). When Socrates was subsequently brought in for questioning, he was forbidden by Critias and Charicles "to speak at all with the young" or "to speak of shoemakers, carpenters, smiths ... or herdsmen". If he did he might have an accident (Xen. *Mem.* 1.2.37). For Socrates to ask Polus to suppress his wordiness (461d) is ironic: mirroring the suppression of freedom of speech with a stylistic criticism. For Socrates to greet Polus as a visitor to Athens (461e) is a clever way of alluding to Critias' status as a returned exile, and for him to say that it would be "a terrible thing if [Polus], of all people, should be deprived of the power of speech [in the city] which has the most freedom of speech in Greece" (461e) would be ironic if Critias was really in question.

On another occasion, Socrates was closely involved in the arrest of Theramenes, a relatively moderate member of the Thirty whom Critias had accused of betraying the cause. Put on trial before the *Boule*, Theramenes won the sympathy of most present, but "Critias, fearing that Theramenes might dissolve the oligarchy, surrounded him with soldiers carrying drawn swords" (Diod. 14.4.5–6; cf. Xen. *Hell.* 2.4.55). Socrates and two of his attendants tried in vain to intervene when Theramenes was forcibly dragged from the altar in the Bouleuterion and through the middle of the Agora complaining loudly at his treatment (Diod. 14.5.1–3; cf. Xen. *Hell.* 2.4.55-6).[69] This perhaps lies behind the image Plato puts into Socrates' mouth when he says:

Suppose that I go into the Agora when it is crowded, and take a dagger under my arm. Polus, I say to you, I have just acquired rare power and become a tyrant; for if I think that any of these men whom you see ought to be put to

---

69. This may be the altar illustrated in H. A. T. Thompson & R. E. Wycherley, *The Agora of Athens, The Athenian Agora* 14 (Princeton, NJ: Princeton University Press, 1972), pl. 30b.

death, he is as good as dead; and if I am disposed to break his head or tear his garment, he will have his head broken or his garment torn in an instant. Such is my great power in the city. (469d–e)

Theramenes was in effect put to death at Critias' bidding, and this passage gives the essence of what occurred.

In two places in his speech at 464b–466a, Socrates draws special attention to Polus. Thus, at 464e–465a, when he says that he considers κολακεία (fawning) to be a shameful thing because it aims at pleasure instead of good, he makes a point of saying, "I am addressing this to you, Polus". If Critias is indeed in question, there may be a reference here to the incident that had brought about a breach between him and Socrates. Critias was making a fool of himself over the youthful Euthydemus, and Socrates pointed out to him that it was both demeaning and unseemly for a gentleman to beg for favours from someone he wanted to impress. Critias took no notice, and so Socrates said "in the presence of many others 'Critias seems to me to have the feelings of a pig, wanting to rub against Euthydemus as a pig rubs against stones'" (Xen. *Mem.* 1.2.29–30).[70] It was a similar kind of κολακεία with which the young Alcibiades was beset by his admirers, and which drove Socrates to take steps to protect him (Plut. *Alc.* 4.1–4). And if Critias did indeed write a treatise *On the Nature of Love and Virtue* (Critias 88 B 42 DK), Plato's implicit jibe might have even more point. It is certainly one that he drives home hard.[71]

In the same speech (465d) Socrates again tells Polus that he is talking to him in particular. He quotes Anaxagoras on chaos – everything mixed up together – and goes on to say that the themes of the previous discussion, "medicine, health and cookery" would be ἀκρίτων (a confused mess). If directed at Critias, these words may be full of *emphasis*, of "additional meanings ... put there for the reader or listener to find".[72] Critias, like Polus (462b–c), was a writer. Some of his works have survived in an extremely fragmentary state, and while they appear to bear out the verdict of antiquity that Critias was "an amateur among philosophers and a philosopher among amateurs" (Schol. Pl. *Ti.* 20a), all of the concerns mentioned by Socrates at *Gorgias* 465d – medicine, health and cookery – seem to have been his.

---

70. Not in T. K. Hubbard, *Homosexuality in Greece and Rome: A Sourcebook of Basic Documents* (Berkeley, CA: University of California Press, 2003).
71. Cf. κολακεία *vel sim.* at 463b, 463d, 464c, 465b, 466a (× 3).
72. Ahl, "The Art of Safe Criticism", 177–9; Ahl also discusses the Demetrian analysis (*Eloc.* 288) of the "emphasis" of Plato, *Phd.* 59c. One sympathizes with Ahl's remark: "Since the Romantic era, classicists have tended to find such innuendo morally repugnant and to balk at the suggestion that Plato might have engaged in its use" (ibid.: 179). For a refreshing change, see Brock, "Plato and Comedy".

Critias is thus quoted as stating that "The blood around the heart is, they say, for men the [source of] thought [νόημα]" (Critias 88 A 23.26–8 DK). This bespeaks an interest in both medicine and Anaxagoras, for whom Νοῦς (Mind) was one of the central concepts of his teaching.[73] It may be significant too that Galen cites Critias three times (Critias 88 B 39–40 DK). One of the aphorisms Galen quotes mentions health: "Men are accustomed to recognise health [ὑγιαίνειν] in the will" (Critias 88 B 39, 22–3 DK). Finally, Critias appears to have written about cookery (what Plato calls ὀψοποιία) as well; at least Pollux has the hitherto mysterious line "Critias said ὀψωνίας and ὀψωνεῖν, the latter he called ὀψωνεῖν and ὀψονομεῖν" (Poll. 6.38; Critias 88 B 60 DK).

But the real riches lie in ἀκρίτων (465d). Not only is this a near anagram of Critias' name,[74] but the word ἄκριτος actually survives among Critias' writings (Critias 88 B 19.4 DK). There it is used to describe the "countless" stars, but ἄκριτος was more usually used to mean "unjudged" or "untried". Now this was Critias' especial foible: to put the victims of his tyrannical rule to death without trial. The most outstanding example in terms of the numbers involved was the judicial massacre of 300 Eleusinians in order to create a bolt-hole at Eleusis for the Thirty (Xen. *Hell.* 2.4.8–9; Diod. 14.32.4; Lys. 12.52). What made matters worse in the eyes of contemporaries was that the Eleusinians were condemned μιᾷ ψήφῳ (with a single vote; Lys. 12.52), rather than being judged individually. Critias was the prime mover in these irregular proceedings (Xen. *Hell.* 2.4.9). The immediate precedent was the condemnation of the generals after Arginusae, a trial that Socrates considered to be improper even before it began (Xen. *Mem.* 1.7.15), and with the memory of which Plato's Socrates upbraids Polus in the *Gorgias* (at 473e–474a).

There are many aspects of the Polus section of the *Gorgias* that have a potentially Critian significance. The adjective νομοθετική (legislative), for example, which occurs at 464b (twice) and 465c (twice) may have something to do with the fact that Critias was designated a νομοθέτης (lawmaker) of the Thirty.[75] Plato's Polus is said to have written a *Techne* (462a–b) on rhetoric, and although we do not knowingly possess anything of such a work by Critias, the sentiments expressed in his aphorism "More people become virtuous through study than from nature" (Stob. 3.29.11; Critias 88 B 9) bear on themes Plato makes Socrates discuss. We know a little about Critias' literary style from Philostratus; that it was characterized by

---

73. G. Kirk, J. E. Raven & M. Schofield, *The Presocratic Philosophers: A Critical History with a Selection of Texts*, 2nd edn (Cambridge: Cambridge University Press, 1983), 362–5.

74. See F. Ahl, *Metaformations: Soundplay and Wordplay in Ovid and Other Classical Poets* (Ithaca, NY: Cornell University Press, 1985), 45–7, on the anagrammatizing wordplay in Pl. *Cra.*

75. Together with Charicles: Xen. *Mem.* 1.2.31; cf. D. Chr. 21.3; Munn, *The School of History*, 221–2.

inter alia the use of *asyndeton:* the absence of the connecting words customary in Greek prose (Philostr. *VS* 16.4).[76] For what it is worth, in his chapter on *asyndeton* J. D. Denniston uses as an example a sentence from Polus' speech at 471b.[77] The rancorous tone Polus adopts towards Socrates is a commonplace; the rancour of Critias as a member of the Thirty, and especially in his dealings with Socrates, is equally well known.

But this was part of Plato's objective: to make his Polus admit to using such an expression as an "unjust attempt to become tyrant", and to show Socrates disagreeing with him vehemently – twice (471d and 472b), in case anyone missed the point. Similarly, despite the fact that Callicles is prepared to say that he is well disposed towards Socrates (485e), Socrates is shown to hold a very low opinion of Callicles' views (527e). Far from honouring "Critias' memory in the Dialogues",[78] in the *Gorgias* at least Plato distances himself from the excesses of Critias' tyrannical regime. The *Gorgias* is indeed Plato's equivalent of the passages in the *Memorabilia*, where Xenophon tries to exculpate Socrates from the later careers of Critias and Alcibiades.[79] Plato is far more subtle, however, and even has Gorgias making a long speech in which he suggests that the individual wrongdoer should receive blame and punishment, and not his teacher (457b–c). Plato is in fact arguing the opposite case to that of Xenophon, but by representing Polus and Callicles in Gorgias' thrall, he suggests by indirect means that the excesses of Critias and Alcibiades should be laid at the door of a teacher other than Socrates, namely Gorgias.

Plato in fact cleverly makes his Gorgias refer to these very excesses at 456e, where he remarks that the trained rhetorician should not "strike or goad or kill" (τύπτειν οὐδε κεντεῖν τε καὶ ἀποκτεινύναι) his friends. These three words are full of *emphasis* in the technical sense of the word. (i) "Striking" recalls Alcibiades, and Plato's Gorgias in effect says as much in the next sentence in speaking of "a man who has been the pupil of a palaestra and is a skilful boxer, and in the fullness of his strength he goes and strikes his father or mother ...", which may allude to Alcibiades' historically attested attack on his future father-in-law (Plut. *Alc.* 8.1). (ii) "Killing" was Critias' forte, as we have seen, and Gorgias expands on the tyrant's career by speaking of a hypothetical teacher who is detested (μισεῖν) and expelled

76. W. C. Wright, *Philostratus and Eunapius: The Lives of the Sophists* (London: Heinemann, 1922), 573 suggests that figure had its origins in the style of Gorgias.

77. J. D. Denniston, *Greek Prose Style* (Oxford: Clarendon Press, 1952), 102.

78. *OCD*² 299.

79. The *Gorgias* thus corresponds to the category of "Alkibiadesliteratur" as defined by H. Meier, Die ganze sokratische Alkibiadesliteratur scheint ein Reaktion auf die Invektive des Polykrates gewesen zu sein' (*Sokrates, sein Werk und sein geschichtliche Stellung* [Tübingen: Mohr (Paul Siebeck), 1913], 138 n.1); cf. Gribble, *Alcibiades and Athens*, 226–30.

from the city (457b). Critias ἐμίσει τὸν Σωκράτην (came to detest Socrates; Xen. *Mem.* 1.2.31), and although Socrates himself was merely threatened and not exiled by the Thirty, many others were. (iii) "Goading" calls to mind a Greek proverb used to describe "impetuous haste": κεντεῖν τὸ πῶλον περὶ τὴν νύσσαν (to goad the colt around the turning post; LSJ s.v. κεντεῖν). If there were such an allusion, it would apply to both Alcibiades and Critias, for both were devoted to chariot racing,[80] and perhaps account for the Critias' characterization as Polus. An equation between Polus (Πῶλος) and a colt (πῶλος) is in any case made clear in the pun at 463e. Plato is thus not only implying that "Gorgias' teaching is the seed of which the Calliclean way of life is the poisonous fruit",[81] but that Critias' failings have their source there as well. Plato is indeed suggesting that "Gorgias set men's feet on the road to tyranny without warning them that the tyrant is of all men the most unhappy".[82]

Two principal concerns of Socrates in the *Gorgias* are δικαιοσύνη (justice) and σωφροσύνη (sobriety of conduct). These are reminiscent of the virtues that Socrates attempted to instil in the young Critias and Alcibiades according to Xenophon. For as long as they associated with Socrates, they "were able, with the assistance of his example, to maintain a mastery over their immoral inclinations" (Xen. *Mem.* 1.2.24). In the event, they turned their backs on him. Critias, having fled to Thessaly, fell prey to men who did not respect δικαιοσύνη, while Alcibiades was corrupted by "many men who were able flatterers" (Xen. *Mem.* 1.2.25). Xenophon then reasons with the imaginary accuser, asking whether perhaps Socrates deserved some credit for having kept Critias and Alcibiades σώφρονε (well-behaved; Xen. *Mem.* 1.2.26; cf. 27–8). This is what Plato is also attempting to do in the *Gorgias*. The stress on σωφροσύνη in *Charmides* may, moreover, have had the same objective (although with application to Critias alone).

---

80. Critias' devotion to chariot-racing is, it is true, less well-known than that of Alcibiades, but evidence exists in the form of *IG* I³ 1022, an inscribed statue-base dedicated to the Twelve Gods, but found in Salamis (and subsequently lost), rather than near the Altar in the Athenian Agora. It was dedicated by a certain [-]ς Καλαίσχρο to commemorate victories at the Isthmian and Nemean Games (two at each). A. E. Raubitschek, "Leagros", *Hesperia* **8** (1979), 157–8, restored the name of Critias the tyrant (= Kritias [IV]; Davies, *Athenian Propertied Families 600–300 BC*, 157–8). Davies notes that "if Kritias (IV) had in fact gained these four victories there would have been some unmistakable echo of them in the literary tradition". Perhaps Polus is the missing echo. (In making this suggestion, I withdraw the view I once held that someone other than Critias was mentioned on the relevant inscription: E. D. Francis & M. Vickers, "Leagros kalos", *Proceedings of the Cambridge Philological Society* n.s. **27** (1981), 97–136, 122).
81. Dodds, *Plato: Gorgias*, 15.
82. Dodds, *Plato: Gorgias*, 10.

Last judgements

There are many loose ends still, and many outstanding questions. Is there, for example, any significance in the fact that Critias may have written a *Rhadamanthys* (Critias 88 B 13–15 DK), given that the last part of the dialogue is devoted to this myth? Or that Gorgias wrote a study Περὶ φύσεως (On Nature; Gorgias 82 B 1 DK),[83] given the long discussion in *Gorgias* of νόμος (customary law) and φύσις (nature)?[84] Could the theme of "dressing up" (cf. κομμωτική; 465b–c) have something to do with Gorgias' liking for fine clothes?[85] Could Callicles' deme, supposedly of Acharnae, be an "emphatic" allusion to the fact that the Thirty made their final camp at Acharnae in September 403?[86] Could the need to conceal Alcibiades beneath a fictional identity have been a precaution against a reaction from Alcibiades' descendants (Alcibiades Jr. came of age in *c*.397)? Could the concealment of Critias beneath a pseudonym have had something to do with the fact that he was a relative of Plato's?[87] And could the choice of pseudonym – the name of an overly technical Acragantine rhetorician (cf. Pl. *Phdr.* 267b–c) – have been intended as a deliberate criticism of Critias' writings, and perhaps too of Gorgias' teaching? Further research may provide some answers.

Socrates, Critias and Alcibiades were all dead by the time the *Gorgias* was composed. Like the *Menexenus*, where Socrates discourses with Aspasia in 386, and like the portrayals of Aeschylus and Euripides in Aristophanes' *Frogs*, the *Gorgias* is technically an example of *idolopoieia*, or a "dialogue of the dead" (Aristid. 3.487; Hermog. *Prog.* 9; Aphth. *Prog.* 11; cf. Aristid. 2.322). It is helpful to bear this in mind when considering the myth that Socrates addresses to Callicles at the end of the dialogue. There was a time, it seems, when people could be judged on the basis of the finery they wore, and σώματα ... καλὰ καὶ γένη καὶ πλοῦτος (beautiful bodies, noble birth and wealth) were what counted. Alcibiades' fine clothes were legendary

---

83. The subject was a fashionable one at the time, however: cf. F. Heinimann, *Nomos und Physis: Herkunft und Bedeutung einer Antithese im griechischen Denken des 5. Jahrhunderts* (Basle: F. Reinhardt, 1945); Guthrie, *A History of Greek Philosophy*, 3.55–134.

84. Cf. Alcibiades' general παρανομία (lawlessness) (Ath. 5.220c [= Antisth. *Fr.* 29 Caizzi]), and the exploitation by Socratic writers of the magnificence of Alcibiades' φύσις (Bruns, *Das literarische Porträt der Griechen*, 512; Gribble, *Alcibiades and Athens*, 139).

85. Ael. *VH* 12.32 describes Gorgias (and Hippias) "dressed in purple".

86. "The Thirty, seeing many revolting from them because of hatred and the exiles growing ever more numerous, despatched ambassadors to Sparta for aid, and meanwhile themselves gathered as many troops as they could and pitched a camp in open country near Acharnae, as it is called" (Diod. 14.32.6).

87. He was a cousin of Plato's mother; cf. Davies, *Athenian Propertied Families 600–300 BC*, 326–7.

(Plut. *Alc.* 16.1, 23.3; Ath. 12. 534c),[88] as was his physical beauty (Plut. *Alc.* 1.4).[89] Plutarch speaks of τοῦ τε γένους καὶ τοῦ πλούτου (noble birth and wealth) among the advantages Alcibiades possessed on entering politics (Plut. *Alc.* 10.3).

Plato, however, makes Socrates posit an afterlife in which this system of judgement has been replaced by one in which people are judged naked and dead by three judges, "two for Asia, Minos and Rhadamanthys, and one for Europe, Aeacus", who pass judgement in a meadow (λειμῶνι; 524a). "Meadows" were part of the geography of the afterlife from Homeric times (e.g. Hom. *Od.* 11.539), but if Callicles is intended to be Alcibiades, this may be an additional reference to the garden in Caria full of λειμώνων (meadows) and health-giving waters, which his Persian host Tissaphernes decreed should be called "Alcibiades" (Plut. *Alc.* 24.7).[90] The dramatic need for Asiatic judges becomes apparent when it is recalled that Alcibiades died in northern Asia Minor, having been forced naked out of the house in which he was sleeping (Plut. *Alc.* 39.3–7; Diod. 14.11; Nep. *Alc.* 10.2–6; Just. *Epit.* 5.8). Rhadamanthys, the Asiatic judge, is mentioned twice again at 524e, and the person he beholds is full of αἰσχρότητος (ugliness) on account of his "abuse of authority, luxury, hubris, and incontinence (ἀκρατίας)" (525a). Αἰσχρότητος throws back at Callicles a word he used ten times.[91] Abuse of authority, luxury and *hubris* are familiar failings of Alcibiades, but ἀκρατίας (incontinence) is a very neat sidethrust at Critias, in that it is another near anagram of his name,[92] and also recalls the cause of the original breach between him and Socrates.[93] Among those suffering dire punishment in the prison in Hades – and the dead Socrates knew all about prisons – will be "Archelaus, if the truth is being told by Polus, and any other who is such a tyrant" (525c–d). "Archelaus" is revealed to be a speaking name, "Leader of the people", as was Critias, and there is a deliberate ambiguity as to which tyrant – Polus or Archelaus (or both) – is in question.[94] Plato's wit may also extend to

---

88. Cf. Pritchett, "Attic Stelai, Part II" and "Five New Fragments", 23.
89. Cf. Plut. *Alc.* 4.1, 16.4; Pl. *Smp.* 216c–219e; *Prt.* 309a; Ath. 12.534c; Ael. *VH* 12.14; Dio Chrys. 64.27; cf. Gribble, *Alcibiades and Athens*, 39.
90. See pp. 80, 87, above.
91. At 482d, 482d, 482e, 482e, 483a (× 2), culminating in αἰσχρόν four times (483c [× 2]), 485a and 486a).
92. Cf. ἀκρίτων at 465d. There is thus no need to amend the text with Dodds, *Plato: Gorgias, ad loc.* Xen. *Mem.* 1.2.12 similarly, but less subtly, applies an Alcibiadean adjective to Critias and vice versa: Alcibiades is called ἀκρατέστατος (the most intemperate) and Critias βιαιότατος (the most violent).
93. See above, p. 168.
94. The precise authorship of the speech Περὶ πολιτείας often attributed to Herodes Atticus (U. Albini (ed.), *[Erode Attico] Peri Politeias* [Florence: Le Monnier, 1968]) is, thankfully, not germane to the argument; but whether it is by Critias (e.g. H. T. Wade-Gery, *Essays in Greek History* [Oxford:

Alcibiades here: his allusions are frequently like assonant chords, harmoniously striking several notes at once. It seems very likely that Alcibiades was the proposer of a decree granting *proxenia* and *euergesia* to Archelaus.[95]

When Rhadamanthys gets such an individual, he knows that he is a villain and sends him off to Tartarus (526b). The individual who is sent to the isles of the blest, however, is set up by Plato in the image of Socrates himself; or rather of a Socrates who has lived a "holy" life (526c), thus meeting the accusation that Socrates had been guilty of impiety (Pl. *Ap.* 26–7). Plato's anonymous philosopher is devoted to the truth, and has not been a πολυπράγμων (a person overly active in politics).[96] Socrates hankered after the truth, and in the *Apology* tells the jury how his *daemon* prevented him from entering public life; had he done so, he would long ago have perished, to the advantage of no one (Pl. *Ap.* 31c–32a).[97] This again is to put a different spin on the view put forward by Aristophanes to the effect that Socrates was simply a layabout (Ar. *Ra.* 1498).

Then Plato remembers his geography, and having realized that the Asiatic Rhadamathys would not have judged Socrates, quickly brings in Aeacus, who was responsible for Europeans and was also Alcibiades' legendary ancestor.[98] The Socrates of the dialogue addresses Callicles in historical time, as it were, threatening him with an adverse judgement from Aeacus if and when he died: presumably at home in Greece, as opposed to Asia. When in court, Callicles will be giddy and gawping, as he earlier had said Socrates would be (cf. 486b), and as he perhaps was, when he went on trial in 399. Callicles will even be given a "crack on the jaw" of an Alcibiadean nature (cf. 486c). Finally, for Socrates to call Callicles, Polus and Georgias "the wisest of the Greeks" (527a–b) is surely ironic,[99] and intended to recall the story recounted by Plato in the *Apology* that the Delphic oracle had stated that no one was wiser than Socrates (Pl. *Ap.* 21a), although no commentator seems to have made the connection.

Blackwell, 1957], [1945]; Albini, *[Erode Attico] Peri Politeias*, 11–12) or a good later imitation of Critias (e.g. G. Anderson, *Philostratus* [London: Croom Helm, 1986], 113; Albini, *[Erode Attico] Peri Politeias*), it is of more than passing interest to note that it concerns an alliance against Archelaus of Macedon, who figures large in Polus' part of Plato's *Gorgias* (471a–472d; cf. 525d).

95. Walbank, *Athenian Proxenies of the Fifth Century* BC, 460–69; ML 91.

96. Cf. Carter, *The Quiet Athenian*, 117–18.

97. Cf. *ibid.*, 183; "ἀπραγμοσύνη was viewed with ironic scorn by ... Alcibiades (Thuc. 6.18.6)" (Dodds, *Plato: Gorgias*, 383).

98. Alcibiades was supposedly descended from Eurysaces (Plut. *Alc.* 1.1), Aeacus' great-grandson; cf. Chapter 4, above.

99. Contrast: "It is a great honour for Callicles and is a recognition at least of the fame of Gorgias" (C. O. Zuretti, *Platone: Gorgia* [Palermo: Sandron, 1931], 240).

***

This has merely scratched the surface of what is clearly a very rich field of study. Plato's purpose can easily be read once it is acknowledged that he knew the art of safe criticism,[100] and once it is accepted that, at least where the *Gorgias* is concerned, "classical simplicity" might give way to classical duplicity: Gorgias was said by Quintilian to have been unrestrained (*immodicus*) in the matter of word-play (Quint. *Inst.* 9.3.74), and he even gave his name to a feeble kind of pun (Syn. *Ep.* 83 and 134).[101] Isocrates, himself a student of Gorgias (Cic. *Orat.* 52.176), put matters very neatly when he said that employing λόγους ἀμφιβόλους (ambiguous words) was shameful in legal contexts, but "when one discourses on the nature of man and of things, is fine and philosophical" (Isoc. 12.240).[102] There are stories that are, however, perhaps fictional[103] concerning the historical Gorgias' reaction to Plato's work. He is said to have remarked, "What fine satire Plato knows how to write!" Gorgias also claimed never to have spoken any of the lines attributed to him by Plato (Ath. 11.505d–e). Whether or not these anecdotes are true, Plato's playfulness with words, his skilful literary parodies, his satire on individuals and certain echoes of Aristophanes in his treatment of political matters have recently won him the title of a "second Plato Comicus".[104] The story of the discovery of a copy of Aristophanes' plays in his bed after his death (Olymp. *Vit. Pl.* 5) suggests that he had learnt the art of political allegory from a good authority, for Aristophanes was in no way inferior to his tragic contemporaries in weaving the politics of the day into his dramas.[105]

---

100. Cf. Ahl, "The Art of Safe Criticism".
101. Cf. Stanford, *Ambiguity in Greek Literature*, 3.
102. Cf. *ibid.*, 13.
103. Cf. Riginos, *Platonica*, no. 37; cf. 17 and 58.
104. Brock, "Plato and Comedy", 50.
105. See my *Pericles on Stage*; *Alcibiades on Stage*.

Epilogue

Even when specific attention was not drawn to the fact, constant use has been made throughout this book of the "wigwam argument", according to which "each pole would fall down by itself, but together the poles stand up, by leaning on each other; they point roughly in the same direction and circumscribe 'truth'".[1] Another guiding principle has been to follow W. S. Heckscher's injunction to disregard what he called "the academic frontier police" and to employ any fact, no matter how small or apparently insignificant, in reconstructing the intellectual framework within which artists and writers of the past may have worked.[2] The working hypothesis, about the essentially Alcibiadean nature of many of the surviving plays of Sophocles seems to hold good, and to be supported by Euripides' even subtler approach, as well as by the ingenious allusions that Thucydides and Plato make to Athens' most notorious son.

Many problems with which criticism has been beset have vanished: whether the problems arising from Antigone's quirky speech at *Antigone* 904–20 to which Goethe took exception, or the problematic First Stasimon in the same play (332–75); the apparent inconsistencies in the plotting of *Oedipus Tyrannus* that so disturbed Voltaire and misled Freud's acolytes; the problem of Ajax's madness and mutability, or his impiety and untruthfulness; the problem of Odysseus' needless advertisement of his own amorality in *Philoctetes*, or that of Philoctetes' puzzling submission to Heracles' will; the problem of Oedipus' venomous rejection of his son Polyneices, or the reason for the Eleusinian allusions in *Oedipus at Colonus*, to name but a few.

---

1. Hopkins, *Conquerors and Slaves*, 19.
2. "'Il faut penser à côté' he maintains: rectilinear thinking is inimical to creativity. The straight path, the well-charted route taken by the specialist, leads inevitably to a trivial end ... Disconnected observations – *petites perceptions* – arising from a patiently tended reserve of knowledge, will in time resolve themselves into a mosaic which makes sense" (E. Sears, "The Life and Work of William S. Heckscher", *Zeitschrift für Kunstgeschichte* **53** (1990), 107–33, esp. 107).

Together, the substantial poles that result from this work suggest that Sophocles and Euripides created not another wigwam, but a soaring cathedral of literary achievement, now infinitely richer for having its lost historical aspect restored.[3] The poetry is still magnificent, and the drama still powerful, but now that we can safely go "outside the play", the dramatic works discussed in these pages can be seen against the background of the day-to-day events of the second half of the fifth century, and when viewed in context they make a good deal more sense.

---

3. There is much more on Euripides in my *Alcibiades on Stage*.

Bibliography

Adam, J. 1963. *The Republic of Plato*, 2nd edn. Cambridge: Cambridge University Press.

Adcock, F. E. 1963. *Thucydides and His History*. Cambridge: Cambridge University Press.

Adeleye, G. 1974. "Critias: Member of the Four Hundred?" *Transactions of the American Philological Association* **104**: 1–9.

Ahl, F. 1984. "The Art of Safe Criticism in Greece and Rome". *American Journal of Philology* **105**: 174–208.

Ahl, F. 1985. *Metaformations: Soundplay and Wordplay in Ovid and Other Classical Poets*. Ithaca, NY: Cornell University Press.

Ahl, F. 1991. *Sophocles' Oedipus: Evidence and Self-Conviction*. Ithaca, NY: Cornell University Press.

Ahl, F. 2008. *Two Faces of Oedipus: Sophocles'* Oedipus Tyrannus *and Seneca's* Oedipus. Ithaca, NY: Cornell University Press.

Albini, U. (ed.) 1968. *[Erode Attico] Peri Politeias*. Florence: Le Monnier.

Alt, K. 1961. "Schicksal und φύσις in Sophokles' Philoktet". *Hermes* **89**: 141–79.

Altmeyer, M. 2001. *Unzeitgemässes Denken bei Sophokles*. Stuttgart: Franz Steiner.

Amit, M. 1968. "The Melian Dialogue and History". *Athenaeum* **46**: 216–35.

Amit, M. 1974. "A Peace Treaty Between Sparta and Persia". *Rivista storica dell' antichità* **4**: 55–63.

Anderson, G. 1986. *Philostratus*. London: Croom Helm.

Apelt, O. 1912. *Platonische Aufsätze*. Leipzig: B. G. Teubner.

Apelt, O. 1922. *Platon Gorgias*. Leipzig: Felix Meiner.

Appel, W. (ed.) 1999. *Origine Cujavus. Beiträge zur Tagung anläßlich des 150. Geburtstags Ulrich von Wilamowitz-Moellendorffs (1848–1931)*. Toruń: Wydawnictwo Uniwersytetu Mikołaja Kopernika.

Aurenche, O. 1974. *Les Groupes d'Alcibiade, de Léogoras et de Teucros: remarques sur la vie politique athénienne en 415 avant J.C.* Paris: Belles Lettres.

Avery, H. C. 1963. "Critias and the Four Hundred". *Classical Philology* **58**: 166–7.

Badian, E. 1971. "Archons and *strategoi*". *Antichthon* **5**: 1–34.

Badian, E. 1992. "Thucydides on Rendering Speeches". *Athenaeum* **80**: 187–90.

Badian, E. 1993. *From Plataea to Potidaea: Studies in the History and Historiography of the Pentecontaetia*. Baltimore, MD: Johns Hopkins University Press.

Bicknell, P. J. 1989. "Themistokles, Phrynichos, Aischylos, Ephialtes and Perikles: Political Dimensions of Attic Tragedy". *Ancient History: Resources for Teachers* **19**: 120–30.

Bishop, S. 2004. "An American Antigone: Seamus Heaney's Version of Antigone". *Harvard Book Review* **6**(1) (Winter). www.hcs.harvard.edu/~hbr/issues/winter04/articles/heaney.shtml (accessed Mar. 2008).

Blanckenhagen, P. von 1992. "Stage and Actors in Plato's *Symposium*". *Greek, Roman and Byzantine Studies* **33**: 51–68.

179

Blaydes, F. H. M. 1886. *Aristophanis Plutus*. Halle: Orphanotrophei Libraria.

Bleckmann, B. 1998. *Athens Weg in die Niederlage: Die letzten Jahre des Peloponnesischen Krieges*. Beiträge zur Altertumskunde 99. Stuttgart: B. G. Teubner.

Bloedow, E. F. 1972. *Alcibiades Reexamined*. Wiesbaden: Steiner.

Bloedow, E. F. 1975. "Aspasia and the Mystery of the Menexenos". *Wiener Studien* (new series) 9: 32–48.

Bloedow, E. F. 1990. "'Not the Son of Achilles, but Achilles Himself': Alcibiades' Entry on the Political Stage at Athens, 2". *Historia* **39**: 1–19.

Bloedow, E. F. 1991. "Alcibiades, A Review Article". *Ancient History Bulletin* **5**: 17–29.

Bloedow, E. F. 1991. "On Nurturing Lions in the State: Alcibiades' Entry on the Political Stage in Athens". *Klio* **73**: 49–65.

Bloedow, E. F. 1992. "Alcibiades 'Brilliant' or 'Intelligent'?". *Historia* **41**: 139–57.

Blundell, M. W. 1987. "The Moral Character of Odysseus in *Philoctetes*". *Greek, Roman and Byzantine Studies* **28**: 307–49.

Blundell, M. W. 1989. *Helping Friends and Harming Enemies: A Study in Sophocles and Greek Ethics*. Cambridge: Cambridge University Press.

Blundell, M. W. 1993. "The *phusis* of Neoptolemus in Sophocles' *Philoctetes*". In *Greek Tragedy*, I. McAuslan & P. Walcot (eds), 104–15. Oxford: Oxford University Press.

Blundell, M. W. 1993. "The Ideal of Athens in Oedipus at Colonus". In *Tragedy, Comedy and the Polis: Papers from the Greek Drama Conference, Nottingham, 18-20 July 1990*, A. H. Sommerstein, S. Halliwell, J. Henderson & B. Zimmermann (eds), 287–306. Bari: Levante Editori.

Boegehold, A. 1982. "A Dissent at Athens ca. 424–421 BC". *Greek, Roman and Byzantine Studies* **23**: 147–56.

Bowie, A. M. 1997. "Tragic Filters for History: Euripides' *Supplices* and Sophocles' *Philoctetes*". In *Greek Tragedy and the Historian*, C. B. R. Pelling (ed.), 39–61. Oxford: Clarendon Press.

Bowra, C. M. 1944. *Sophoclean Tragedy*. Oxford: Clarendon Press.

Bremmer, J. N. 1999. "Transvestite Dionysus". In *Rites of Passage in Ancient Greece*, M. W. Padilla (ed.), 183–200. Lewisburg, PA: Bucknell University Press.

Briant, P. 1985. "Dons de terres et de villes: l'Asie Mineure dans le contexte achéménide". *Revue des études anciennes* **87**: 53–71.

Briant, P. 1998. "Droaphernès et la statue de Sardes". In *Studies in Persian History: Essays in Memory of David M. Lewis*, M. Brosius & A. Kuhrt (eds), 205–26. Leiden: Nederlands Instituut voor het Nabjie Oosten.

Briant, P. 2002. *From Cyrus to Alexander: A History of the Persian Empire*. Winona Lake, IN: Eisenbrauns.

Briant, P. forthcoming. "Histoire et archéologie d'un texte: la *Lettre de Darius à Gadates* entre Perses, Grecs et Romains". In *Licia e Lidia prima dell'ellenizzazione. Atti del Convegno internazionale, Roma 11–12 ottobre 1999*, M. Gorgieri, M. Salvini, M.-C. Trémouille, P. Vannicelli (eds). Rome: Consiglio Nazionale delle Ricerche (www.achemenet.com/ressources/souspresse [accessed Feb. 2008]).

Broadhead, H. D. (ed.) 1960. *The Persae of Aeschylus*. Cambridge: Cambridge University Press.

Brock, R. 1990. "Plato and Comedy". In *"Owls to Athens": Essays on Classical Subjects Presented to Sir Kenneth Dover*, E. M. Craik (ed.), 39–49. Oxford: Clarendon Press.

Brown, A. (ed.) 1987. *Sophocles: Antigone*. Warminster: Aris & Phillips.

Bruns, I. 1896. *Das literarische Porträt der Griechen im fünften und vierten Jahrhundert vor Christi Geburt*. Berlin: W. Hertz.

Brunt, P. A. 1952. "Thucydides and Alcibiades". *Revue des études grecques* **65**: 59–96.

Bultrighini, U. 1999. *"Maledetta democrazia": studi su Crizia*. Alessandria: Edizioni dell'Orso.

Burkert, W. 1966. "Greek Tragedy and Sacrificial Ritual". *Greek, Roman and Byzantine Studies* **7**: 87–121.

Burton, R. W. B. 1980. *The Chorus in Sophocles' Tragedies*. Oxford: Clarendon Press.

Bury, J. B. 1909. *The Ancient Greek Historians*. London: Macmillan.

Butler, J. 2000. *Antigone's Claim: Kinship between Life and Death*. New York: Columbia University Press.

Buxton, R. G. A. 1984. *Sophocles*. Oxford: Clarendon Press.

Buxton, R. 2003. "Time, Space and Ideology: Tragic Myths and the Athenian Polis". In *Mitos en la literatura griega arcaica y clásica*, J. López Férez (ed.), 175–89. Madrid: Ediciones clásicas SA.

Calder, W. M., III. 1962. "The Staging of the Exodus: *Oedipus Tyrannus* 1515–30". *Classical Philology* 57: 219–29.

Calder, W. M., III. 1968. "Sophokles' Political Tragedy, *Antigone*". *Greek, Roman and Byzantine Studies* 9: 389–407.

Calder, W. M., III. 1971. "Sophoclean Apologia: *Philoctetes*". *Greek, Roman and Byzantine Studies* 12: 153–74.

Calder, W. M., III. 1981. "The Anti-Periklean Intent of Aeschylus' *Eumenides*". In *Aischylos und Pindar: Studien zu Werk und Nachwirkung*, E. G. Schmidt (ed.), 217–23. Berlin: Akademie-Verlag.

Calder, W. M., III. 1985. "The Political and Literary Sources of Sophocles' *Oedipus Coloneus*". In *HYPATIA: Essays in Classics, Comparative Literature, and Philosophy presented to Hazel E. Barnes on her Seventieth Birthday*, W. M. Calder III, U. K. Goldsmith & P. B. Kenevan (eds), 1–14. Boulder, CO: Associated University Press.

Calder, W. M., III. 2005. *Theatrokratia: Collected Papers on the Politics and Staging of Greco-Roman Tragedy*, R. Scott Smith (ed.). Hildesheim: George Olms.

Cameron, A. 1968. *The Identity of Oedipus the King*. New York: New York University Press.

Canfora, L. 1971. "Per una storia del dialogo dei Melii e degli Ateniesi". *Belfagor* 26: 409–26.

Cantarella, R. 1974. "Dioniso, fra *Baccanti* e *Rane*". In *Serta Turyniana*, J. L. Heller (ed.), 291–310. Urbana, IL: University of Illinois Press.

Carey, C. 1986. "The Second Stasimon of Sophocles' *Oedipus Tyrannus*". *Journal of Hellenic Studies* 106: 175–9.

Carnicke, S. M. 1991. *The Theatrical Instinct: Nicolai Evreinov and the Russian Theater of the Early Twentieth Century*. Frankfurt: Lang.

Carter, D. M. 2007. *The Politics of Greek Tragedy*. Bristol: Phoenix.

Carter, L. B. 1986. *The Quiet Athenian*. Oxford: Clarendon Press.

Cartledge, P. A. 1987. *Agesilaos*. London: Duckworth.

Cartledge, P. A. 1990. *Aristophanes and his Theatre of the Absurd*. Bristol: Bristol Classical Press.

Cartledge, P. A. 2003. *The Spartans: The World of the Warrior-heroes of Ancient Greece, from Utopia to Crisis and Collapse*. Woodstock, NY: Overlook.

Cawkwell, G. 1997. *Thucydides and the Peloponnesian War*. London: Routledge.

Centanni, M. 1997. *Atene Assoluta: Crizia dalla Tragedia alla Storia*. Padua: Esedra.

Chroust, A. H. 1957. *Socrates, Man and Myth: The Two Socratic Apologies of Xenophon*. London: Routledge.

Cobetto Ghiggio, P. 1995. *[Andocide] Contro Alcibiade: introduzione, testo critico, traduzione e commento*. Pisa: Edizioni ETS.

Cohen, D. 1991. *Law, Sexuality and Society: The Enforcement of Morals in Classical Athens*. Cambridge: Cambridge University Press.

Collard, C. (ed.) 1975. *Euripides Supplices*. Groningen: Bouma's Boekhuis.

Collard, C. 2004. "Musgrave, Samuel". In *Dictionary of British Classicists*, R. B. Todd (ed.), vol. 2, 694–6. Bristol: Thoemmes Continuum.

Collinge, N. E. 1962. "Medical Terms and Clinical Attitudes in the Tragedians". *Bulletin of the Institute of Classical Studies* 9: 45–53.

Colvin, S. 1999. *Dialect in Aristophanes and the Politics of Language in Ancient Greek Literature*. Oxford: Clarendon Press.

Connor, W. R. 1984. *Thucydides*. Princeton, NJ: Princeton University Press.

Cornford, F. 1907. *Thucydides Mythistoricus*. London: Edward Arnold.

Crane, G. 1990. "Ajax, the Unexpected and the Deception Speech". *Classical Philology* 85: 89–101.

Crews, F. C. 1998. *Unauthorized Freud: Doubters Confront a Legend*. New York: Viking.

Currie, B. 2005. *Pindar and the Cult of Heroes*. Oxford: Oxford University Press.

Daiches, D. 1969. *Some Late Victorian Attitudes*. London: Deutsch.

Dale, A. M. 1956. "Seen and Unseen on the Greek Stage: A Study in Scenic Conventions". *Wiener Studien* **69**: 96–106. Reprinted in his *Collected Papers*, 119–29 (Cambridge: Cambridge University Press, 1969).

Davidson, J. 2001. "Dover, Foucault and Greek Homosexuality: Penetration and the Truth of Sex". *Past and Present* **170**: 3–51.

Davies, J. K. 1971. *Athenian Propertied Families 600–300* BC. Oxford: Clarendon Press.

Dawe, R. D. 1974–78. *Studies on the Text of Sophocles*. Leiden: Brill.

Dawe, R. D. (ed.) 1982. *Sophocles* Oedipus Rex. Cambridge: Cambridge University Press.

Delebecque, E. 1965. *Thucydide et Alcibiade*. Aix-en-Provence: Éditions Ophrys.

Denniston, J. D. 1952. *Greek Prose Style*. Oxford: Clarendon Press.

Denton, M. 2004. Review of *Antigone*, 27 July, www.nytheatre.com/nytheatre/archweb/arch2005_02.htm (accessed Feb. 2008).

Denyer, N. (ed.) 2001. *Plato* Alcibiades. Cambridge: Cambridge University Press.

Develin, R. 1985. "Age Qualifications for Athenian Magistrates". *Zeitschrift für Papyrologie und Epigraphik* **61**: 149–59.

Develin, R. 1989. *Athenian Officials 684–321* BC. Cambridge: Cambridge University Press.

Dodds, E. R. (ed.) 1959. *Plato: Gorgias*. Oxford: Clarendon Press.

Dodds, E. R. (ed.) 1960. *Euripides Bacchae*. Oxford: Clarendon Press.

Dodds, E. R. 1966. "On Misunderstanding the *Oedipus Rex*". *Greece and Rome* **13**: 37–49. Reprinted in his *The Ancient Concept of Progress and other Essays on Greek Literature and Belief*, 64–77 (Oxford: Clarendon Press, 1973) and in *Oxford Readings in Greek Tragedy*, E. Segal (ed.), 177–88 (Oxford: Clarendon Press, 1983).

Donaldson, J. W. 1860. *Theatre of the Greeks*, 7th edn. London: Longman.

Dover, K. J. (ed.) 1968. *Aristophanes Clouds*. Oxford: Clarendon Press.

Dover, K. J. 1978. *Greek Homosexuality*. London: Duckworth.

Duff, T. 2003. "Plutarch on the Childhood of Alkibiades (*Alk.* 2–3)". *Proceedings of the Cambridge Philological Society* **49**: 89–117.

Eagleton, T. 1983. *Literary Theory: An Introduction*. Minneapolis, MN: University of Minnesota Press.

Earle, M. L. 1901. *The Oedipus Tyrannus*. New York: American Book Company.

Easterling, P. E. 1967. "Oedipus and Polyneices". *Proceedings of the Cambridge Philological Society* **13**: 1–13.

Easterling, P. E. 1978. "*Philoctetes* and Modern Criticism". *Illinois Classical Studies* **3**: 27–38. Reprinted in *Oxford Readings in Greek Tragedy*, E. Segal (ed.), 217–28 (Oxford: Oxford University Press, 1983).

Easterling, P. E. 1996. "Tragedy, Greek". In *OCD*[3], 1540–42. Oxford: Clarendon Press.

Easterling, P. E. 2005. "The Image of the *Polis* in Greek Tragedy". In *The Imaginary Polis*, M. H. Hansen (ed.), 49–72. Copenhagen: Royal Danish Academy of Sciences & Letters.

Edmunds, L. 1996. *Theatrical Space and Historical Place in Sophocles' Oedipus at Colonus*. Lanham, MD: Rowman & Littlefield.

Edwards, M. (ed.) 1995. *Greek Orators 4: Andocides*. Warminster: Aris & Phillips.

Ehrenberg, V. 1954. *Sophocles and Pericles*. Oxford: Blackwell.

Ellenberger, H. 1970. *The Discovery of the Unconscious: The History and Evolution of Dynamic Psychiatry*. New York: Basic Books.

Ellis, W. 1989. *Alcibiades*. London: Routledge.

Eucken, C. 1991. "Die thematische Einheit des Sophokleischen Aias". *Würzburger Jahrbücher für die Altertumswissenschaft* (new series) **17**: 119–33.

Finley, J. H. 1942. *Thucydides*. Cambridge, MA: Harvard University Press.

Finley, J. H. 1967. *Three Essays on Thucydides*. Cambridge, MA: Harvard University Press.

Finley, M. 1981. *The Legacy of Greece: A New Appraisal*. Oxford: Clarendon Press.

Fisher, N. R. E. 1992. *Hybris: A Study in the Values of Honour and Shame in Ancient Greece*. Warminster: Aris & Phillips.

Fisher, N. R. E. 1993. "Multiple Personalities and Dionysiac Festivals: Dicaeopolis in Aristophanes' *Acharnians*". *Greece and Rome* **40**: 31–47.

Foley, H. P. 1996. "Antigone as Moral Agent". In *Tragedy and the Tragic: Greek Theatre and Beyond*, M. S. Silk (ed.), 49–73. Oxford: Clarendon Press.

Forde, S. 1989. *The Ambition to Rule: Alcibiades and the Politics of Imperialism in Thucydides*. Ithaca, NY: Cornell University Press.

Foucart, P. 1893. "Le Poète Sophocle et l'oligarchie des Quatre Cents". *Revue Philologique* **17**: 1–10.

Francis, E. D. 1980. "Greeks and Persians: The Art of Hazard and Triumph". In *Ancient Persia, the Art of an Empire*, D. Schmandt-Besserat (ed.), 53–86. Malibu, CA: Undena Publications.

Francis, E. D. 1991–3. "Brachylogia Laconica: Spartan Speeches in Thucydides". *Bulletin of the Institute of Classical Studies* **38**: 198–212.

Francis, E. D. 1992. "Oedipus Achaemenides". *American Journal of Philology* **113**: 333–57.

Francis, E. D. & M. Vickers 1981. "Leagros kalos". *Proceedings of the Cambridge Philological Society* n.s. **27**: 97–136.

Frey, K. 1878. "Der Protagonist in der Antigone des Sophokles". *Neue Jahrbücher* 1, **117**: 460–64.

Friis Johansen, H. 1962. "Sophocles 1939–1959". *Lustrum* 7: 94–288.

Fritz, K. von 1967. *Die griechische Geschichtsschreibung*. Berlin: de Gruyter.

Furley, W. D. 1989. "Andokides iv ('Against Alkibiades'): Fact or Fiction?". *Hermes* **117**: 138–56.

Furley, W. D. 1996. *Andokides and the Herms: A Study of Crisis in Fifth-Century Athenian Religion*. London: Institute of Classical Studies.

Garvie, A. F. 1969. *Aeschylus' Supplices: Play and Trilogy*. Cambridge: Cambridge University Press.

Garvie, A. F. 1972. "Deceit, Violence and Persuasion in the Philoctetes". In *Studi classici in honore di Quintino Cataudella*, 213–32. Catania: Università di Catania, Facoltà di lettere e filosofia.

Garvie, A. F. (ed.) 1998. *Sophocles Ajax*. Warminster: Aris & Phillips.

Gaston Hall, H. 1984. *Comedy in Context: Essays on Molière*. Jackson, MI: University Press of Mississippi.

Gazzano, F. 1999. *Contro Alcibiade*. Genova: Il melangolo.

Gibert, J. C. 1995. *Change of Mind in Greek Tragedy*. Göttingen: Vandenhoek & Ruprecht.

Goldhill, S. 1987. "The Great Dionysia and Civic Ideology". *Journal of Hellenic Studies* **107**: 58–76.

Goldhill, S. 2006. "The Thrill of Misplaced Laughter". In *ΚΩΜΩΙΔΟΤΡΑΓΩΙΔΙΑ: intersezioni del tragico e del comico nel teatro del V secolo a.C.*, E. Medda, M. S. Mirto & M. P. Pattoni (eds), 83–102. Pisa: Edizioni della Normale.

Gomme, A. W. 1938. "Aristophanes and Politics", *Classical Review* **52**: 97–109.

Gomme, A. W., A. Andrewes & K. J. Dover 1948–81. *A Historical Commentary on Thucydides*. Oxford: Clarendon Press.

Grégoire, H. & P. Orgels 1953. "L'*Ajax* de Sophocle, Alcibiades et Sparte". *Annuaire de l'Institut de Philologie et d'histoire orientales et slaves* **13**: 653–63.

Grégoire, H. 1955. "La Date de l'*Ajax* de Sophocle". *Academie Royale de Belgique, Bulletin de la Classe des Lettres* **41**: 187–98.

Gribble, D. 1997. "Rhetoric and History in [Andocides]-4, 'Against Alcibiades'". *Classical Quarterly* **47**: 367–91.

Gribble, D. 1999. *Alcibiades and Athens: A Study in Literary Presentation*. Oxford: Clarendon Press.

Griffin, J. 1999. "Sophocles and the Democratic City". In *Sophocles Revisited: Essays Presented to Sir Hugh Lloyd-Jones*, J. Griffin (ed.), 73–108. Oxford: Oxford University Press.

Griffith, M. (ed.) 1999. *Sophocles Antigone*. Cambridge: Cambridge University Press.

Grote, G. 1870. *A History of Greece*, new edn. London: John Murray.

Grunbaum, A. 1984. *The Foundations of Psychoanalysis: A Philosophical Critique*. Berkeley, CA: University of California Press.

Gurchiani, K. (forthcoming). "Sophocles on the Georgian Stage". In *Proceedings of the 1st International*

Symposium "The Theatre and Theatrical Studies at the Beginning of the Twenty-first Century", Athens 2005.

Guthrie, W. K. C. 1969. *A History of Greek Philosophy*. Cambridge: Cambridge University Press.

Halliwell, S. 1986. "Where Three Roads Meet: A Neglected Detail in the *Oedipus Tyrannus*". *Journal of Hellenic Studies* **106**: 187–90.

Handley, E. W. 1993. "Aristophanes and the Generation Gap". In *Tragedy, Comedy and the Polis: Papers from the Greek Drama Conference, Nottingham 18–20 July 1990*, A. H. Sommerstein *et al.* (eds), 417–30. Bari: Levante editori.

Harsh, P. W. 1960. "The Role of the Bow in the Philoctetes of Sophocles". *American Journal of Philology* **81**: 408–14.

Hatzfeld, J. 1951. *Alcibiade: étude sur l'histoire d'Athènes à la fin du Ve siècle*, 2nd edn. Paris: Presses Universitaires de France.

Havelock, E. A. 1957. *The Liberal Temper in Greek Politics*. New Haven, CT: Yale University Press.

Heath, M. 1987. *The Poetics of Greek Tragedy*. Palo Alto, CA: Stanford University Press.

Heath, M. 1999. "Sophocles' *Philoctetes*: A Problem Play?". In *Sophocles Revisited: Essays Presented to Sir Hugh Lloyd-Jones*, J. Griffin (ed.), 137–60. Oxford: Oxford University Press.

Heftner, H. 1995. "Ps.-Andokides' Rede gegen Alkibiades ([And.] 4) und die politische Diskussion nach dem Sturz der 'Dreissig' in Athen". *Klio* **77**: 75–104.

Heftner, H. 2001. "Die pseudo-andokideische Rede 'Gegen Alkibiades' ([And.] 4) – ein authentischer Beitrag zu einer Ostrakophoriedebatte des Jahres 415 v. Chr.?". *Philologus* **145**: 39–56.

Heinimann, F. 1945. *Nomos und Physis: Herkunft und Bedeutung einer Antithese im griechischen Denken des 5. Jahrhunderts*. Basle: F. Reinhardt.

Henderson, J. (ed.) 1987. *Aristophanes Lysistrata*. Oxford: Clarendon Press.

Henderson, J. 1993. "Problems in Greek Literary History: The Case of Aristophanes *Clouds*". In *Nomodeiktes: Greek Studies in Honor of Martin Ostwald*, R. Rosen & J. Farrell (eds), 591–601. Ann Arbor, MI: University of Michigan Press.

Henderson, J. 2007. "Drama and Democracy". In *The Age of Pericles*, L. J. Salamons II (ed.), 179–95. Cambridge: Cambridge University Press.

Henry, A. S. 1974. "Bios in Sophocles' *Philoctetes*". *Classical Review* (new series) **24**: 3–4.

Henry, M. M. 1995. *Prisoner of History: Aspasia of Miletus and her Biographical Tradition*. Oxford: Oxford University Press.

Hertzberg, G. F. 1853. *Alkibiades: Der Staatsmann und Feldherr*. Halle: C. E. M. Pfeffer.

Hesk, J. 2003. *Sophocles Ajax*. London: Duckworth.

Hester, D. A. 1971. "Sophocles the Unphilosophical". *Mnemosyne* **24**: 11–59.

Hignett, C. 1952. *A History of the Athenian Constitution to the End of the Fifth Century* BC. Oxford: Clarendon Press.

Hopkins, K. 1978. *Conquerors and Slaves: Sociological Studies in Ancient History*. Cambridge: Cambridge University Press.

Hopkins, K. 1993. "Novel Evidence for Roman Slavery". *Past and Present* **138**: 3–27.

Hornblower, S. 1987. *Thucydides*. London: Duckworth.

Hornblower, S. 1991. *A Commentary on Thucydides* 1. Oxford: Clarendon Press.

Hubbard, T. K. 2003. *Homosexuality in Greece and Rome: A Sourcebook of Basic Documents*. Berkeley, CA: University of California Press.

Hunter, V. 1990. "Gossip and the Politics of Reputation in Classical Athens". *Phoenix* **44**: 299–325.

Hunter, R. 2004. *Plato's Symposium*. Oxford: Oxford University Press.

Iannucci, A. 2002. *La parola e l'azione: i frammenti simposiali di Crizia*. Bologna: Edizioni Nautilus.

Jacob, A. L. W. 1821. *Sophocleae quaestiones; praemittuntur disputationes de tragoediae origine et De tragicorum cum republica necessitudine*. Warsaw.

Jameson, M. H. 1956. "Politics and the Philoctetes". *Classical Philology* **51**: 217–27.

Jameson, M. H. 1971. "Sophocles and the Four Hundred". *Historia* **20**: 541–68.

Jebb, R. C. (ed.) 1898. *Sophocles, the Plays and Fragments 4: The Philoctetes*. Cambridge: Cambridge University Press.

Jebb, R. C. (ed.) 1900. *Sophocles, the Plays and Fragments 2: Oedipus Coloneus.* Cambridge: Cambridge University Press.

Kagan, D. 1990. *Pericles of Athens and the Birth of Democracy.* London: Secker & Warburg.

Kennedy, R. F. 2003. "Athena/Athens on Stage: Athena in the Tragedies of Aeschylus and Sophocles". PhD dissertation, Department of Classics, Ohio State University.

Kiberd, D. 1995. *Inventing Ireland.* London: Cape.

Kirk, G., J. E. Raven & M. Schofield. 1983. *The Presocratic Philosophers: A Critical History with a Selection of Texts,* 2nd edn. Cambridge: Cambridge University Press.

Kirkwood, G. M. 1965. "Homer and Sophocles' Ajax". In *Classical Drama and its Influence; Essays Presented to H. D. F. Kitto,* M. J. Anderson (ed.), 51–70. London: Methuen.

Knox, B. M. W. 1956. "The Date of the *Oedipus Tyrannus* of Sophocles". *American Journal of Philology* 77: 133–47.

Knox, B. M. W. 1957. *Oedipus at Thebes: Sophocles' Tragic Hero and his Time.* New Haven, CT: Yale University Press.

Knox, B. M. W. 1964. *The Heroic Temper: Studies in Sophoclean Tragedy.* Berkeley, CA: University of California Press.

Knox, B. M. W. 1979. *Word and Action: Essays on the Ancient Theater.* Baltimore, MD: Johns Hopkins University Press.

Knox, B. M. W. 1983. "Sophocles and the *Polis*". In *Sophocle,* J. de Romilly (ed.), 1–37. Geneva: Fondation Hardt.

Konstan, D. 2001. "Introduction". In *Euripides Cyclops,* H. McHugh (trans.). Oxford: Oxford University Press.

Kriegbaum, S. 1913. *Der Ursprung der von Kallikles in Platons Gorgias vertretenen Anschauungen.* Paderborn: F. Schöningh.

Landucci Gattinoni, F. 1997. *Duride di Samo.* Rome: 'L'Erma' di Bretschneider.

Lattimore, R. 1958. *The Poetry of Greek Tragedy.* Baltimore, MD: Johns Hopkins University Press.

Lear, J. 1995. "A Counterblast in the War on Freud: The Shrink is In". *New Republic* (25 December): 18–25.

Lebeau le cadet, M. 1770. "Mémoires sur les tragiques grecs". *Mémoires de littérature; tirés des registres de l'Académie des Inscriptions* 35: 432–74.

Lefèvre, E. 2001. *Die Unfähigkeit, sich zu erkennen: Sophokles' Tragödien.* Leiden: Brill.

Lenormant, C. 1855. "Du Philoctète de Sophocle: á propos de la représentation de cette tragédie à Orléans". *Le Correspondant* (25 July): 6.

Leonard, M. 2003. "Antigone, the Political and the Ethics of Psychoanalysis". *Proceedings of the Cambridge Philological Society* 49: 130–54.

Levi, M. A. 1967. *Quattro studi spartani e altri scritti di storia greca.* Milan: Istituto Editoriale Cisalpino.

Lewis, D. M. 1966. "After the Profanation of the Mysteries". In *Ancient History and its Institutions: Studies Presented to Victor Ehrenberg on his 75th birthday,* 177–91. Oxford: Blackwell.

Lewis, D. M. 1977. *Sparta and Persia.* Leiden: Brill.

Lewis, R. G. 1988. "An Alternative Date for *Antigone*". *Greek, Roman and Byzantine Studies* 29: 35–50.

Lintott, A. 1982. *Violence, Civil Strife and Revolution in the Classical City, 750–330 BC.* London: Croom Helm.

Lippold, A. 1965. "Pausanias von Sparta und die Perser". *Rheinisches Museum* (new series) 108: 320–41.

Littmann R. J. 1970. "The Loves of Alcibiades". *Transactions of the American Philological Association* 101: 263–76.

Lloyd-Jones, H. 1957. "Notes on Sophocles' *Antigone*". *Classical Quarterly* 7: 12–27.

Lloyd-Jones, H. 1971. *The Justice of Zeus,* 2nd edn. Los Angeles, CA: University of California Press.

Lloyd-Jones, H. (ed.) 1994. *Sophocles: Ajax, Electra, Oedipus Tyrannus.* Cambridge, MA: Harvard University Press.

Long, A. A. 1968. *Language and Thought in Sophocles: A Study of Abstract Nouns and Poetic Technique*. London: Athlone.

Loraux, N. 1981. *L'Invention d'Athènes: histoire de l'oraison funèbre dans la "cité classique"*. Paris: Mouton.

Luschnat, O. 1971. *Thukydides der Historiker*. Stuttgart: J. B. Metzler.

MacDowell, D. M. 1962. *On the Mysteries*. Oxford: Clarendon Press.

Mackenzie, C. 1937. *Pericles*. London: Hodder & Stoughton.

Macleod, C. W. 1974. "Form and Meaning in the Melian Dialogue". *Historia* **23**: 385–400.

Macleod, C. W. 1983. *Collected Essays*. Oxford: Clarendon Press.

Macmillan, M. B. 1991. *Freud Evaluated: The Completed Arc*. Amsterdam: North Holland.

MacNeice, L. 1967. *The Poetry of W. B. Yeats*. London: Faber & Faber.

Macurdy, G. H. 1942. "References to Thucydides, Son of Milesias, and to Pericles in Sophocles *OT* 863–910". *Classical Philology* **37**: 307–10.

Mader, G. 1993. "Rogues' Comedy at Segesta (Thukydides 6.46): Alcibiades Exposed?". *Hermes* **121**: 181–95.

Maehly, H. 1853. "De Aspasia Milesia". *Philologus* **9**: 213–30.

Maidment, K. J. (ed.) 1941. *Minor Attic Orators* 1. London: Heinemann.

Marcus, S. 1966. *The Other Victorians*. London: Weidenfeld & Nicolson.

Markantonatos, A. 2002. *Tragic Narrative: A Narratological Study of Sophocles' Oedipus at Colonus*. Berlin: de Gruyter.

Markantonatos, A. 2007. *Oedipus at Colonus: Sophocles, Athens, and the World*. Berlin: de Gruyter.

Marshall, M. 1990. "Pericles and the Plague". In *"Owls to Athens": Essays on Classical Subjects Presented to Sir Kenneth Dover*, E. M. Craik (ed.), 163–70. Oxford: Clarendon Press.

Maurer, K. 1995. *Interpolation in Thucydides*. Leiden: Brill.

Meiggs, R. 1972. *The Athenian Empire*. Oxford: Clarendon Press.

Meiggs, R. & D. Lewis 1988. *A Selection of Greek Historical Inscriptions to the End of the Fifth Century BC*, rev. edn. Oxford: Clarendon Press.

Meier, H. 1913. *Sokrates, sein Werk und sein geschichtliche Stellung*. Tübingen: J. C. B. Mohr.

Meir, C. 1996. "Classical and Political Analogues in Heaney's *The Cure at Troy*". In *The Classical World and the Mediterranean*, G. Serpillo & D. Badin (eds), 256–60. Cagliari: Tema.

Milio, V. 1928–9. "Per la cronologia dell' Edipo Re". *Bolletino di Filologia Classica* **35**: 203–5.

Miller, P. A. 2007. "Lacan's Antigone: The Sublime Object and the Ethics of Interpretation". *Phoenix* **61**: 1–14.

Mills, S. 1997. *Theseus, Tragedy, and the Athenian Empire*. Oxford: Clarendon Press.

Missiou, A. 1992. *The Subversive Oratory of Andokides: Politics, Ideology and Decision-making in Democratic Athens*. Cambridge: Cambridge University Press.

Missiou, A. 1993. "ΔΟΥΛΟΣ ΤΟΥ ΒΑΣΙΛΕΩΣ: The Politics of Translation." *Classical Quarterly* **43**: 377–91.

Montuori, M. 1974. *Socrate: fisiologia di un mito*. Florence: G.C. Sansoni.

Moore, J. 1977. "The Dissembling Speech of Ajax". *Yale Classical Studies* **25**: 47–66.

Moorton, R. F. 1988. "Aristophanes on Alcibiades". *Greek, Roman and Byzantine Studies* **29**: 345–59.

Morrison, B. 2003. "Femme Fatale". *Guardian* (4 October), http://arts.guardian.co.uk/features/story/0,11710,1055507,00.html (accessed Mar. 2008).

Morrison, J. S. 1941. "Protagoras in Athenian Public Life". *Classical Quarterly* **35**: 1–16.

Müller, G. (ed.) 1967. *Sophokles, Antigone*. Heidelberg: Winter.

Münsterberg, R. 1902. "Zum Renstallprozess des Alkibiades (Isokrates περὶ τοῦ ζεύγους)". In *Festschrift Theodor Gomperz dargebracht zum siebzigsten Geburtstage am 29 März 1902 von Schülern, Freunden, Collegen*, 298–9. Vienna: Alfred Hölder.

Munn, M. 2000. *The School of History: Athens in the Age of Socrates*. Berkeley, CA: University of California Press.

Murray, G. 1933. *Aristophanes, a Study*. Oxford: Clarendon Press.

Musgrave, S. (ed.) 1800. *Sophoclis tragoediae septem*. Oxford: Clarendon Press.

Nesselrath, H.-G. 2000. "Eupolis and the Periodization of Athenian Comedy". In *The Rival of Aristophanes: Studies in Athenian Old Comedy*, D. Harvey & J. Wilkins (eds), 233–46. London: Duckworth and the Classical Press of Wales.

North, H. 1966. *Sophrosyne*. Ithaca, NY: Cornell University Press.

Norwood, G. 1931. *Greek Comedy*. London: Methuen.

Ober, J. 1989. *Mass and Elite in Democratic Athens*. Princeton, NJ: Princeton University Press.

Okell, E. 2002. "Does Themistocles 'Hero of Salamis' Lie behind Sophocles' *Ajax*?". Paper delivered to the joint Classical Association and Classical Association of Scotland conference, 4–7 April, University of Edinburgh.

O'Neill, Y. V. 1980. *Speech and Speech Disorders in Western Thought before 1600*. Westport, CT: Greenwood.

Osborne, R. 1985. "The Erection and Mutilation of the Hermai". *Proceedings of the Cambridge Philological Society* **211**: 47–73.

Ostwald, M. 1958. "Aristotle on Hamartia and Sophocles' Oedipus Tyrannus". In *Festschrift Ernst Kapp zum 70. Geburtstag am 21. Januar 1958 von Freunden und Schülern überreicht*, 93–108. Hamburg: M. von Schröder.

Ostwald, M. 1986. *From Popular Sovereignty to the Sovereignty of Law: Law, Society and Politics in Fifth-Century Athens*. Berkeley, CA: University of California Press.

Ostwald, M. 1988. *ANAΓKH in Thucydides*. Atlanta, GA: Scholars Press.

Ostwald, M. 1990. "On Interpreting Sophocles' *Oedipus Tyrannus*". In *The Verbal and the Visual: Essays in Honor of William S. Heckscher*, K.-L. Selig & E. Sears (eds), 133–49. New York: Italica Press.

Otto, R. & P. Wersig. 1982. *Gespräche mit Goethe in den letzten Jahren seines Lebens/Johann Peter Eckermann*. Berlin: Aufbau-Verlag.

Parry, M. 1930. "Studies in the Epic Technique of Oral Verse-Making, I: Homer and Homeric Style". *Harvard Studies in Classical Philology* **41**: 73–147. Reprinted in *The Making of Homeric Verse: The Collected Papers of Milman Parry*, A. Parry (ed.), 266–324 (Oxford: Clarendon Press, 1971).

Patin, H. 1913. *Études sur les tragiques grecs: Sophocle*, 9th edn. Paris: Hachette.

Patterson, C. 1993. "'Here the Lion Smiled': A Note on Thuc. 1.127–38". See Rosen & Farrell (1993), 145–52.

Pavese, C. 1987. "The New Heracles Poem of Pindar". *Harvard Studies in Classical Philology* **72**: 45–88.

Pelling, C. B. R. 1992. "Plutarch and Thucydides". In *Plutarch and the Historical Tradition*, P. A. Stadter (ed.), 10–40. London: Routledge.

Pelling, C. B. R. (ed.) 1997. *Greek Tragedy and the Historian*. Oxford: Clarendon Press.

Pelling, C. B. R. 2002. *Plutarch and History: Eighteen Studies*. London: Duckworth.

Perrin, B. 1906. "The Death of Alcibiades". *Transactions of the American Philological Association* **37**: 25–37.

Petit, T, 1997. "Alcibiade et Tissapherne". *Les Études Classiques* **65**: 137–51.

Petit, T. 2004. "Xenophon et la vassalité achéménide". In *Xenophon and his World; Papers from a Conference held in Liverpool in July 1999*, C. J. Tuplin (ed.), 175–99. Stuttgart: Franz Steiner.

Piazza, S. 1896. *La politica in Sofocle*. Padua: Tipografia del Seminario.

Podlecki, A. J. 1966. *The Political Background of Aeschylean Tragedy*. Ann Arbor, MI: University of Michigan Press.

Podlecki, A. J. 1975. *The Life of Themistocles: A Critical Survey of the Literary and Archaeological Evidence*. Montreal: McGill-Queen's University Press.

Podlecki, A. J. 1998. *Perikles and his Circle*. London: Routledge.

Pohlenz, M. 1930. *Die griechische Tragödie*. Leipzig: B. G. Teubner.

Pollitt, J. J. 1972. *Art and Experience in Classical Greece*. Cambridge: Cambridge University Press.

Pope, M. 1991. "Addressing Oedipus". *Greece and Rome* **38**: 156–70.

Prandi, L. 1992. "Introduzione". In Plutarch, *Vite parallele, Coriolano/Alcibiade*, 255–317. Milan: Biblioteca Universale Rizzoli.

Pritchett, W. K. 1953. "The Attic Stelai". *Hesperia* **22**: 225–99.

Pritchett, W. K. 1956. "Attic Stelai, Part II". *Hesperia* 25: 167–210.

Pritchett, W. K. 1961. "Five New Fragments of the Attic Stelai". *Hesperia* 30: 23–9.

Raaflaub, K. 1987. "Herodotus, Political Thought, and the Meaning of History". *Arethusa* 20: 221–48.

Radermacher, L. 1951. *Artium Scriptores (Reste der voraristotelische Rhetorik)*. Sitzungsberichte der Akademie der Wissenschaften in Wien, Philosophisch-Historische Klasse 227/3.

Raubitschek, A. E. 1939. "Leagros", *Hesperia* 8: 155–64.

Raubitschek, A. E. 1948. "The Case against Alcibiades (Andocides IV)". *Transactions of the American Philological Society* 79: 191–210. Reprinted in *The School of Hellas: Essays on Greek History, Archaeology, and Literature*, D. Obbink & P. A. Vander Waerdt (eds), 116–31 (New York: Oxford University Press, 1991).

Rawlings, H. R. 1981. *The Structure of Thucydides's History*. Princeton, NJ: Princeton University Press.

Reinhardt, K. 1947. *Sophokles*. Frankfurt: V. Klostermann.

Reinhardt, K. 1979. *Sophocles*. Oxford: Blackwell.

Rhodes, P. J. 1981. *A Commentary on the Aristotelian* Athenaion Politeia. Oxford: Clarendon Press.

Rhodes, P. J. 1985. "What Alcibiades Did or What Happened to Him". Inaugural lecture, University of Durham.

Richardson, N. J. 1974. *The Homeric Hymn to Demeter*. Oxford: Clarendon Press.

Richter, G. M. A. 1965. *Portraits of the Greeks*. London: Phaidon.

Riginos, A. 1976. *Platonica: The Anecdotes Concerning the Life and Writings of Plato*. Leiden: Brill.

Ritter, F. 1861. "Sieben unechten Schlussstellen in den Tragödien des Sophokles". *Philologus* 17: 422–36.

Roaf, M. 1983. "Sculpture and Sculptors at Persepolis". *Iran* 21: 1–164.

Robert, L. 1980. *À travers l'Asie Mineur: poètes et prosateurs, monnaies grecques, voyageurs et géographie*. Athens/Paris: École française d'Athènes/de Boccard.

Robinson, D. 1969. "Topics in Sophocles' Philoctetes". *Classical Quarterly* (new series) 19: 34–56.

Rodríguez Blanco, M. E. 1988. *Alcibíades: Antología de textos con notas y comentarios*. Madrid: *Ediciones de la Universidad Autónoma*.

Roisman, H. M. 1997. "The Appropriation of a Son: Sophocles' *Philoctetes*". *Greek, Roman and Byzantine Studies* 38: 127–71.

Romilly, J. de 1963. *Thucydides and Athenian Imperialism*. Oxford: Blackwell.

Romilly, J. de 1993. *Alcibiade, ou, Les dangers de l'ambition*. Paris: Editions de Fallois.

Root, M. C. 1979. *The King and Kingship in Achaemenid Art*. Leiden: Brill.

Rose, H. J. 1957. *A Commentary on the Surviving Plays of Aeschylus*. Verhandelingen der Koninklijke Nederlandse Akademie van Wetenschappen, Afd. Letterkunde 64. Amsterdam.

Rose, P. 1995. "Historicizing Sophocles' *Ajax*". In *History, Tragedy, Theory: Dialogues in Athenian Drama*, B. Goff (ed.), 59–90. Austin, TX: Texas University Press.

Rose, P. W. 1976. "Sophocles' *Philoctetes* and the Teachings of the Sophists". *Harvard Studies in Classical Philology* 80: 49–105.

Rosen, R. & J. Farrell (eds) 1993. *Nomodeiktes: Greek Studies in Honor of Martin Ostwald*. Ann Arbor, MI: University of Michigan Press.

Rosenbloom, D. 2002. "From *Ponéros* to *Pharmakos*: Theatre, Social Drama and Revolution in Athens, 428–404 BCE". *Classical Antiquity* 21(2): 283–346.

Russell, D. A. 1966. "Plutarch, 'Alcibiades' 1–16". *Proceedings of the Cambridge Philological Society* 12: 37–47.

Russell, D. A. 1972. *Plutarch*. London: Duckworth.

Sandys, J. E. (ed.) 1897. *The Bacchae of Euripides with Critical and Explanatory Notes*. Cambridge: Cambridge University Press.

Schadewaldt, W. 1929. *Die Geschichtschreibung des Thukydides: Ein Versuch*. Berlin: Weidmann.

Schaeffer, A. 1949/50. "Alkibiades und Lysander in Ionien". *Würzburger Jahrbücher für die Altertumswissenschaft* 4: 287–308.

Schein, S. L. 1988. "The Chorus in Sophocles' *Philoctetes*". *Studi italiani di filologia classica* **81**: 196–204.

Schmidt, E. F. 1957. *Persepolis*, vol. 2. Chicago, IL: Oriental Institute.

Schöll, A. 1842. *Sophokles, sein Leben und Wirken*. Frankfurt: Hermann.

Schneider, W. J. 1999. "Eine Polemik Polemons in den Propyläen: Ein Votivgemälde des Alkibiades – Kontext und Rezeption". *Klio* **81**: 18–44.

Schouler, A. 1984. *La Tradition hellénique de Libanius*. Lille/Paris: Atelier national reproduction des thèses. Université de Lille III/Belles Lettres.

Schroff, A. 1901. *Zur Echtheitsfrage d. vierten Rede des Andokides*. Inaugural dissertation, University of Erlangen. Erlangen: Hof- und Univ.-Bucherei.

Schwartz, E. 1919. *Das Geschichtswerk des Thukydides*. Bonn: F. Cohen.

Scodel, R. 2003. "The Politics of Sophocles' *Ajax*". *Scripta Classica Israelica* **22**: 31–42.

Seaford, R. A. S. 1982. "The Date of Euripides' Cyclops". *Journal of Hellenic Studies* **102**: 161–72.

Seaford, R. A. S. (ed.) 1984. *Euripides Cyclops*. Oxford: Clarendon Press.

Seaford, R. A. S. 1994. "Sophokles and the Mysteries". *Hermes* **122**: 275–88.

Seager, R. 1967. "Alcibiades and the Charge of Aiming at Tyranny". *Historia* **16**: 6–18.

Seager, R. & C. Tuplin 1980. "The Freedom of the Greeks of Asia: On the Origins of a Concept and the Creation of a Slogan". *Journal of Hellenic Studies* **100**: 141–54.

Sears, E. 1990. "The Life and Work of William S. Heckscher". *Zeitschrift für Kunstgeschichte* **53**: 107–33.

Seidensticker, B. 1978. "Comic Elements in Euripides' *Bacchae*". *American Journal of Philology* **99**: 303–20.

Seidensticker, B. 1982. *Palintonos Harmonia: Studien zu komischen Elementen in der griechischen Tragödie*. Göttingen: Vandenhoeck & Ruprecht.

Sheard, W. S. 1979. "Antique Subjects and their Transformations". In her *Antiquity in the Renaissance*. Northampton, MA: Smith College.

Sheffield, F. C. C. 2001. "Alcibiades' Speech: A Satyric Drama". *Greece and Rome* **48**: 193–209.

Sicherl, M. 1977. "The Tragic Issue in Sophocles' *Ajax*". *Yale Classical Studies* **25**: 67–98.

Siewert, P. 1977. "The Ephebic Oath in Fifth-Century Athens". *Journal of Hellenic Studies* **97**: 102–11.

Siewert, P. 1979. "Poseidon Hippios am Kolonos und die athenischen Hippeis". In *Arktouros: Hellenic Studies Presented to Bernard M. W. Knox on the Occasion of His Sixty-fifth Birthday*, G. W. Bowersock *et al.* (eds), 280–89. Berlin: de Gruyter.

Sifakis, G. M. 1995. "The One-actor Rule in Greek Tragedy". In *Stage Directions: Essays in Ancient Drama in Honour of E. W. Handley*, A. Griffiths (ed.), 13–24. London: Institute of Classical Studies.

Smereka, J. 1936. *Studia Euripidea: De Sermone. De Vocabulorum copia. De Elocutionis consuetudinibus. De Genere dicendi sive "Stilo"*. Lwow: Sumptibus Societatis Litterarum.

Smith, R. R. R. 1990. "Late Roman Philosopher Portraits from Aphrodisias". *Journal of Roman Studies* **80**: 127–55.

Sommerstein, A. H. (ed.) 1981. *The Comedies of Aristophanes 2: Knights*. Warminster: Aris & Phillips.

Sourvinou-Inwood, C. 1989. "Assumptions and the Creation of Meaning: Reading Sophocles' *Antigone*". *Journal of Hellenic Studies* **109**: 134–48.

Spacks, P. M. 1985. *Gossip*. Chicago, IL: University of Chicago Press.

Spathari, E. 1992. *The Olympic Spirit*. Athens: Adam Publications.

Spielvogel, J. 2003. "Die politische Position des athenischen Komödiendichters Aristophanes". *Historia* **52**: 1–22.

Stadter, P. A. 1989. *A Commentary on Plutarch's Pericles*. Chapel Hill, NC: University of North Carolina Press.

Stahl, H.-P. 1966. *Thukydides: Die Stellung des Menschen im geschichtlichen Prozess*. Munich: Beck.

Stallbaum, G. 1861. *Platonis Gorgias*, 3rd edn. Göttingen: Hennings.

Stanford, W. B. 1939. *Ambiguity in Greek Literature*. Oxford: Blackwell.

Stanford, W. B. (ed.) 1963. *Sophocles* Ajax. London: Macmillan.

Stanford, W. B. 1967. *The Sound of Greek: Studies in the Greek Theory and Practice of Euphony*. Berkeley, CA: University of California Press.

Stanford, W. B. (ed.) 1973. *Aristophanes Frogs*, 2nd edn. London: Macmillan.

de Ste. Croix, G. 1972. *The Origins of the Peloponnesian War*. London: Duckworth.

Steiner, G. 1961, 1995. *The Death of Tragedy*. London: Faber & Faber.

Steiner, G. 1984. *Antigones*. Oxford: Clarendon Press.

Stinton, T. C. W. 1975. "Hamartia in Aristotle and Greek Tragedy". *Classical Quarterly* **25**: 237–46.

Stoneman, R. 2008. *Alexander the Great: A Life in Legend*. London: Yale University Press.

Strauss, B. S. 1990. "*Oikos/Polis*: Towards a Theory of Athenian Paternal Ideology 450–399 BC". *Classica et Mediaevalia* **40**: 101–27.

Strauss, B. S. 1993. *Fathers and Sons in Athens: Ideology and Society in the Era of the Peloponnesian War*. Princeton: NJ: Princeton University Press.

Stupperich, R. 1982. "Das Statuenprogramm in den Zeuxippos-Thermen". *Istanbuler Mitteilungen* **32**: 210–35.

Sulloway, F. J. 1979. *Freud, Biologist of the Mind: Beyond the Psychoanalytic Legend*. New York: Basic Books.

Sutton, D. F. 1980. *The Greek Satyr Play*. Meisenheim am Glan: Hain

Svenbro, J. 1993. *Phrasikleia: An Anthropology of Reading in Ancient Greece*. Ithaca, NY: Cornell University Press.

Taplin, O. 1978. *Greek Tragedy in Action*. Berkeley, CA: University of California Press.

Taplin, O. 1979. "Yielding to Forethought: Sophocles' Ajax". In *Arktouros: Hellenic Studies, presented to Bernard M. W. Knox on the Occasion of his Sixty-fifth Birthday*, G. W. Bowersock *et al.* (eds), 122–9. Berlin: de Gruyter.

Taplin, O. 1983. "Sophocles in his Theatre". In *Sophocle*, 155–74. Geneva: Fondation Hart.

Taylor, A. E. 1926. *Plato, the Man and his Work*. London: Methuen.

Taylor, C. C. W. 1976. *Plato Protagoras*. Oxford: Clarendon Press.

Thomas, R. 1989. *Oral Tradition and Written Record in Classical Athens*. Cambridge: Cambridge University Press.

Thompson, H. A. T. & R. E. Wycherley. 1972. *The Agora of Athens, The Athenian Agora* 14. Princeton, NJ: Princeton University Press.

Thumb, A. & E. Kieckers 1932. *Handbuch der griechischen Dialekte*, 2nd edn. Heidelberg: C. Winter.

Tompkins, D. P. 1972. "Stylistic Characterization in Thucydides: Nicias and Alcibiades". *Yale Classical Studies* **22**: 181–214.

Tompkins, D. P. 1993. "Archidamus and the Question of Characterization in Thucydides". See Rosen & Farrell (1993), 99–111.

Tuplin, C. 1987. "The Administration of the Achaemenid Empire". In *Coinage and Administration in the Athenian and Persian Empires: The Ninth Oxford Symposium on Coinage and Monetary History*, I. Carradice (ed.), 109–66. Oxford: British Archaeological Reports.

Turolla, E. 1948. *Saggio sulla poesia di Sofocle*. Bari: G. Laterza.

Tyrrell, W. B. & L. J. Bennett, 1998. *Recapturing Sophocles' Antigone*. Lanham, MD: Rowman & Littlefield.

Ugolini, G. 2000. *Sofocle e Atene: Vita politica e attività teatrale nella Grecia classica*. Rome: Carocci.

Untersteiner, M. 1957. *The Sophists*. Oxford: Blackwell.

Ussher, R. G. (ed.) 1978. *Euripides* Cyclops: *Introduction and Commentary*. Rome: Edizioni dell' Ateneo e bizzarri.

Ussher, R. G. (ed.) 1990. *Sophocles Philoctetes*. Warminster: Aris & Phillips.

Vandvik, E. 1942. "Ajax the Insane". *Symbolae Osloenses, Supplement* **11**: 169–75.

Vickers, M. 1987. "Alcibiades on Stage: *Philoctetes* and *Cyclops*". *Historia* **36**: 171–97.

Vickers, M. 1991. "A Contemporary Account of the Athenian Plague? Aristophanes *Clouds* 694–734". *Liverpool Classical Monthly* **16**: 64.

Vickers, M. 1993. "Alcibiades in Cloudedoverland". See Rosen & Farrell (1993), 603–18.

Vickers, M. 1994. "Alcibiades and Critias in the *Gorgias*: Plato's 'Fine Satire'". *Dialogues d'histoire ancienne* **20**: 85–112.

Vickers, M. 1995. "Thucydides 6.53.3–59: not a 'digression'". *Dialogues d'histoire ancienne* **21**: 193–200.

Vickers, M. 1995. "Heracles Lacedaemonius: The Political Dimensions of Sophocles *Trachiniae* and Euripides *Heracles*". *Dialogues d'histoire ancienne* **21**: 41–69.

Vickers, M. 1997. *Pericles on Stage: Political Comedy in Aristophanes' Early Plays*. Austin, TX: University of Texas Press.

Vickers, M. 1999. "Alcibiades and Melos: Thucydides 5.84–116". *Historia* **48**: 265–81.

Vickers, M. 2000. "Alcibiades and Aspasia: Notes on the *Hippolytus*". *Dialogues d'histoire ancienne* **26**: 7–17.

Vickers, M. 2001. "Aristophanes *Frogs*: Nothing to do with Literature". *Athenaeum* **89**: 187–201.

Vickers, M. 2004. "Aspasia on Stage: Aristophanes' *Ecclesiazusae*". *Athenaeum* **92**: 431–50.

Vickers, M. 2005. *Oedipus and Alcibiades in Sophocles*. Toruń: Wydawnictwo Uniwersytetu Mikołaja Kopernika.

Vickers, M. 2005. "Sophocles' *Antigone* in Ancient Greece and Modern Georgia". *Phasis: Greek and Roman Studies* **8**: 134–51.

Vickers, M. 2005–6. "The *Dramatis Personae* of Alma-Tadema's *Phidias* and the *Frieze of the Parthenon, Athens*". *Assaph: Studies in Art History* **10–11**: 235–9.

Vickers, M. 2007. "Art or Kitsch?". *Apollo* (January): 98–9.

Vickers M. 2007. "A Legend of Wild Beauty: Sophocles' *Antigone*". *Classics Ireland* **14**: 44–77.

Vickers, M. in preparation. *Alcibiades on Stage: Political Comedy in Aristophanes*.

Vickers, M. & D. Briggs 2007. "Juvenile Crime, Aggression and Abuse in Classical Antiquity: A Case Study". In *Children and Sexuality: The Greeks to the Great War*, G. Rousseau (ed.), 41–64. Basingstoke: Palgrave Macmillan.

Vickers, M. & D. Gill. 1996. *Artful Crafts: Ancient Greek Silverware and Pottery*, 2nd edn. Oxford: Clarendon Press.

Vidal-Naquet, P. 1972. "Le *Philoctète* de Sophocle et l'Éphébie". In *Mythe et Tragédie en Grèce Ancienne*, J. P. Vernant & P. Vidal-Naquet (eds), 161–84. Paris: F. Maspero.

Visser, T. 1998. *Untersuchungen zum Sophokleischen Philoktet: Das auslösende Ereignis in der Stückgestaltung*. Stuttgart: B. G. Teubner.

Wade-Gery, H. T. 1957. *Essays in Greek History*. Oxford: Blackwell.

Wade-Gery, H. T. 1996. "Thucydides". In *Oxford Classical Dictionary*, 3rd edn, S. Hornblower & A. Spawforth (eds), 1516–19. Oxford: Clarendon Press.

Walbank, M. 1978. *Athenian Proxenies of the Fifth Century BC*. Toronto: Samuel Stevens.

Waldock, A. J. A. 1951. *Sophocles the Dramatist*. Cambridge: Cambridge University Press.

Wallace, R. W. 1985. *The Areopagus Council to 307 BC*. Baltimore, MD: Johns Hopkins University Press.

Wallace, R. W. 1993. "Private Lives and Public Enemies: Freedom of Thought in Classical Athens". In *Athenian Identity and Civic Ideology*, A. Scafuro & A. Boegehold (eds), 127–55. Baltimore, MD: Johns Hopkins University Press.

Webster, R. 1996. *Why Freud was Wrong: Sin, Science and Psychoanalysis*. London: Harper-Collins.

Welcker, F. G. 1829. "Über den Aias des Sophokles". *Rheinisches Museum* **3**: 43–92, 229–364. Reprinted in *Kleine Schriften 2*, 264–340 (Bonn: E. Weber, 1845).

Westlake, H. D. 1938. "Alcibiades, Agis and Spartan Policy". *Journal of Hellenic Studies* **58**: 31–40.

Westlake, H. D. 1968. *Individuals in Thucydides*. Cambridge: Cambridge University Press.

Westlake, H. D. 1980. "The *Lysistrata* and the War". *Phoenix* **34**: 38–54.

Westlake, H. D. 1989. *Studies in Thucydides and Greek History*. Bristol: Bristol Classical Press.

Whitby, M. 1996. "The Origins of Neoptolemus in *Philoctetes*". *Greece and Rome* **43**: 31–42.

Whitman, C. 1951. *Sophocles: A Study of Heroic Humanism*. Cambridge, MA: Harvard University Press.

Wiesehöfer, J. 1980. "Die 'Freunde' und 'Wohltäter' des Grosskönigs". *Studia Iranica* **9**: 7–21.

Wilamowitz-Moellendorff, T. von 1917. *Die dramatische Technik des Sophokles*. Berlin: Weidmannsche Buchhandlung.

Wilamowitz-Moellendorff, U. von 1893. *Aristoteles und Athen* 1. Berlin: Weidmann.

Wilamowitz-Moellendorff, U. von 1897. "Die Xenophontische Apologie". *Hermes* **36**: 99–106.

Wilamowitz-Moellendorff, U. von 1899. "Excurse zum Oedipus des Sophokles". *Hermes* **34**: 55–80.

Wilamowitz-Moellendorff, U. von 1982. *History of Classical Scholarship*. London: Duckworth.

Wilson, P. 2003. "The Sound of Cultural Conflict: Critias and the Culture of *Mousike* in Athens". In *The Cultures within Ancient Greek Culture: Contact, Conflict, Collaboration*, C. Dougherty & L. Kurke (eds), 181–206. Cambridge: Cambridge University Press.

Wilson, P. 2004. Review of Iannucci 2002. *Bryn Mawr Classical Review* (16 September).

Winnington-Ingram, R. P. 1971. "The Second Stasimon of the Oedipus Tyrannus". *Journal of Hellenic Studies* **91**: 124–7.

Wohl, V. 1999. "The Eros of Alcibiades". *Classical Antiquity* **18**: 349–85.

Woodhead, A. G. 1960. "Thucydides' Portrait of Cleon". *Mnemosyne* **13**: 289–317.

Woodhead, A. G. 1970. *Thucydides on the Nature of Power*. Cambridge, MA: Harvard University Press.

Wright, W. C. 1922. *Philostratus and Eunapius: The Lives of the Sophists*. London: Heinemann.

Wunder, E. (ed.) 1831. *Sophoclis Tragoediae*. Göttingen and Erfurt: W. Hennings.

Zierl, A. 1999. "Erkenntnis und Handlung im Oidipus Tyrannos des Sophokles". *Rheinisches Museum* **142**: 127–48.

Zimmermann, B. 2002. "Der tragische Homer: Zum Aias des Sophokles". In *Epea pteroenta: Beiträge zur Homerforschung. Festschrift W. Kullmann*, M. Reichel & A. Rengakos (eds), 239–46. Stuttgart: Steiner.

Zuntz, G. 1963. *The Political Plays of Euripides*. Manchester: Manchester University Press.

Zuretti, C. O. 1931. *Platone: Gorgia*. Palermo: Sandron.

Index Locorum

Literary texts

Inscriptions and papyri

General index

201